UNSTEADY STATE

The 1997 Canadian Federal Election

Neil Nevitte • André Blais

Elisabeth Gidengil • Richard Nadeau

OXFORD
UNIVERSITY PRESS

OXFORD
UNIVERSITY PRESS

70 Wynford Drive, Don Mills, Ontario M3C 1J9
www.oupcan.com

Oxford University Press is a department of the University of Oxford.
It furthers the University's objective of excellence in research, scholarship,
and education by publishing worldwide in

Oxford New York

Athens   Auckland   Bangkok   Bogotá   Buenos Aires   Calcutta
Cape Town   Chennai   Dar es Salaam   Delhi   Florence   Hong Kong   Istanbul
Karachi   Kuala Lumpur   Madrid   Melbourne   Mexico City   Mumbai
Nairobi   Paris   São Paulo   Singapore   Taipei   Tokyo   Toronto   Warsaw

with associated companies in Berlin   Ibadan

Published in Canada
by Oxford University Press

Canadian Cataloguing in Publication Data
Main entry under title:
Unsteady state : the 1997 Canadian federal election
Includes bibliographical references and index.
ISBN 0-19-541466-7
1. Canada. Parliament — Elections, 1997. I. Nevitte, Neil.

JL193.U48 1999   324.971'0648   C99-931926-4

Cover Image: Robert Stanton/Tony Stone Images
Cover & Text Design: Tearney McMurtry

1 2 3 4 - 03 02 01 00
This book is printed on permanent (acid-free) paper ∞
Printed in Canada

Table of Contents

List of Figures

List of Tables

Acknowledgements

The 1997 Canadian Election Study has been a team effort in many senses of the phrase and we have been extremely fortunate to receive support and encouragement from a variety of organizations and individuals. No research project of this scale could have been undertaken without significant financial backing. On this front, our greatest debt is to the Social Sciences and Humanities Research Council of Canada (SSHRCC). This study would not have taken place without the support of the SSHRCC; we thank them for the research grant and also for the timely and professional advice they have provided throughout the course of the project. We would also like to thank Elections Canada for its financial assistance and interest in the project. Election Canada's Tony Coulson was actively involved in various phases of the study, and we thank him for his involvement.

Our own universities were also vital supporters of the project. They helped by providing both financial assistance and by agreeing to allow each of us to take some time away from teaching so that we could complete this book in a more expeditious way. The University of Toronto (Neil Nevitte), the Université de Montréal (André Blais and Richard Nadeau), and McGill University (Elisabeth Gidengil) were all generous and accommodating. We appreciate that.

This Canadian Election Study was unusual in one respect. From the beginning we wanted the project to benefit from the wisdom and experience of other researchers, and so we set about recruiting a variety of scholars to our advisory board. Talented people are usually busy people. The members of our advisory board were extremely generous with their time and energy. Most of them continue to offer their help, and we are extremely grateful to each one of them. They too are a part of the team. In particular, we would like to express our deep appreciation to the following:

Herman Bakvis (Political Science, Dalhousie University)
Keith Banting (School of Policy Studies, Queen's University)
Lynda Erickson (Political Science, Simon Fraser University)
John Fox (Sociology, McMaster University)
Jonathan Freedman (Psychology, University of Toronto)
Larry LeDuc (Political Science, University of Toronto)
Ken Norrie (Economics, University of Alberta)
Vincent Price (The Annenberg School for Communication,
    University of Pennsylvania)
John Zaller (Political Science, University of California, Los Angeles)

Collecting data for the Canadian Election Study is no easy task, but the Institute for Social Research (ISR) at York University did a masterly job. David

Northrup, the project manager, is very much a member of the team. He and Rick Myles are both experts at managing, prodding, and cajoling the principal academic researchers into making decisions and meeting tough deadlines. They have humour, compassion, and good judgement, and we are very grateful for their efforts on our behalf. Anne Oram at ISR, as usual, continues to provide the Canadian Election Studies with expert archival skills and we thank her for her services.

One of the great benefits of involvement in the election study is the research opportunity it provides for the next generation of researchers—our research assistants. In particular, we would like to thank Amanda Ng at the University of Toronto; Antoine Bilodeau, Annie Sabourin, Christopher Kam, Éric Bélanger, and Thierry Giasson at the Université de Montréal; and Tim Sinke at McGill University.

Finally, our thanks go to Laura McLeod and Phyllis Wilson at Oxford University Press. We very much appreciate their advice and editorial skills.

Chapter 1

Setting the Stage

Introduction

This book is about the 1997 Canadian federal election. But since context is vital to the interpretation of any political event, it is important to begin with the most immediate reference point for interpreting an election, namely the preceding election. By most accounts the 1993 federal election was a watershed election, producing one of the most stunning outcomes in Canadian electoral history. Never before had a major political party been so thoroughly defeated as the Progressive Conservatives were in 1993. Never before had a Quebec sovereignist party found itself the Official opposition in the House of Commons. And for the first time in recent memory a new political party, Reform, surged rapidly from obscurity to mount a vigorous challenge to the political status quo. Collectively, these dramatic events seemed to signify that the once stable Canadian party system had come adrift from its moorings.

For citizens, party strategists, and analysts alike, the 1993 election was a disorienting one that introduced new uncertainties and raised a multitude of questions. The approach adopted in this book might best be called a question-centred one. The goal is not to test a single unified theory of electoral behaviour; instead, it is to present, and to try to answer, the kinds of common-sense questions that were being asked about the 1997 election by interested voters and observers. Those questions can be assembled into two very broad categories. First, there are those that concern the context of the 1997 election most broadly conceived; they apply to the entire electoral landscape of the country. An understanding of these system-wide factors helps to situate more precisely the challenges facing the parties, and the voters for that matter, and for that reason we begin by investigating these larger themes. They include such issues as electoral consolidation, regionalism, strategic voting, non-voting, campaign dynamics, ideological belief systems, and the media. These themes are the subject of chapters 2 to 5.

The second set of questions apply more particularly to the relationship between voters and political parties. For some of the parties, many of their most urgent tasks came into sharp focus as a direct consequence of their performance at the polls in the 1993 federal election. For others, their 1993 performance opened up new opportunities. The combination of challenges and opportunities was different for each of the parties, and in the second half of the book we consider these from the standpoint of each of the parties. The questions central to the second part of the book deal with themes that are common to all the parties. What did each party hope to achieve in the 1997 election? How did it go about trying to achieve those goals? To what extent was it successful and why? Where did it fall short and why? As we address these questions, such considerations as issue positions and platforms, leadership, and socio-demographic bases of support all feature prominently.

To answer these questions, the 1997 Canadian Election Study makes use of an extremely rich body of survey evidence. The data come from three waves of surveys. The first wave, telephone interviews with a stratified random sample of 3,949 eligible voters, collected data on each day (there were 110 cases a day) of the election campaign. The second wave, the post-election component of the study, involved re-interviewing 3,170 people from the first wave immediately *after* the election. The third wave of survey data come from a mail-back survey of 1,857 of the same respondents. (Some of the technical features of the surveys are reported in Appendix A.)

The analysis of such rich databases as these is a painstaking business. It is more difficult still to present the results in ways that make sense to readers. The approach adopted here is, wherever possible, to present the data in graphic form, because visual presentations of findings, if done well, make the central findings easily comprehensible. More than that, graphic presentations make fewer demands on, and assumptions about, the technical background of readers. Not all of the evidence, however, can be easily represented in graphic format. It turns out that some of the crucial findings to emerge in the following pages only surface after much detailed statistical digging and poking. In these cases, the essential findings are reported in the text and readers are referred to the technical information, which we report either in notes or in technical appendices. Research results should be clear, and readers ought to be able to judge for themselves the more detailed technical evidence that provides the foundation for some of the conclusions. For that reason, Appendix C offers some guidance about how the results from the most commonly used analytic tool, regression analysis, are interpreted. It also summarizes some of the main results.

To set the stage for the analysis that follows, we begin by fleshing out the organizing questions that the book aims to answer. We make no claim that the questions raised throughout the book completely exhaust the entire range of possibilities, but they do address some of the most central ones.

Questions of Context

At the beginning of the 1997 election, one matter at issue concerned the status and stability of the entire Canadian party system. Before election day, no one knew whether the 1997 election result would produce a consolidation of the novel 1993 alignment, a return to the pre-1993 status quo, or something else. The only way to answer that question is to compare distributions and turnover in 1993 and 1997. Geographic factors also qualify as systemic. Geography has always been an important feature of Canadian electoral behaviour, and the changes in election results between 1988 and 1993 provide a vivid illustration of just how quickly regional considerations can come to the fore. But what about the 1993-7 interlude? Was regionalism a stronger force in 1997 than in 1993?

System-wide factors, of course, can also have a direct influence on individual voters. The emergence of new political parties, for example, not only expands the range of choices for the voters, but also makes outcomes more difficult to predict, particularly when the relative strength of the parties is such that small swings in popular support can produce large shifts in the distribution of seats. In 1997, did citizens just vote for the party they liked the most? Or did voters think about possible outcomes? And is there any evidence that voters' calculations about outcomes played any role at all in how they cast their ballot in 1997? In other words, was there any evidence of strategic voting?

The 1993 election result demonstrated most vividly that voters do not always cast their ballots in the same way from one election to the next. Who are the mobile voters and who are the consistent ones? Which citizens changed their minds during the course of campaigns? And did such campaign events as the leadership debates have any effect at all on people's vote intentions?

Other broad questions that are addressed in the first part of the book concern the media, ideology, and non-voting. It is easy to see why people attribute considerable influence to the media particularly during elections. Nowhere is the power of the media more evident than in such events as the TV leadership debates. But just how does the influence of the media work? Were the media unduly critical of political parties? Is there any evidence that some parties got more exposure or better treatment? And are there any systematic differences between the anglophone and francophone media?

One possible explanation for the apparent fluidity of partisan attachments is ideology. Shifting ideological winds can give new momentum to some parties while leaving others stranded. Is there any evidence of any ideological shifts? If so, what were they? And were some parties better positioned than others to capitalize on these changes? How nimble or stubborn were the political parties in reacting to shifts in the ideological climate?

Voter turnout was low in 1997: fully one in three eligible voters failed to cast a ballot. Much post-election commentary fixed on the issue of voter turnout, and for good reason, for voting is an important barometer of the democratic health of a society; elections are infrequent participatory opportunities that require little effort on the part of citizens. Who, then, did not vote and why? Was the low turnout fuelled by public cynicism about politicians and the political process?

Political Parties and Voters

The Liberals had reason to be optimistic about their chances of being returned as the government party in the 1997 election, and the prospect of making significant electoral advances beyond their 1993 showing was not out of the question. There were at least three reasons for that optimism.

First, there was the possibility of a battle for votes between the two parties that flanked the Liberals to the right. The Liberals' traditional rivals, the Progressive Conservatives, were so badly defeated in 1993 that the chances appeared slim that, in the space of one election, they could haul themselves back from the brink of extinction and restore their former levels of support. Better yet, for the Liberals, the Conservatives were down but not completely out. So the Liberal strategists could hope, given Conservative defections to Reform in 1993, that any Conservative comeback in 1997 might largely eat into Reform support. With any luck, then, the right-wing vote would be divided.

The second reason for optimism had to do with the economy. Voters pay attention to the economy, and at the beginning of the campaign the economy seemed to be performing reasonably well. If Canadians asked themselves the classic question about retrospective economic perceptions: 'Are you better off now than you were four years ago?' then informed voters may well have been able to say yes. And, after reaching that conclusion, the reasonable expectation may have been that voters would go on to reward the governing party.

A third possible reason for optimism had to do with the mixture of factors contributing to the uneven distribution of support for other political parties. Part of that mixture concerned Quebec and regionalism. The Bloc spoke eloquently for the sovereignist forces, but who could most effectively represent federalist ones in that province? Then again, Reform was articulate and forceful on Western issues and grievances, but which party was best positioned to speak for the whole country? In effect, the Liberals looked like the only party that had a real chance of meeting these needs.

The Liberals, of course, *were* returned to power in 1997, but for optimistic Liberal strategists and supporters, the election outcome fell far short of expectations on two fronts. First, the total Liberal vote was just 38 per cent, that is, three percentage points short of its 1993 performance. And second, the seats that they did win were distributed in such a way that the Liberal party of Canada came out of the election looking more like the Liberal party of Ontario.

When the Liberal electoral performance in 1997 is viewed in that light, several puzzles emerge. First, how did the Liberals manage to lose votes when the economy appeared to be performing better? There are several possibilities. Although governing parties have many advantages when running for re-election, they have the disadvantage of often being measured against their record. Did the voters think the Liberals had performed poorly in office? Were they punishing them for, for example, breaking their promise to abolish the GST? Was it a matter of leadership? Was Jean Chrétien unpopular? These and other closely related questions are explored in Chapter 6.

The 1993 election delivered the sharpest and most painful message to the Progressive Conservatives. Going into the 1997 election they had the clear task of putting the party back on the electoral map. The very briefest survey of the debris from 1993 indicates that the task would be enormous. They had only two seats in the House of Commons, and support for the party in 1993 was dangerously low. Even the most optimistic party stalwarts must have had diffi-culty imagining a bright future. Nevertheless, party strategists did have some opportunities available to them. If the most significant cause of the Conservative collapse in 1993 was the unpopularity of the preceding Mulroney government, the Conservatives could hope that with the passage of time Canadians' irritations with the Mulroney era might have subsided. And they could also hope that those voters who had defected from the party in huge numbers in 1993 might conclude that the Conservatives had been punished enough and that it was time to return to the fold.

But defecting voters had to be lured back with something, and what the Conservative party offered was their platform and an attractive leader. But recognizing opportunities is one thing; finding ways to maximize them in practice is quite another. As it happens, the Conservatives did make some inroads; their 1997 results were an improvement over the débâcle of 1993. But their 1997 share of the vote amounted to an increase of only three percentage points over 1993. The possible reasons for that are examined in Chapter 7.

For Reform, the results of the 1993 election launched the party into an entirely different trajectory. More than anything else, the 1997 election presented Reform with an opportunity to build upon its electoral success. The party now had more than three years of legislative experience under its belt, it had a profile, and it seemed to have carved out a niche in the ideological landscape. Like other parties, Reform's ambition was to expand its electoral base. But more than that, its goal was to extend the reach of the party beyond the confines of the West, particularly, to secure an electoral foothold in Ontario. If along the way Reform could also bury its rival on the right by driving a stake through the heart of the Conservatives, so much the better. But the main goal was to establish an electoral beachhead in Ontario.

Having no electoral seats east of Manitoba was partly an image problem for the Reform party because its opponents could dismiss it as just another manifestation of Western protest. And how could a party with roots and electoral support only in the West make a credible claim to speak for something more than the West? Historical experience suggests that federal protest parties whose origins are in the West usually follow one of two career paths. When they spring to life in the West and stay in the West, they tend to wither shortly thereafter. On the other hand, when they spring to life in the West and success- fully build support in other parts of the country, like the NDP, they tend to be long-lived. The challenge for Reform was to transform itself into a country- wide electoral force. Since the party ran only token candidates in Quebec in 1997, its potential constituency was limited to English-speaking Canada. The party did run candidates in the Atlantic provinces, but the chances of a pro- free enterprise party that touted the virtues of less government were never reckoned to be very good in an economically deprived region so reliant on government largesse. And so if Reform was going to achieve such a break- through and lay claim to be a credible cross-country party, *pace* Quebec, then it had to win in Ontario. Reform failed to achieve that vital Ontario foothold in 1997. Why it failed and whether its failure on the Ontario front tells us anything about the prospects for a united right are questions that will be considered in Chapter 8.

Clearly, each party drew its optimism from different sources going into the 1997 election. The hopes of the New Democratic Party were perhaps the most conventional of all, or at least they were the easiest to anticipate. New Democrats claim, with some justification, that they are the party of conscience in Canada. Their mandate has been to protect the rights of the needy, and to defend the social safety net that gives substance to social rights in the country. The Liberal record in office presented the New Democrats with more than enough ammunition for the 1997 election campaign. In 1993 the governing Liberals had gone to Canadians with the promise to create more jobs; their record on jobs was mixed. No party in Canada has spoken about jobs longer, louder, or with more conviction than the New Democrats. In 1993 the Liberals campaigned on the need to protect social programs; when in office, they cut social spending. Then there was the promise to abolish the GST issue. The Liberals, it seemed, had broken promises and drifted to the ideological right. Broken promises, unemployment numbers stuck in the high range, and cuts to welfare programs—what more could the New Democrats hope for? And in the 1997 election they did increase their share of the vote. But given what looked like optimal conditions, why did they attract only 11 per cent of the vote? That question is examined in Chapter 9.

The results of the 1993 federal election were a major victory for the Bloc Québécois. Unlike the Conservatives, the New Democrats, and to a lesser extent the Liberals, the Bloc did not pay the penalties that the electoral system imposes on parties with thinly distributed popular support. Indeed, it was precisely because Bloc support was so concentrated that the party ended up as the official Opposition in Ottawa. In 1993 the Bloc attracted the votes of half the Quebec electorate, and it did so by efficiently tapping the reservoir of sover- eignist sentiment in the province. The challenge for them in 1997 was to repeat that success. But instead, Bloc support slumped and the party lost a substantial number of seats. What explains this reversal? Was it a matter of leadership? Did voters prefer Jean Charest and Jean Chrétien to Gilles Duceppe? Did Quebec voters think the economy was getting better and credit federalist forces with the improvements? Or was there a waning in enthusiasm for the sovereignist project? Chapter 10 discusses several possibilities.

Some of the findings that emerge in the course of the following analysis cannot be folded into questions that fit neatly into the system-wide or party-centred categories around which most of the book is organized. Some concern the visibility of political parties during the campaign and the tone of media coverage. Others have to do with voter information, the relevance of issues, and how the issues were framed. In addition to providing a broader interpretation of the system-wide and party-specific findings, the conclusions bring together some of the findings that shed new light on larger questions about the Canadian party system and about Canadian voting behaviour more generally.

Chapter 2

The Vote

On 2 June 1997, 67 per cent of Canadians who had the right to vote went to the polls. Of those, 38 per cent voted for the Liberals, 19 per cent for Reform, 19 per cent for the Conservative party, 11 per cent for the Bloc Québécois, and 11 per cent for the NDP. These results, or indeed the results of any election, can be interpreted from a variety of vantage points. The aim of this chapter is to sketch a broad context for evaluating the 1997 election results. The place to begin is with an assessment of five vantage points that set the stage for the analysis that follows.

First there is history. The most immediate benchmark for evaluating the 1997 election outcome is to compare the 1997 results with those of previous elections. In many respects, the 1993 federal election marked a shift towards a new electoral order, and against that backdrop the 1997 vote seemed to signal a consolidation of that new order. From this historical perspective, the central questions to ask are how similar or different the distribution of the vote was from that of previous elections in general and of 1993 in particular.

Then there is geography. There are few advanced industrial states in which geography has such a profound effect on the political representation of citizens as in Canada. In fact, not to consider the effect of geography on a Canadian election would be an extraordinary omission. Indeed, the regionalization of the vote was perhaps the most striking feature of the 1997 election outcome. But just how regionalized was the 1997 vote? And was this regionalization really much stronger than before? Which party's support was the most regionalized and which the least?

Most analysts assume that people vote for the party they like the most, but the empirical evidence does not always support this proposition. There is evidence that for strategic reasons some voters will support a party that is not their favourite. It is important to know whether some voters did that in 1997 and, if so, why? The vital question here is to what extent the distribution of the vote corresponds to the distribution of preferences.

The last part of the chapter deals with two aspects of what might be called the dynamics of the vote. First, there is the campaign to consider. Political parties expend enormous amounts of money and energy during campaigns because that is the last opportunity to solidify their support and persuade non-supporters to change allegiance. But do campaigns actually matter? Did people's vote intentions shift during the campaign? How much? Which parties gained or lost ground? When and why? Then there is a longer perspective from which to examine change and stability. If we look at the 1993 and 1997 elections together, how many voters qualified as 'consistent' in the sense that they voted for the same party in both elections? How many switched party allegiances between 1993 and 1997? Who went where? Which parties benefited most from this volatility? Which suffered the greatest defections and why?

The 1997 Election in Perspective

From 1968 to 1988, the Canadian party system corresponded to what political scientists often call the 'two-party plus' system. The two major parties—the Liberals and the Conservatives—each had a good chance of winning enough seats to form the government. The 'plus' component, represented by the NDP, usually managed to attract between 15 per cent and 20 per cent of the vote. Table 2.1 reports the vote and seat shares of the various parties in federal elections since 1968. During that 19-year period, the three federal parties forming the core of this 'two-party plus' system obtained, on average, 94 per cent of the total vote.

In 1993 this long-standing configuration was shattered by the emergence of two new parties, the Bloc and Reform. The three 'traditional' parties were able to attract only 64 per cent of the vote. And in 1997 those same three parties recovered only very slightly, taking 68 per cent of the total vote. It should be noted, however, that the traditional parties have not all been equally affected by this reconfiguration of the party system. The Liberals' share of the vote in both 1993 and 1997 turned out to be close to their mean share (39 per cent) between 1968 and 1988.

At first glance, then, the 1997 election appears to represent a consolidation of the shift that had taken place in 1993. But there are reasons to be cautious about jumping to the conclusion that the 1997 election was a mere repeat of 1993. From 1993 to 1997, the Liberals and the Bloc each lost three points, and the NDP and the Conservatives gained four and three points respectively. Together, this represents a total shift of some 13 points. As it happens, this 13-point shift corresponds exactly to the median shift in Canadian elections since 1945. Again, context is important. In comparative terms, the mean shift in votes from one election to the next in Western democracies runs at about 9 points (Dalton, Beck, and Flanagan 1984, 10). From that standpoint, the 1993–7 Canadian vote shift looks substantial. In effect, these results mean that we need

Table 2.1: Election Outcomes, 1968–1997

	Liberals		Conservatives		NDP		Social Credit		Other		Reform		Bloc	
	% votes	% seats	% votes	% seats	% votes	% seats	% votes	% seats	% votes	% seats	% votes	% seats	% votes	% seats
1968	45.5	(58.7)	31.4	(27.3)	17.0	(8.3)	4.4	(5.3)	1.7	(0.4)	—	—	—	—
1972	38.5	(41.3)	35.0	(40.5)	17.7	(11.7)	7.6	(5.7)	1.2	(0.8)	—	—	—	—
1974	43.2	(53.4)	35.4	(36.0)	15.4	(6.1)	5.1	(4.2)	0.9	(0.4)	—	—	—	—
1979	40.1	(48.2)	35.9	(40.4)	17.9	(9.2)	4.6	(2.1)	1.5	(0.0)	—	—	—	—
1980	44.3	(52.1)	32.5	(36.5)	19.8	(11.3)	1.7	(0.0)	1.7	(0.0)	—	—	—	—
1984	28.0	(14.2)	50.0	(74.8)	18.8	(10.6)	0.1	(0.0)	3.0	(0.4)	—	—	—	—
1988	31.9	(28.1)	43.0	(57.3)	20.4	(14.6)	—	—	4.7	(0.0)	—	—	—	—
1993	41.3	(60.0)	16.0	(0.7)	6.9	(3.1)	—	—	3.6	(0.3)	18.7	(17.6)	13.5	(18.3)
1997	38.5	(51.5)	18.8	(6.6)	11.0	(7.0)	—	—	1.8	(0.3)	19.4	(19.9)	10.5	(14.6)

to account for two things. On the one hand, there is evidence of stability—the consolidation of a new multi-party system; on the other hand, there is evidence of change—a significant 13-point vote shift between 1993 and 1997.

An election is first and foremost an opportunity for citizens to have a say about who will form the government. In 1997 the Liberal party was returned to power, but with fewer votes than in 1993. Is this an unusual outcome? The simple answer is no. In the 16 Canadian federal elections since 1949, the party in power lost votes 11 times and the median loss was three percentage points, which is exactly what the Liberals lost in 1997. Nor is this pattern peculiar to Canada. Strom (1990, 124), who examined the electoral performance of government parties in 15 democracies, found that the mean shift in their vote share is minus three points.

Why do parties in power tend to lose votes? There are two kinds of explanations. The first is that since their vote in the previous election may have been exceptionally high—the result of a 'surge'—they are likely to lose some ground. Indeed, the four Canadian governments that had won 45 per cent or more of the vote in the previous election all lost votes in the next election and the median drop in these cases turned out to be 7.5 points.

That does not explain the fate of the other 12 governments that had been elected with less than 45 per cent of the vote. These governments fared better electorally. Still, 8 times out of 12, parties lost ground, and their median loss was two and a half points. According to Strom (1990, 45–6) the main reason is that 'incumbents have their reliability and responsibility more severely tested'. The extent to which this explanation holds in the case of the Liberal vote is considered in Chapter 6.

The Regional Vote

The evidence considered so far has been limited to aggregate results, the overall vote for the whole country, but that is only a starting point because aggregate findings reveal nothing about possible variations among regions. Table 2.2 provides a more detailed perspective; it shows the provincial breakdown of the vote in 1997 and 1993. The Liberals' stronghold was of course Ontario, where they claimed almost 50 per cent of the vote. Note, however, that in 1997 they lost three points in Ontario, compared to 1993. And the Liberals performed poorly west of Manitoba, where they obtained only 27 per cent of the vote. But the Liberals lost most in the Atlantic provinces, where their 1997 score (33 per cent) fell a very substantial 24 points from their 1993 performance. Quebec was the only province where the Liberals made some gains. Finally, they lost 11 points in Manitoba, much more than in Ontario and Saskatchewan, an indication that the decision to call an election at the time of the Red River flood may have cost them some votes (and seats) in that province.

Table 2.2: Regionalization of the Vote, 1993 and 1997

	Liberals % votes		Conservatives % votes		NDP % votes		Reform % votes		Bloc % votes	
	1997	(1993)	1997	(1993)	1997	(1993)	1997	(1993)	1997	(1993)
Nfld	37.9	(67.3)	36.8	(26.7)	22.0	(3.5)	2.5	(1.0)	0.0	(0.0)
PEI	44.8	(60.1)	38.3	(32.0)	15.1	(5.2)	1.5	(1.0)	0.0	(0.0)
NS	28.4	(52.0)	30.8	(23.5)	30.4	(6.8)	9.7	(13.3)	0.0	(0.0)
NB	32.9	(56.0)	35.0	(27.9)	18.4	(4.9)	13.1	(8.5)	0.0	(0.0)
PQ	36.7	(33.0)	22.2	(13.5)	2.0	(1.5)	0.3	(0.0)	37.9	(49.3)
Ont.	49.5	(52.9)	18.8	(17.6)	10.7	(6.0)	19.1	(20.1)	0.0	(0.0)
Man.	34.3	(45.0)	17.8	(11.9)	23.2	(16.7)	23.7	(22.4)	0.0	(0.0)
Sask.	24.7	(32.1)	7.8	(11.3)	30.9	(26.6)	36.0	(27.2)	0.0	(0.0)
Alta	24.0	(25.1)	14.4	(14.6)	5.7	(4.1)	54.6	(52.3)	0.0	(0.0)
BC	28.8	(28.1)	6.2	(13.5)	18.2	(15.5)	43.1	(36.4)	0.0	(0.0)
NWT	43.1	(65.4)	16.7	(16.2)	20.9	(7.7)	11.7	(8.4)	0.0	(0.0)
Yukon	22.0	(23.3)	13.9	(17.8)	28.9	(43.3)	25.3	(13.1)	0.0	(0.0)

For their part, the Conservatives were strongest in the East and weakest in the West. They won a plurality of the votes in Nova Scotia and New Brunswick, but less than 10 per cent in Saskatchewan and British Columbia. They gained eight points in the East, where they were already stronger, and lost three points in the West, where they were already quite weak. In British Columbia, their support plummeted to 6 per cent. Their strongest gains came in Quebec, the province of their leader.

In the case of Reform, it is useful to distinguish among six regions. Reform's stronghold remained Alberta, where it obtained 55 per cent of the votes. Then came neighbouring British Columbia and Saskatchewan, with about 40 per cent of the vote; these were the two provinces where Reform made substantial progress. In Ontario and Manitoba, Reform support stood at about 19 or 20 per cent, about the national average. And it was much weaker (about 10 per cent) in Nova Scotia and New Brunswick and extremely weak in Newfoundland and Prince Edward Island.

The shifting regional bases of partisan support are most striking in the case of the NDP. In 1993 the NDP managed to win more than 10 per cent of the vote in only three provinces, Manitoba, Saskatchewan, and British Columbia. In each of these three provinces the party made small gains. The most spectacular gains, of course, were in the Atlantic provinces, but even there, it is useful to distinguish between Nova Scotia, home of the NDP leader, from the other three provinces. The NDP gained 23 points in Nova Scotia, but only 15 points elsewhere in the region. Finally, the party lost votes in the Yukon, home of their former leader.

The story for the Bloc is simple: the party ran candidates only in Quebec and so all its votes were concentrated in that province.

The picture that emerges is that unquestionably the vote was strongly regionalized in the 1997 federal election. But how strongly? Social scientists assess the degree of regionalization by using such measures of association as Cramer's V. This is a simple and useful summary measure because it has a 'natural range', zero to one, that is easy to understand. When a Cramer's V has a value of 0, it means that all parties get exactly the same share of the vote in each region. When Cramer's V has a value of 1 it means that each party gets either 100 per cent of the vote or no vote at all in each region. For 1997, Cramer's V has a value of .33, which, being closer to 0 than to 1, is a reminder that regionalization is certainly not as extreme as it could have been.

In relative terms, regionalization was quite strong in 1997, but the important point is that it was also about the same as it had been in 1993.[1] However, regionalization is much stronger in the 1990s than it was in the 1980s. In 1988, for example, Cramer's V was equal to .20. And, as far as can be determined, the vote is more strongly regionalized in Canada than in any other Western democracy, except perhaps Belgium (see Dalton 1996, 325).

The scope and scale of regionalism can also be judged from the standpoint of the parties. For each party, we can compute a specific Cramer's V to measure the degree of regionalization in its own vote.[2] Such analysis indicates that the Bloc vote was the most regionalized, followed by Reform, the NDP, the Liberals, and the Conservatives.[3] The clear pattern here is that new parties were more regionalized than traditional ones.

Finally, we know that regional differences in the vote are real and cannot be explained away by socio-economic factors such as income, education, or religion (Gidengil, Blais, Nadeau, and Nevitte 1999). Regression analyses show that in vote choice the sharpest cleavage is the regional one (see Appendix C). The most crucial cleavage is, of course, between Quebec and the rest of the country, but regional differences are also huge outside Quebec. For instance, the probability of voting Liberal is 20 points higher in Ontario than in either the East or the West, even after a host of socio-economic factors have been controlled for.

Do Voters Vote Strategically?

In trying to understand why people vote for a particular party, analysts look for reasons that may have made that party more attractive than other parties. In doing so, the operating assumption is usually that people vote for the party they like the most. The problem is that people are sometimes moved by less straightforward motives. For instance, it is possible to cast what is sometimes called a 'strategic' vote. Consider the following example. Suppose there are three parties, A, B, C, in a riding and that a given voter likes A very much, likes B only slightly, and strongly dislikes C. Suppose also that this voter thinks that party A has practically no chance of winning the election and that there is a close race between B and C. That person might decide to vote 'strategically' for B. A strategic vote is thus a vote for a party that is not the most preferred because of their expectations about the likely outcome of the election.

There is a large body of research probing the question of strategic voting (see, especially, Abramson et al. 1992, Blais and Nadeau 1996, Cox 1997). This research clearly establishes, first, strategic voting exists, and second, that it is relatively rare. Usually, somewhere between 5 and 10 per cent of the voters vote strategically, and between 90 and 95 per cent vote sincerely. Nevertheless, if those strategic votes systematically benefit some parties at the expense of others, the combined effect may be quite substantial. And it could be that in some elections and under some conditions, the amount and direction of strategic voting is particularly important.

What about the 1997 election? Is there any evidence that some Canadians voted strategically in that election? And if they did, which parties gained and which ones lost ground in the process? Recall that when people vote strategically, they not only vote on the basis of their preferences but they also consider the various parties' chances of winning the election. The Canadian Election Study included questions about the respondents' perceptions of the race in their local constituency.[4] Detailed analysis shows that perceptions of the parties' chances of winning in one's riding did affect the vote,[5] even when voters' ratings of the parties and of the leaders and their party identification are taken into account. In short, there is evidence of strategic voting in the 1997 election.

At the same time, however, strategic voting occurred on a modest scale. According to our estimates, only 4 per cent of voters voted for a party different from the one they would have supported if they had not taken into account their perceptions of the race in their constituency, and such strategic voting had very little overall effect on the vote.

Some observers did raise the possibility that another kind of strategic voting may have taken place in 1997. Since it is not hard to imagine that many Canadians disliked the idea of a sovereignist party being the official Opposition, it is plausible that voters who strongly disliked the Bloc may have been inclined to vote for the party that seemed the most likely to finish second in the country and to unseat the Bloc as the official Opposition. Though there is evidence that such strategic behaviour took place, once again, it was on a modest scale. Outside Quebec,[6] those who thought that Reform had good chances of forming the official Opposition were less likely to vote Liberal and more likely to vote Reform, even after we take into account their ratings of the parties and of the leaders and their party identification (as well as their perceptions of the race in their local constituency). But detailed analysis indicates that only 1 per cent of the voters changed their vote for that reason. The net effect of these strategic considerations gave Reform an extra one point, which came at the expense of the Liberals.

First and Second Choices

Under the current electoral rules, Canadians are asked to vote for a candidate in their local constituency, a candidate who represents a particular party. In other systems, such as the alternative vote that is used in Australia, voters are asked to rank the candidates in order from the one they like the most to the one they like the least. What would have been Canadians' second choices in the election? That question becomes particularly relevant given the debate about a potential unification of the right, because the proposals for unification rest on the belief that Reformers and Conservatives form a kind of ideological family, and so Reform voters' second choice might well be the Conservative party and vice versa.

The Canadian Election Study survey evidence suggests that the basis for such a belief is weak (Table 2.3). Outside Quebec, the Liberals were the most frequent second choice of PC, Reform, and NDP voters alike.[7] The situation is more complex in Quebec. There, the Liberals were the most popular second choice of Conservative and NDP voters, but they had only a slight edge over the Bloc. As for Bloc voters, their second choices went to the Conservatives.

Table 2.3: Second Choice by Vote, 1997

			Vote			
Second Choice						
Quebec	*Liberals*	*Conservatives*	*NDP*	*Reform*	*Bloc*	*Other*
	%	%	%	%	%	%
Liberals	—	50.4	29.4	—	14.5	27.3
Conservatives	67.0	—	11.8	—	37.4	18.2
NDP	5.3	6.5	—	—	9.8	9.1
Reform	1.4	0.0	0.0	—	0.0	0.0
Bloc	8.6	33.3	23.5	—	—	18.2
Other	0.0	1.6	5.9	—	0.9	0.0
None / Don't Know	17.7	7.3	29.4	—	37.4	27.3
N = 595	209	123	17	—	235	11
Outside Quebec	*Liberals*	*Conservatives*	*NDP*	*Reform*	*Bloc*	*Other*
Liberals	—	44.0	48.9	30.8	—	45.2
Conservatives	38.2	—	17.8	27.3	—	6.5
NDP	26.8	19.5	—	11.9	—	12.9
Reform	16.1	17.7	8.9	—	—	12.9
Other	0.0	0.0	4.0	2.0	—	3.2
None / Don't know	18.9	18.8	20.4	28.1	—	19.4
N = 1,726	671	293	225	506	—	31

These findings help to establish three basic points. First, it is not certain at all that Conservative voters would be willing to support the Reform party or vice versa. In fact, more Conservative voters gave the NDP than Reform as their second choice, a finding that challenges the view that the supporters of the two parties 'on the right' really do see themselves as part of a single ideological family. The reasons why Reform is not the second choice of Conservative voters are investigated in Chapter 8. Second, the Liberal party was acceptable to a definite majority of Canadians: according to our data, as many as 60 per cent of voters would have had the party as their first or second choice. Third, and somewhat surprisingly perhaps, the Conservatives were the most frequent second choice, especially among those who voted Liberal. All in all, 47 per cent of our sample either voted for the Conservatives or picked them as their second choice. The equivalent figure for Reform was 30 per cent. The problem for the Conservatives, of course, was that these second choices do not count. As a consequence, the party that was the second-most preferred overall finished third in terms of votes and fifth in terms of seats.

Campaign Dynamics

Did voters change their mind about how to vote during the election campaign? If they did, is it possible to identify which specific campaign event produced these shifts? And did these effects persist through election day? The objective here is simply to document the presence or absence of such effects. (Chapter 3 explores one thing that may have led some people to revise their vote intentions, that is, the media coverage of the campaign.)

Most observers of the 1997 federal election campaign name two events that had the potential to change the course of the election: the televised leaders' debates that took place on 12 and 13 May,[8] and the 'Quebec' Reform advertisement, which raised the issue of whether the unity question should be left to Quebec politicians.

Figure 2.1 tracks vote intentions during the course of the campaign.[9] The evidence confirms that the TV debates did have an effect on how people intended to vote. In the days immediately following the debates, the Conservatives gained about five points, mostly, it seems, at the expense of the Liberals. Less clear is the matter of whether that gain was permanent or only temporary. Likewise, Reform seemed to pick up three or four points after its commercial was first aired (22 May), but it is not clear whether the effect lasted to the end of the campaign.

The best way to measure the influence of these two events on people's vote intentions is through time-series analysis. These findings[10] indicate that in the ten days that followed the debates the Conservatives gained about five points to the detriment of the Liberals. But by election day, it seems, the effect of the debates had almost completely disappeared.[11] With respect to Reform's Quebec ad, the data suggest that Reform gained about seven points in the five days immediately following the ad, but that the gain had vanished entirely by election day. Both events did have a substantial impact on people's vote intentions, but only temporarily. The final effect on the outcome of the election, according to time-series analysis, was negligible.

Other pieces of evidence corroborate this interpretation. With respect to the debates, for instance, Jean Charest was widely considered to have done the best,[12] and his ratings did increase in the days following them. But it turns out that his winning performance during the leadership debates did not have a lasting effect on the vote. The people who thought that Charest had won the debate were not more likely to vote Conservative, once their pre-debate predispositions were taken into account.

In the case of the Quebec ad, public opinion on such matters as how much should be done to accommodate Quebec, the distinct society clause, and feelings towards the Quebec leaders did not move after the commercial was aired. Nor did they become more strongly related to the vote.[13]

Is this the whole story of the campaign? It does not seem so. A comparison of vote intentions in the first and last ten days of the campaign shows that the

Figure 2.1: Evolution of Vote Intentions (Canada) (five-day moving averages)

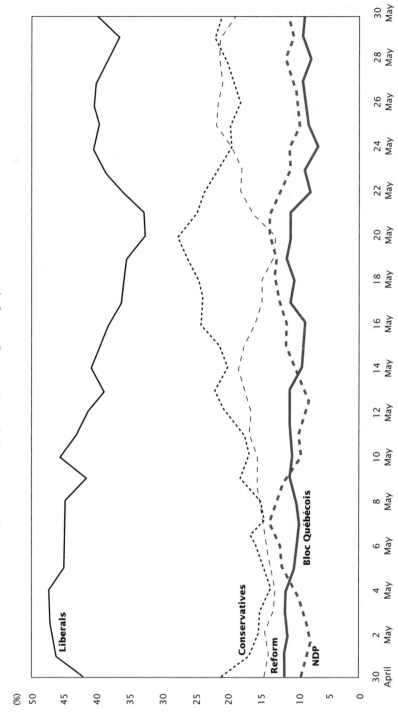

Liberals lost four points (from 43 to 39 per cent). Meanwhile, Reform gained six (from 14 to 20 per cent). The central question here is what caused these changes. The answer is a good deal more difficult, and it is tempting just to attribute these shifts to 'momentum'. As far as we can tell, these particular changes do not seem to be related to any specific campaign event. As the campaign progressed, the Reform party became slightly more attractive to voters and the Liberals slightly less so. Furthermore, the greatest drop in perceived Liberal performance occurred on two issues, national unity and keeping promises.

The burden of 'keeping promises' is the unique challenge to governing parties. During the course of campaigns, all parties make promises, but only government parties are positioned to do anything about them. It comes as no surprise that opposition parties scrutinize the record of governing parties and enthusiastically exploit any shortcomings during election campaigns. The one broken promise that was the most difficult for the Liberals to explain away had to do with the GST affair. Throughout the campaign, 65 per cent of our respondents told us that, in their view, the Liberals had promised to do away with the GST in the 1993 election campaign and that they did not really try to keep their promise. In the first ten days of the campaign, 39 per cent of those who thought the Liberals had not kept their promise were still willing to vote Liberal, whereas 25 per cent intended to vote Reform. In the last ten days of the campaign, the Liberals lost and Reform gained five points in that group.[14]

All in all, there is evidence that the 1997 election campaign did influence the voters; both the leaders' debates and the Quebec ad had an effect on people's vote intentions, but neither effect was a lasting one. By election day, neither the Reform party nor the Conservatives were able to capitalize on either of these events. Nonetheless, Reform evidently did achieve some gains among the electorate during the campaign, mostly at the expense of the Liberals. Reform was particularly successful in attracting the support of those who did not trust the Liberals to keep their promises.

The Flow of the Vote

To many analysts, the 1997 election represented a consolidation of the new pattern established in the election of 1993. The Liberals and the Bloc each lost three points, at the expense of the NDP and the Conservatives. Since these changes can be construed as relatively marginal, they feed the impression that most voters simply voted the same way in 1997 as they had done in 1993. But is that impression correct?

To address this question we must take a close look at the evidence provided by individual voters. The 1993 and 1997 aggregate election results look very similar and stable, but they may hide volatility at the individual level. The very first step is to construct a flow-of-the-vote table, that is, one that links individual voting behaviour in 1993 and 1997. The approach is based on similar analyses performed in Britain (Butler and Stokes 1969; Sarlvik 1983) and Canada (Johnston, Blais, Brady, Gidengil, and Nevitte 1996b).[15]

The full table (Table 2.4) has eight categories in both 1993 and 1997. The first five categories correspond to a vote for each of the five main parties, the sixth to support for other parties, and the seventh to the cases where people abstained from voting. The eighth category simply captures those who were in the electorate in only one of the two elections. According to our estimates, there is some population replacement to consider; about 4 per cent of the 1993 electors had died or left the country at the time of the 1997 election, and 8 per cent of the 1997 electors did not have the right to vote in 1993, either because they were too young or because they were not Canadian citizens.

The starting point for estimating the flow of the vote is the respondents' reported voting behaviour in 1997 and 1993. Now, these data do not quite correspond to the actual outcome of the two elections. For instance, surveys often exaggerate the voter turnout. To get a more accurate read on the findings, it is common practice to resort to a statistical adjustment procedure—known as 'Mostellarization'—to correct for discrepancies between survey data and the actual outcome of the election.[16]

Table 2.4 begins by indicating the sources of the 1997 vote.[17] It shows that the majority (68 per cent) of those who had voted in 1993 voted for the same party in 1997. The reverse of this, of course, is that as many as one voter out of three switched from one party to another. Clearly, voter stability in 1997 was much greater than it had been in 1993, when the surge of two new parties led as many as 56 per cent of voters to switch their vote from 1988 (see Johnston, Blais, Brady, Gidengil, and Nevitte 1996a). Still, the findings above show that there was a substantial amount of individual-level movement between 1993 and 1997.

Table 2.4 also shows that Reform was the most successful in retaining its core of party supporters from the 1993 federal election, and the Conservatives the least successful. The Conservatives' inability to retain their 1993 support base is particularly striking since the party did gain ground in 1997. Note too that the Bloc, the party that, proportionately lost the most in 1997, was still as successful as the Liberals and NDP in retaining much of its 1993 support.

Vote switching, that is, voting for one party in 1993 and a different one in 1997, is crucial for understanding the shape and scope of stability and change in support for the various parties. Among vote switchers, a plurality of former Liberals and Reformers went to the Conservatives, and a plurality of former Conservatives and NDPers ended up supporting the Liberals. Most, though not all, of these switches are consistent with the traditional left-right cleavage. As for those who deserted the Bloc, they overwhelmingly voted Conservative. This is undoubtedly the major source of the Conservative surge in Quebec.

Finally, a number of Canadians voted for the very first time in 1997; they either came of voting age or acquired Canadian citizenship in the 1993–7 inter-

Table 2.4: Sources of the 1997 Vote

1997	1993							
	Liberals	Conservatives	NDP	Reform	Bloc	Other	Abstain	Entering
	%	%	%	%	%	%	%	%
Liberals	68	19	14	5	7	19	48	46
Conservatives	11	57	5	10	21	0	20	16
NDP	10	7	70	2	2	24	9	8
Reform	9	15	10	82	0	23	12	7
Bloc	1	1	0	0	70	13	8	19
Other	1	1	0	0	1	21	2	5
Total	100	100	100	100	100	100	100	100

lude. As indicated before, this group represents 8 per cent of the electorate but only 6 per cent of voters; these eligible voters were more likely to abstain. For these new voters, the Liberals and the Bloc turn out to be the most attractive parties, and as will become clearer later on, these findings are attributable to strong Liberal support from recent immigrants and strong Bloc support among young voters. At the other end, Reform did very poorly among new voters, especially recent immigrants.

The major sources of gains and losses for each of the political parties can be summarized as follows:

1. The Liberals lost about equally to the Conservatives, Reform, and the NDP.[18] These losses were only partly offset by the Liberals' success in attracting the support of new voters.

2. Reform gains came mostly at the expense of the Liberals, but Reform did poorly among new voters.

3. The Conservatives made substantial inroads into the 1993 Bloc electorate, but were unable to retain many of their 1993 supporters.

4. The NDP's gains came mostly at the expense of the Liberals. Almost as many 1997 NDP voters had voted Liberal in 1993 as had voted NDP.

5. The Bloc was unable to sway those who had voted for other parties in 1993, but was very successful in attracting those people who qualified as new voters.

In effect, the total vote shift between 1993 and 1997 was 13 points. As many as one voter in three voted differently in the two elections. Some of the individual shifts cancelled each other out. Some voters switched from the Liberals to the Conservatives and others went from the Conservatives to the Liberals. And the net benefit of these shifts to any party was small.

Did the same pattern occur during the campaign itself? Did many people change their mind during the campaign? In this case it is particularly interesting to compare vote intentions expressed before the debates and actual voting behaviour. Among those who indicated a vote intention before the debates, one out of four settled for a different party on election day. And at the centre of much of this movement was the Conservative party: the Conservatives were able to attract the support of 10 per cent of those who intended to vote Liberal or Bloc, but 38 per cent of those who said they were going to vote for the Conservatives eventually deserted the party. Most of these turned either to the Liberals or Reform.

Reform did well during the campaign, but not because the party was particularly successful in converting supporters of other parties—in fact it was proportionately less successful than the Liberals and the Conservatives. Behind Reform's success was the fact that only 11 per cent of those who intended to vote Reform before the debates deserted the party, compared to 23 per cent for the Liberals and 38 per cent for the Conservatives.[19]

Two findings plainly illustrate the scope of individual-level change between 1993 and 1997. One out of three voters switched their vote from 1993 to 1997, and one out of four changed their mind in the last three weeks of the campaign. These changes were not all in the same direction, of course, so the net effect was not concentrated.

What is also clear from these findings is that similar total shifts in the vote can have very different sources. For example, both the Conservatives and the NDP gained ground in 1997, the former mostly from former Bloc supporters and the latter from former Liberal voters. The Liberals and the Bloc both lost votes, the former about equally to three parties and the latter almost exclusively to the Conservatives.

Conclusion

The 1997 election featured elements of both continuity and change. Two out of three voters voted for the same party they had supported in 1993, and the outcome was the consolidation of the multi-party system that had emerged in that election. But there was also volatility. One out of three voters switched from one party to another. The total 13-point shift has to be considered relatively high, at least when compared to the shifts that usually take place in elections in other Western democracies.

There was also movement during the campaign. The debates and the 'Quebec' ad did boost support for the Conservatives and Reform respectively, but these effects proved to be only temporary and their final influence on the vote was practically nil. Irrespective of these two events, Reform made some gains at the expense of the Liberals among those who were angry with the Liberals' broken promise on the GST.

The 1997 federal election vote was strongly regionalized, especially when it came to the vote for the new parties. Indeed, one of the most crucial questions of this election is why Reform performed so much better in the West than in Ontario, a question that is tackled in Chapter 8.

Finally, there was evidence of strategic voting, and of a special nature. Traditionally, strategic voting involves supporters of weak parties deserting their party because it is thought to have little chance of winning in their riding. There was relatively little such strategic voting in 1997. But there is evidence of another, more unusual, type of strategic voting, in which a few Liberal supporters voted Reform to help unseat the Bloc as the official Opposition.

Given the evidence of electoral dynamics, the next chapter considers the media as one possible source of change.

Chapter 3

Television Coverage in the 1997 Election

Television is so central to modern electoral campaigns that elections are becoming 'contests of television performance' (Fletcher and Everett 1991, 198). The growing importance of television has been accompanied by a noticeable shift in the coverage of the parties and their leaders. The largely positive tone of coverage in the 1960s and early 1970s (Clarke et al. 1984; Qualter and MacKirdy 1964) has progressively given way to an increasingly negative tone (Capella and Jamieson 1997; Fletcher and Everett 1991; Frizzell et al. 1990; Frizzell and Pammett 1994; Mendelsohn and Nadeau 1999).

Was this negative tone particularly evident in the television coverage of the 1997 federal election? Voters were certainly in a cranky mood. The Liberals' failure to do away with the Goods and Services Tax fed the perception that politicians were ready to lie to get elected, and cynicism about politics and politicians was widespread (see Chapter 4). Did this negative attitude colour the media coverage of the campaign as well?

The answer may well depend on the party being covered. Differential treatment of political parties raises questions about fairness that lie at the heart of studies of elections and media coverage: are the parties all treated fairly or do the media systematically favour some parties over others? There are different ways that media biases can show up, the two most obvious being the amount of coverage that parties receive, and the tone of the coverage. There is evidence, for example, that the media give the governing party extra visibility (Crête 1984, but see Monière 1994). But was this incumbency advantage apparent for the Liberals in 1997? And did the NDP suffer from the practice of 'hopeless cases get[ting] hopeless coverage' (Robinson and Shehan 1980, 76)? Media coverage may also be biased in partisan or ideological directions (Dalton et al. 1998). Research in the United States, for example, has documented the liberal leanings of that country's journalists (Rothman and Lichter 1981, 1987). These might show up in Canada in the form of systematically favourable coverage of the NDP and systematically negative coverage of Reform.

The tone of coverage, of course, may simply be due to the parties' own campaigns. Since campaign gaffes will naturally elicit negative stories, it is important to ask whether the parties' images in the media changed noticeably during the course of the campaign, and, if they did, to identify events that may have caused these shifts.[1] In a similar vein, there is the question whether a systematic link can be found between the highs and lows of the parties' media coverage and the fluctuation of vote intentions.[2]

One way to answer these questions is through a content analysis of the television coverage of the parties during the campaign. In this study, we did that by counting the number of stories that each party received and having coders independently rate the tone of each story. The content analysis undertaken here is based on the late-night news bulletins broadcast by Radio-Canada (for Quebec), and by the CBC and CTV (for the rest of Canada). Television network news was chosen because televised news is the main source of political information for citizens in Canada (Fletcher and Everett 1991), as is the case elsewhere (Ansalobehere et al. 1993).[3]

Evaluating the tone of the media coverage first involved locating the campaign stories in each night's newscast and then identifying the party that was the principal subject of the story. A total of 486 news stories were examined, 152 for Radio-Canada, 156 for the CBC, and 178 for CTV. The stories were analysed by three groups of coders, one for each network. The groups were made up of undergraduate university students, and included an equal number of men and women. To allow us to evaluate the impact of partisanship, the coders were selected on the basis of their support for each of the different parties; non-voters were also included.[4] The coders' task was relatively simple. Each one was shown the news stories and then they were asked to rate each story on a three-point scale, depending on whether the treatment of the party in question was favourable (+1), neutral (0), or unfavourable (–1). This coding was done for each night's television news coverage.[5]

This research design has two advantages. First, the groups were sufficiently large (18 for the English networks and 14 for Radio-Canada) that any idiosyncrasies in the individual coding would tend to cancel out when the individual scores were aggregated. The strategy has the merit of minimizing the effect of unusually extreme coding. Second, the design approximated real-world conditions. Unlike trained coders using a pre-established analytical grid, these coders responded 'spontaneously' to the news, much as the typical viewer might.[6]

Getting Visibility

The results indicate some evidence of an incumbency advantage for the Liberals, who were the subject of more news items than any other party on all three networks (see Table 3.1). The higher visibility of the other parties seems mainly linked to their competitiveness. This could explain the Bloc Québécois's

Table 3.1: Television Coverage of Parties in 1997 Federal Election

Network	Newscasts	Number of Stories					
		Liberals	Conservatives	NDP	Reform	Bloc	Total
CBC	36	44 (28%)	28 (18%)	23 (15%)	34 (22%)	27 (17%)	156 (100%)
CTV	36	42 (24%)	40 (22%)	29 (16%)	31 (17%)	36 (20%)	178 (99%)
Radio-Canada	36	41 (27%)	32 (21%)	19 (13%)	25 (16%)	35 (23%)	152 (100%)

second-place ranking in Quebec on the Radio-Canada network (followed closely by the Conservatives), the good showing of the Reform party (on the CBC, at least) and the Conservatives on the English-language networks, and the limited attention given to the NDP. The exception to this pattern, namely, the Bloc's visibility on the English-language networks, is undoubtedly related to the party's separatist agenda.

The overall conclusion to be drawn from these figures on party visibility is that the Liberals benefited from slightly greater coverage because of their status as the governing party, and that the attention given to the other parties was generally linked either to their competitive character (the Reform and Conservative parties) or to the nature of their fundamental political project (the Bloc). The NDP was at a disadvantage in terms of visibility, perhaps attributable to its peripheral place in the campaign (see Chapter 9). Recall that the New Democratic Party had not set its sights even on the title of official Opposition, still less that of governing party.

The NDP's difficulty in getting its message across becomes even clearer from an examination of the evolution of its visibility across the campaign (see Figure 3.1). The party remained in a relative media shadow throughout the heart of the campaign (namely, weeks two to four).[7] This low visibility may be linked to the fact that, unlike the other parties, the NDP did not enjoy even a single

Figure 3.1: News per Party and per Week, English-Speaking Television Networks

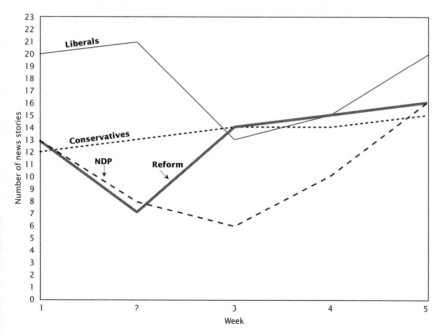

period of intense media coverage. During the first half of the campaign, the Liberals benefited from superior visibility over their opponents on the English-language networks, as well as on Radio-Canada in Quebec (see Figure 3.2). But unlike the NDP, the other parties caught up with the Liberals, and both the Conservatives and Reform benefited from an intense period of media coverage. For the Conservatives, this emerged after the televised debates, and for the Reform party in the wake of their negative campaign advertisement.

Media Statics: The Winners and the Losers

The overall tone of the coverage of the parties does not seem to have been particularly negative during the 1997 election (see Table 3.2).[8] Media coverage does appear to have been a little more negative in Quebec, though, than in the rest of Canada. Whereas two of the three parties (namely, the Liberals and the Bloc) received unfavourable treatment on the Quebec Radio-Canada network, only Reform suffered a similar fate on the English-speaking networks outside Quebec.

The overall tone may not have been negative, but the small number of items judged neutral in their treatment of the parties (36 per cent in Quebec and 42 per cent outside Quebec) indicates that the evaluative content of television news in Canada is important. This is a characteristic that the Canadian media

Figure 3.2: News per Party and per Week, French-Speaking Television Network

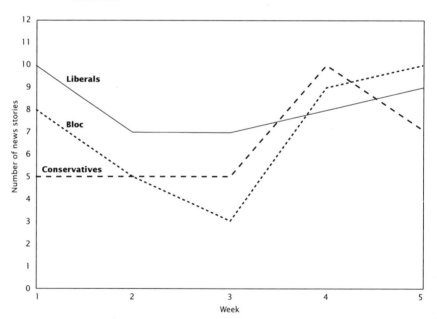

Table 3.2: Tone of Television Coverage of Parties in 1997 Federal Election

A. Average Scores

	French-Speaking Network					
	Week 1	Week 2	Week 3	Week 4	Week 5	Whole Campaign
Liberals	-.08	-.10	-.22	-.17	-.34	-.18
Conservatives	.33	.36	.59	.08	-.18	.20
Bloc	-.37	-.40	-.21	-.29	.29	-.15

	English-Speaking Networks					
	Week 1	Week 2	Week 3	Week 4	Week 5	Whole Campaign
Liberals	-.06	-.17	.03	.10	.13	.00
Conservatives	-.02	.14	.53	.15	.16	.20
NDP	.32	.21	.22	.11	.47	.30
Reform	-.38	-.29	-.24	-.55	-.23	-.34

B. Distribution of Evaluations

	French-Speaking Network				English-Speaking Networks				
	All	Liberals	Conservatives	Bloc	All	Liberals	Conservatives	NDP	Reform
Positive	29%	22%	39%	28%	30%	28%	40%	42%	15%
Neutral	36	40	40	30	42	45	40	46	36
Negative	35	40	21	43	28	28	20	12	49
Balance	-6	-18	18	-15	2	0	20	30	-34

seem to share with their American counterparts, and it stands in contrast with the more neutral tone of the broadcast news in the United Kingdom and Germany (see Dalton et al. 1998).

The tone of the media coverage was not the same for all the parties. The most striking example is the marked contrast between the very positive coverage given to the NDP and the very negative coverage given to the Reform party on the English-language networks. It is difficult to explain these differences on the basis of the two parties' campaigns. Unlike the Bloc's campaign, the Reform campaign was relatively free of the kind of mistakes that might have elicited negative coverage. Indeed, the party's gains in support during the campaign (see Chapter 2) point to the effectiveness of its electoral strategy. It is equally difficult to explain the favourable treatment accorded to the NDP on the basis of the quality of the party's campaign, not least of all because support for the NDP remained virtually unchanged from the time the election was called until voting day.

It is a different matter for the Bloc Québécois and for the two parties that have often been in power, namely, the Conservatives and the Liberals. In all three of these cases, there is a plausible link between the tone of their coverage and the character of their campaigns. The generally negative tone of the coverage of the Bloc Québécois is hardly surprising considering the catastrophic first two weeks of its campaign. Similarly, the generally positive tone of the Conservatives' coverage, on Radio-Canada in Quebec and on the English-language networks alike, seems to reflect the effectiveness of the party's electoral campaign in general and its leader's strong performance during the televised debates in particular. Finally, the neutral tone of the coverage of the Liberals on the CBC and CTV, and the negative tone on the Quebec network, seem to fit well with the impression that Jean Chrétien led a rather laborious campaign, particularly in his home province.

As far as the tone of coverage goes, then, the story is one of contrasts rather than pervasive negativism. On the one hand, the coverage of the NDP was very positive and that of the Conservatives' was fairly positive. On the other hand, the Reform party received very negative coverage and the Bloc Québécois fairly negative coverage. As for the Liberals, their coverage was relatively neutral on CTV and the CBC, but negative in Quebec. In the case of the Conservatives, the Liberals, and the Bloc, the quality of their campaigns can explain the tone of the coverage, but this does not seem to be the case for the two parties occupying the opposite ends of Canada's ideological spectrum. The NDP enjoyed positive coverage but suffered from low visibility, whereas Reform suffered the opposite fate. This pattern suggests that any media biases in Canada operate not so much in favour of parties of the left as against parties of the right.

Media Dynamics: Gaining and Losing Ground

These conclusions about the tone of media coverage are based on the election campaign taken as a whole. Do the patterns continue to hold when we examine shifts in the tone of coverage across the campaign for each of the parties? Certainly, the dynamics of the media coverage of the parties in Quebec seem to correspond fairly closely to the highs and lows of the Bloc, Conservative, and Liberal campaigns (see Table 3.2 and Figure 3.3).

The case of the Bloc Québécois is particularly intriguing, if only for the disasters it endured during the first week of the campaign (the front-page photo of Duceppe wearing a bonnet during a visit to a cheese factory and the lost campaign bus, to name the most obvious). The extremely difficult start to the campaign produced very negative coverage for the party. During this initial period, the front pages of the mainstream Quebec newspapers regularly highlighted the Bloc's organizational gaffes and the contradictory declarations of its leader. The media also played up the contrast between Lucien Bouchard's campaign as Bloc leader in 1993 and Gilles Duceppe's poor performance four years later.[9]

It is important to understand what happened during this first episode for two reasons. First, voters acquire more information about parties and their leaders at the beginning of a campaign and these first impressions weigh heavily in the balance (Holbrook 1996). Second, messages about parties have more influence if they are clear and if they are contrasted. This was precisely the situation at the beginning of the 1997 campaign in Quebec: the Bloc received very negative coverage, while its opponents reaped the benefits of either neutral (the Liberals) or very positive (the Conservatives) coverage. Consequently, it is reasonable to suppose that negative impressions of the Bloc and its leader crystallized fairly quickly at the beginning of the campaign, helping to derail the party's campaign and ultimately affecting its electoral success.

The second period in the evolution of the Bloc's coverage more or less corresponds to the middle third of the campaign. This period featured the televised debates, which were dominated by Jean Charest. During this period, the tone of coverage of the Bloc remained negative, albeit in a less clear-cut fashion than at the beginning of the campaign. Significantly, the coverage of the Bloc and the Liberals is quite similar during this phase; in both cases it was somewhat negative overall with some brief glimpses of neutral coverage. Given the very positive coverage of the Conservatives after the televised debates, however, the net effects of this second period end up being no more favourable for the Bloc than the first.

The Bloc thus received less favourable coverage than both of its adversaries during the first third of the campaign and continued to receive much less favourable media treatment than its principal adversary, the Conservatives, during the second third of the campaign. It was only in the final ten days that the situation was reversed in favour of the Bloc. Particularly during the last week, the Bloc benefited from very positive coverage, while the Liberals' coverage became even more negative and the Conservatives', for the first time during the campaign, became moderately negative.

The tone of the Bloc's coverage was reversed across the campaign, but the Liberals never succeeded in attracting positive coverage. In the first third of the

Figure 3.3: Tone of Coverage, French-Speaking Television Network (five-day moving averages)

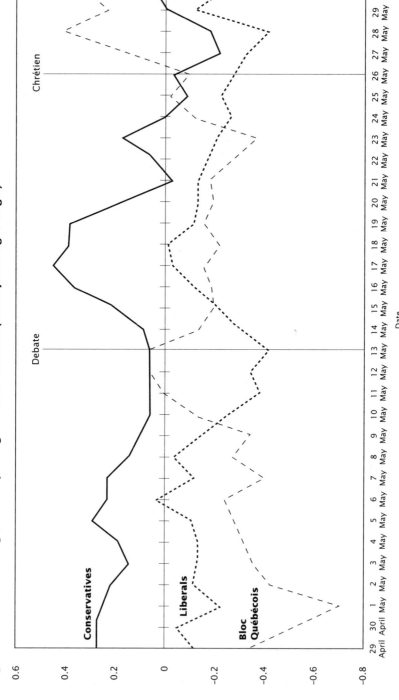

campaign, the party's relatively neutral coverage placed it halfway between the positive treatment of the Conservatives and the negative treatment of the Bloc. After a flurry of negative coverage, the tone continued to be fairly neutral during the second third of the campaign. In this regard, Liberal coverage resembled the treatment given the Bloc, while being clearly less favourable than that accorded the Conservatives in the wake of the leaders' debates. Finally, the tone of the coverage became more negative towards the end of the campaign, perhaps owing to Jean Chrétien's controversial declaration on 26 May concerning the kind of majority that would be required in any future referendum on Quebec sovereignty. In this last phase of the campaign, the Liberals received less favourable coverage than either of their opponents, though they fared only slightly worse than the Conservatives. On balance, the Liberals received relatively negative coverage overall. They never dominated their adversaries, but neither were they ever simultaneously dominated by their two opponents.

The coverage given to the Conservatives in Quebec is also characterized by three distinct periods. The Conservatives started out with a good campaign launch, fairly positive polls, and fairly favourable coverage. The advantage held by Jean Charest's party over its adversaries was reinforced in the period following the televised debates before being overturned to the Bloc's profit in the last part of the campaign. The evolution of the tone of the Conservative coverage suggests that Jean Charest's campaign peaked too soon; the problem was that this positive coverage lacked the momentum necessary to consolidate and maintain the gains made during the televised debates.

The evidence from the content analysis indicates, then, that there were clear links between the media coverage in Quebec and the highs and lows of the parties' campaigns. The Bloc's weak start, the mediocre performance of its leader during the televised debates, and the partial recovery of the party at the end of the campaign are clearly reflected in the tone of the television news. The nature of the Conservative campaign, characterized by a faultless launch, a winning performance by their leader during the debates, and a certain lack of momentum at the end, also seems to have left visible traces in the journalistic treatment of the party. Finally, Jean Chrétien's laborious campaign in Quebec, aggravated by his controversial declaration on the majority required in a referendum, also seems to have been echoed in the media.

Coverage on the two English-language television networks present some similarities, but also notable differences. As in Quebec, the coverage clearly falls into distinct periods. With the significant exception of Reform, however, the overall tone of the journalistic treatment of the parties was more positive than in the Quebec media (see Table 3.2 and Figure 3.4).

The NDP enjoyed the benefits of positive coverage throughout the campaign. It seemed able to take advantage of both the particular indulgence of journalists and the generally positive coverage given to all parties (except Reform). Beyond these elements, the coverage of the NDP falls into three periods. During the first ten days of the campaign, the NDP enjoyed a very clear advantage over the other

Figure 3.4: Tone of Coverage, English-Speaking Television Networks (five-day moving averages)

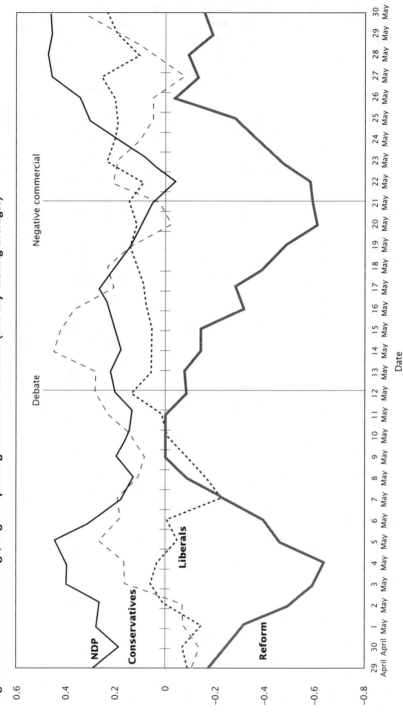

parties, at least when it came to the tone of the coverage. But this initial advantage was lost to the Conservatives in the week following the English-language debate. Then there was a period of stagnation during which the party received relatively little coverage and for the only time during the campaign, the coverage, such as it was, became less favourable than that given to the Conservatives and Liberals. This trend was finally reversed in the last days of the campaign, when the NDP once again enjoyed the most positive coverage.

If the NDP's campaign launch was well received by the media, that was not the case for Reform. Where the coverage of the other parties improved during the campaign's first days, Reform's deteriorated notably. The period leading up to the debates witnessed a recovery, which supports the view that Reform's campaign found its cruising speed after a difficult start. The leaders' debate seemed to mark a complete reversal in the tone of Reform's media coverage. Coverage became increasingly negative until 21 May, when the party released its negative commercial about Québécois political leaders. That marked another reversal in Reform's coverage, which gradually recovered (though staying negative) until election day.

The coverage of the Liberals in the two English-speaking networks exhibited quite a different dynamic. Whereas coverage in Quebec was almost continuously negative, the English-language coverage contained only one brief negative episode. As in Quebec, the beginning of the campaign was marked by fairly neutral coverage, but immediately after the English-language debate, the tone of Liberal TV coverage became positive. This positive trend continued, even as Jean Chrétien's controversial declaration about the majority required in a referendum on sovereignty reinforced the negative tone in Quebec.

Whereas the differences between the coverage of the Liberals by the English networks and Radio-Canada were fairly significant, that was not the case for the Conservatives. The Conservative campaign got off to a slower start on the English networks, but it took flight rapidly and received the most favourable coverage of all of the parties in the immediate aftermath of the debates. As in Quebec, though, there was a visible decline during the campaign's last two weeks. Once again, that change in the tone of the coverage supports the interpretation that Jean Charest peaked too soon.

Apart from the Conservatives, coverage on the English network did not seem to reflect as closely as the French network the ups and downs of the parties' campaigns. This suggests that the link between media coverage and the election results may have been closer in Quebec than elsewhere, a question we examine below.

The Turning Points

Reform's attack ad was one of three possible turning points in the campaign at which the actual media coverage should be scrutinized more closely. The other two episodes were the televised leaders' debates and Jean Chrétien's declaration on the simple majority. In Quebec, the Bloc's stumble across the starting line seems to have weakened the support of its voters and opened the way for the Conservatives to profit from Jean Charest's strong showing in the debates. Chrétien's declaration, though, enabled Gilles Duceppe to limit the damage. Outside Quebec, the leaders' debates in mid-campaign and then, in the last ten days, the intensified attention to national unity provoked by Reform's negative advertisement seem to have unsettled the voters, at least temporarily.

As Table 3.3 shows, the Conservatives benefited not only from favourable coverage after the debates, but also from intense media attention. Jean Charest's performance in the debates became not just the lead campaign story, but the lead story in the news. Media attention heightened once the polls, three or four days after the debates, started to confirm Charest's clear dominance over his opponents.[10]

The evolution of the tone of the news is revealing. Although the CBC did not declare Jean Charest the winner on 12 May, the three reports on the debate insisted that he was the only leader to have received spontaneous applause from the studio audience.[11] On CTV that same evening, it was confirmed that the voters who had been brought together to attend the debate had been more impressed with Jean Charest than by the other leaders. Reporter John Murphy noted 'Jean Charest was quick off the mark to impress these voters', and concluded, 'In the end, most agree on the winner.' In the following days, the coronation of Jean Charest as the winner was complete. Both the CBC and CTV presented voter reactions to reaffirm that Charest dominated the debates, and newspaper analyses and headlines supported this assertion.[12]

Table 3.3: Order of Parties in Television News before and after Debates

	Days Before		Days After	
	4–6	*1–3*	*1–3*	*4–6*
Quebec (Radio-Canada and TVA)				
Liberals	3.8	3.3	2.0	3.3
Conservatives	3.5	4.0	3.5	1.6
Bloc	3.8	2.8	1.6	1.2
English Canada (CBC and CTV)				
Liberals	4.3	4.5	2.6	4.0
Conservatives	5.5	5.7	4.3	1.3
NDP	6.3	4.6	6.0	3.8
Reform	7.1	3.0	3.9	4.3

Content analysis of the francophone data shows that the reaction of the French networks followed a similar pattern. At the beginning they were cautious, but they then became openly favourable towards Jean Charest. On the TVA network, the experts commenting on the night of the debate spoke of a 'three-way tie'. The next day, reporter Paul Larocque noted the success of the Conservative leader, and Normand Rhéaume described Jean Charest as 'the person who came out of the leaders' debate crowned in victory'. On Radio-Canada, Dominique Poirier opened the news item following the debate with the comment: 'As he did yesterday in English, Conservative leader Jean Charest imposed himself.' The next day Bernard Derome said, 'Jean Charest has become the enemy of all the parties.' Michel Cormier, in turn, gave a long commentary, in which he remarked that the Conservative leader had the 'wind in his sails', before concluding: 'at the beginning of the campaign, no one wanted to speak about national unity and no one talked about Jean Charest. Today these questions dominate the election, each in their own manner. It remains to be seen if Jean Charest's apparent momentum will be reflected in the polls and if he can survive the concerted attacks of the Liberal party and the Bloc Québécois.'

What is clear from these reactions is that Jean Charest benefited from a more-or-less ideal media climate in the days following the debate (see Lemert et al. 1991). Proclaimed the winner of both the French and English debates, he enjoyed exceptional visibility and very favourable media coverage. It is hardly surprising that, as the analysis of campaign dynamics demonstrated in Chapter 2, the Conservative party managed to register some gains in the days following the debate.

At the same time, the Reform party's negative commercial presents a paradox. Although the party was condemned by all of its opponents for having resorted to negative advertising, its media image improved in the days after the ad appeared. In tandem with that shift, vote intentions re-established themselves in Reform's favour.

A closer examination of CBC and CTV coverage for 23 and 24 May sheds some light on the commercial and its repercussions. Two features of the television coverage deserve noting: first, as expected, Reform's visibility grew considerably in the days after the commercial was broadcast.[13] Second, Reform's isolation became an advantage. This is particularly clear in the way CTV treated the news. In its first report on the commercial on 23 May, CTV placed the emphasis largely on the very strong reaction of the other leaders towards Preston Manning. The remark that opened journalist Roger Smith's report is revealing: 'The unity issue turned up to a dangerously high pitch when the prime minister accused Preston Manning of extremism.' The next day's reports went on to establish the contrast between the vociferousness of the other leaders' attacks and the relatively favourable reception of the commercial in certain segments of the electorate. It is possible that the sight of all the federal party leaders (themselves Quebeckers, save for the NDP's Alexa McDonough) condemning the Reform commercial produced a boomerang effect, albeit a temporary one, much as we saw in Chapter 2.

The coverage by Quebec television of Jean Chrétien's declaration about a future referendum is a simpler story (see Table 3.4). It resembles the coverage of both the Bloc campaign gaffes and the leaders' debates in two respects: its visibility and the nearly unanimous interpretation of its consequences. In the days following the declaration the Liberals found themselves in the spotlight, a pattern that also characterized the print media.[14] The interpretation of this incident was remarkably similar among media outlets. Michèle Viroly, opening Radio-Canada's 26 May newscast, described the declaration as 'the Bloc's new warhorse'. Daniel L'Heureux, who was covering the Bloc Québécois's campaign, argued, 'it was the view that the BQ hoped to draw [from Jean Chrétien] since the start of the campaign. Gilles Duceppe sank his teeth right in as it involves the issue he needed to relaunch his campaign.' The next day L'heureux concluded, 'the Bloc was given fresh impetus by Jean Chrétien's proposals'. TVA provided a very similar interpretation with newsreader Sophie Thibault affirming that Jean Chrétien's declaration had 'revived the sovereignists' (26 May), and journalist Paul Larocque concluding that Jean Chrétien's declaration was 'what the Bloc was waiting for to whip up the sovereignist activists'.[15]

Jean Chrétien's declaration on the simple majority amounted to a nearly ideal media opportunity for the Bloc Québécois. The evolution of the tone of the Bloc's media coverage is revealing and dramatic; the tone went from -.34 in the six days preceding the declaration to +.17 in the first three days following, and it continued to move up to +.36 in the three days after that.

Table 3.4: Order of Parties in Television News before and after Jean Chrétien's Declaration on Simple Majority

	Days Before		Days After	
	4–6	1–3	1–3	4–6
Quebec (Radio-Canada and TVA)				
Liberals	4.3	5.2	2.8	2.4
Conservatives	4.9	3.9	5.0	4.0
Bloc	4.6	3.1	3.5	3.9
English Canada (CBC and CTV)				
Liberals	5.3	6.7	2.9	1.5
Conservatives	5.0	1.5	4.4	3.0
NDP	3.5	4.5	5.3	6.7
Reform	3.3	2.5	5.3	2.3

The Impact on the Vote

Is it possible to uncover a link between the media coverage and the election results or at least to trace a parallel between media coverage and vote intentions? The answer to these questions is not clear, especially outside Quebec. The party that received the most favourable media coverage overall, namely the NDP, made no gains during the campaign. On the other hand, Reform increased its support, despite receiving the least favourable coverage of any party. And the Liberal party saw its coverage improve at the time of the debates, though its support later bled away to the Conservative party.

Other clues, though, place these findings in a different light. The Liberals largely lost ground in the first part of the campaign, a period during which the Conservatives' media advantage over the Liberals on the English networks was constant and significant. When the Liberals' coverage became more favourable than the Conservatives' at the end of the campaign, they were able to retake part of this lost ground. There are also parallels in the evolution of the Conservatives' coverage on the English networks and the evolution of Conservative vote intentions. The Conservative gains in the post-debate period coincided with a clear media advantage, and the erosion of a significant part of those gains corresponded to a very clear downturn in their coverage. The link may not be very systematic, but all in all, the dynamics of the English-language coverage seem more or less synchronized with the dynamics of vote intentions, the pattern being clearest for the relative fortunes of the Liberals and the Conservatives.

The picture in Quebec is clearer still. The very negative coverage of the Bloc corresponded to a very significant decrease in its support early in the campaign, and the change in tone, after Chrétien's declaration on simple majority, closely mirrored the party's recovery. A similar conclusion seems to apply to the Conservatives. The Conservative gains in the first part of the campaign and, even more, the gains after the televised debates, closely followed the evolution of the party's media advantage. Likewise, the party's decline in the last two weeks coincided with the loss of this advantage to the Bloc. The Liberal case is less clear-cut, but it is also consistent with the big picture: Liberal vote intentions declined only slightly during the campaign despite constantly negative coverage, an outcome that underscores once again a fundamental point, namely, the loyalty of Liberal supporters.

Two pieces of evidence suggest a possible influence of media coverage on the vote in Quebec. The data in Table 3.5 show a marked difference in support for the Bloc and the Conservatives between those who made their decision before and during the campaign, a pattern that suggests that the portrayal by the media of Jean Charest's and Gilles Duceppe's performance had important consequences for their parties. Figures 3.5 and 3.6, which show when these gains and losses took place, provide further evidence of the media's influence

Table 3.5: Reported Voter and Time of Decision, Quebec

	Liberals	*Conservatives*	*Bloc*
Before the campaign	41	9	48
During the campaign	38	28	28

Note: Question about timing was: 'When did you decide that you were going to vote [reported vote]? Was it before the campaign began, before the TV debates, during or just after the TV debates, in the last two weeks of the campaign, or election day?' 51 per cent of voters reported having made their choice before the campaign began and 49 per cent during the campaign or on election day.

in Quebec. Whereas the voting intentions remained stable throughout the campaign, the observed shifts being essentially random, the pattern for voters who made up their minds during the campaign closely followed the parties' highs and lows during the campaign as depicted in the media, namely the Liberal losses, the Bloc's disastrous start and *in extremis* recovery, as well as the Conservative surge right after the debates and partial decline later.

Conclusion

The media coverage of the parties in the 1997 election presents a series of expected and less expected patterns. One intriguing finding is that media coverage does not seem to have been particularly negative, especially on the English networks. It would be difficult to argue that the media fed Canadians' cynicism towards either the electoral process in general or the political parties in particular during the last campaign. This conclusion is surprising, perhaps, given the accusations of opportunism launched against the government concerning the timing of the election, and given the contentious nature of such debates during the campaign as the Liberals' broken promise to abolish the GST and Reform's hard-hitting attacks on the notion of distinct society. Despite all this, the tone of the coverage was not pervasively negative.

Nevertheless, media coverage was not uniformly positive either. In fact, the parties received very different treatment in the media during the campaign. The contrast between the two parties at the opposite ends of Canada's ideological spectrum is the most striking: the NDP received very favourable coverage but suffered from low visibility, while the situation was reversed for Reform. The Liberals reaped a slight incumbency bonus in terms of visibility, especially at the beginning of the campaign, and they enjoyed relatively neutral coverage overall, especially on the English networks. The Bloc's coverage experienced the widest fluctuations; it moved from one extreme to the other over the course of the campaign. Finally, the Conservatives seem to have made gains from the

Figure 3.5: Evolution of Vote Intentions of People Who Decided before Campaign Began, Quebec (seven-day moving averages)

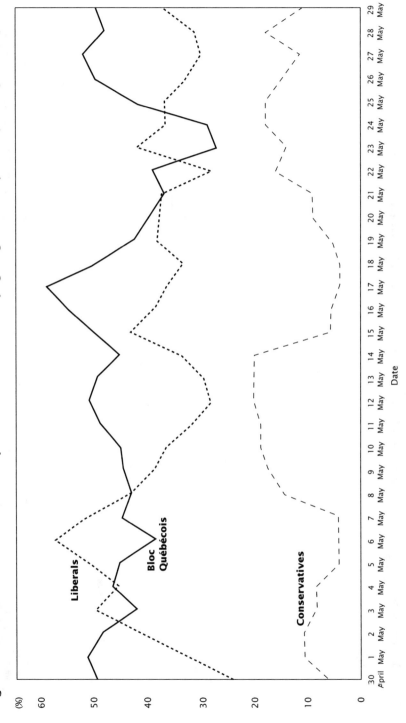

Figure 3.6: Evolution of Vote Intentions of People Who Decided during Campaign, Quebec (seven-day moving averages)

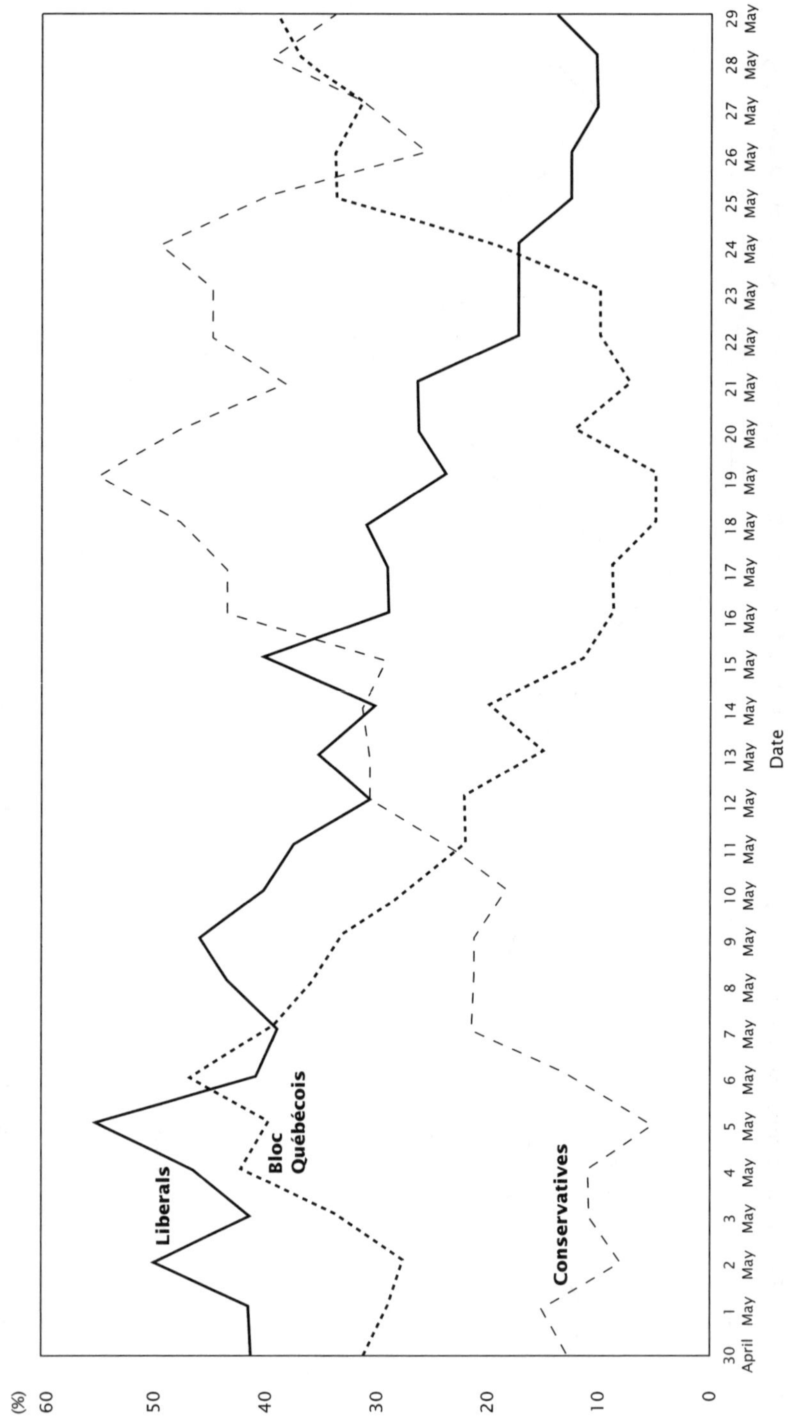

most favourable media environment during the campaign, receiving both significant visibility and favourable coverage.

These findings raise two questions. First, why did the very positive tone of the media coverage of the NDP not translate into increased support for this party? And second, why was the link between coverage and the vote apparently closer in Quebec than elsewhere? The apparent NDP paradox perhaps reflects the influence of another variable, namely, visibility. The NDP coverage may have been more sympathetic, but it was also less intense than that accorded the other parties. This does not explain, though, why the other parties that also received less coverage than the Liberals were less affected by this difficulty. Here, the explanation probably lies in the fact that these parties each benefited from periods of very intense coverage. In other words, they each had their 'hour in the spotlight' of favourable or intense coverage. The NDP, by contrast, was never at the centre of any dramatic events; the same applied to the Conservatives at the end of the campaign. The effect of campaign events adds to the complexity of the link between media coverage and the evolution of vote intentions, and perhaps explains the somewhat ambiguous nature of this link during the 1997 election.

The stronger influence of the media in Quebec is perhaps attributable to the salience of the issue of leadership in the election. In 1997 the leaders of the three main parties in Quebec were from that province and two of them were relatively unknown quantities at the outset of the campaign. Outside of Quebec, on the other hand, the battle was among two 'old' leaders (Chrétien and Manning), one 'invisible' leader (McDonough), and only one fresh face (Charest). From this perspective, the closer link between coverage and the vote in Quebec seems plausible, given the centrality of leaders in the vote (McAllister 1996) and the media's ability to influence voters' opinion about leaders in general and about emerging leaders in particular (Mendelsohn and Nadeau 1999; Zaller and Hunt 1994, 1995).

Media coverage of the campaign as such was also different in Quebec. It was not just that media coverage in Quebec was more negative; the English and French language networks did not always react in the same way to the same events. The televised debates were an exception, providing the Conservatives with the same media advantage on both the English and French networks. This was not the case for Jean Chrétien's declaration on the required majority, which hurt the Liberals in Quebec—and provided the Bloc with its only period of media domination—without damaging the party on the English networks.

Above and beyond these differences, though, the coverage of the parties on the French and English networks alike generally seems to have followed the highs and lows of their campaigns, and some parallels can be drawn with the evolution of their electoral support. These parallels, stronger in Quebec but nevertheless visible on the English networks, point to the links between campaign dynamics and media coverage.

Campaign dynamics depend on what messages political parties send out and on how the media report those messages. How those messages are received and interpreted depend on the citizens themselves. And one major factor that shapes citizens' reactions to these messages is their own ideological frameworks. Ideological orientations qualify as yet another system-wide factor, and it is to this issue that we now turn.

Chapter 4

Ideological Landscape

Some observers suggest that the striking contrast between the outcomes of the 1988 and 1993 federal election indicates that the Canadian party system may have come adrift during this interlude. But the weakening of support bases for old parties and the emergence of new ones are hardly unique to Canada: these are recurring themes throughout many advanced industrial states (Betz and Immerfall 1998; Dalton et al. 1984; Kaase and Newton 1995; King 1987; Kitschelt 1994). A variety of explanations have been supplied for this trend. One suggests that the fluidity of partisan loyalties is a result of a combination of socio-structural and ideological changes (Knutsen and Scarbrough 1995; Müller-Rommel 1990; Offe 1987). In Europe, for example, these transformations have been associated with the emergence of new ideological polarities: new lefts have emerged to challenge old lefts and new rights are challenging old rights (Dalton and Keuchler 1990; Kitschelt 1997; Rucht 1991).

There is no question that Canadians have experienced the same kinds of socio-structural change. Moreover, there is evidence that since the early 1980s Canadians have also experienced the same kinds of value changes that accompany those shifts (Nevitte 1996). It is surely plausible, then, that the joint effects of these forces could well be reordering the links between Canadian voters and parties as they have done in Europe. This chapter investigates the possibility that changes in the ideological landscape may help to account for the ways that Canadians voted in 1997.

Ideological Structures

The power of ideological outlooks to shape party systems depends on certain conditions, one of which is the extent to which, and how, value orientations are organized within a population. If the ideological orientations of Canadians are incoherently organized and lack structure, it would be difficult for political parties to win many votes by trying to appeal to such an inchoate melange of beliefs. Any investigation of the potential for ideological beliefs to shape electoral choices, then, has to begin by addressing a fundamental question: to what extent and in what way are Canadian ideological outlooks, or deep dispositions, systematically organized?

The second condition has to do with whether, and how, citizens' orientations resonate with the political parties. Ideological outlooks may matter to individuals in abstract or private ways, but that in itself is no guarantee that voters will refer to their ideological outlooks as a guide to help them make choices between competing political parties on election day. Private values have to be mobilized and connected to the public domain, and in this respect political parties themselves are a vital part of the equation. It is unlikely that ideology could be decisive in how voters make their decision if the parties make no attempt to appeal to the voters' ideological outlooks, or if all parties end up appealing to the same ones.

One useful means of determining to what extent, and how, Canadian ideological outlooks are coherently organized is factor analysis.[1] As it happens, the results are fairly clear (see Appendix B). The wording of the questions included in the analysis is reported elsewhere (see 'Description of Variables' in Appendix C). The most important initial finding is that Canadians do have coherently structured value orientations and the content of each of the dimensions is meaningful. Two different sorts of dimensions emerge: one concerns what might be called basic outlooks, and the other concerns communal outlooks.

Basic Outlooks

The first and most powerful dimension to emerge is most aptly labelled *cynicism* because it combines standard indicators of efficacy (government does not care what people like me think; those elected to Parliament soon lose touch with the people) together with responses to questions about lying by politicians and the failure of political parties to keep promises. This cynicism factor is identical for respondents both outside and inside Quebec; the items within the factor are ordered in the same way, and it explains a very substantial 23 per cent of the variance in the structure (see Appendix B).

The second dimension identified embraces different aspects of what might be called *moral traditionalism*; it captures a cluster of orientations that are sometimes referred to as traditional 'family values'. These include beliefs about women's place in the family, views of marriage and children, as well as attitudes towards abortion. Once again, there are striking similarities between English Canada and Quebec respondents when it comes to the content and explanatory power of this dimension; the only difference is in the order of the first two components of the factor.

The third factor, which captures a fundamental set of economic beliefs, reflects attitudes towards *free enterprise*. This dimension taps orientations towards business (businesses make money, everyone benefits; feeling positive about business) as well as perspectives about who is to blame when people 'don't get ahead'. Once again, the content and explanatory power of this dimension are identical in Quebec and the rest of the country.

The similarities between the Quebec results and those from the rest of the country are particularly striking given that the exploratory factor analyses were conducted separately for these two groups of respondents. The content, order, and explanatory power of some of these outlooks are almost identical. But that does not mean that Quebec and English Canada share the same beliefs and are located at the same point of the dimension indicated by the factor analysis.

Communal Outlooks

Variations between the ideological structures of those inside and outside of Quebec become more evident when it comes to the second set of factors that tap different kinds of communal orientations. Three communal dimensions emerge outside of Quebec but there are four in Quebec (see Appendix B).

With the communal orientations, the place to start is with the Quebec results and here the most powerful dimension to emerge reflects views regarding *sovereignty*. Notice that this factor alone explains an impressive 20 per cent of the variance in the Quebec factor solution. Respondents outside of Quebec were asked a series of questions about their views on accommodating Quebec. These items cluster together to form a distinct and stable dimension that is in some respects the analogue of the sovereignty factor in Quebec. The *Quebec* factor reflects positive or negative feelings about Quebec, that is whether more or less should be done for Quebec and whether Quebec should or should not be recognized as a distinct society.

There are other differences between Quebec and the rest of Canada. For Quebec, the two other stable orientations to emerge are referred to as *outgroups* and *aboriginal peoples*. A comparison between the items within these two Quebec dimensions and the *outgroups* factor outside Quebec indicates that a similar group of items—those concerned with race and aboriginal peoples—are structured in slightly different ways. Outside Quebec, for example, the *outgroups* factor is the most powerful of all of the communal orientations, accounting for more than 26 per cent of the variance in that structure. But the content of that factor includes two questions that have to do with aboriginal peoples, and one question about how much people think should be done for racial minorities. Quebec's *outgroup* factor is somewhat different; it clusters orientations towards race (two items) with one for immigrants. The *outgroup* factor for respondents outside of Quebec appears as a slightly different combination of the items making up the *outgroups* and *aboriginal peoples* factors in Quebec. The remaining factor, which is identical for respondents inside or outside of Quebec, has to do with continental orientations. This *Canada/US* factor is the weakest of all (8 per cent and 13 per cent of variance explained respectively), but background analysis shows that it is none the less a stable dimension.

The Ideological Distribution of Voters in 1997

The fact that Canadian values are structured coherently and meaningfully along clearly identifiable dimensions means that ideology at least had the potential to matter to the outcome of the 1997 election. What needs to be determined next is whether citizens' orientations on these ideological dimensions were distributed systematically in ways that resonate with distinct partisan positions.

The first step in the analysis involves creating scales from the items contained in each factor, then we shall be able to see if citizens voting for different political parties locate themselves in similar or different places on the scales representing the various dimensions.[2] Factor analysis is a particularly useful tool for examining responses to large numbers of survey questions. But single questions can also reveal dimensions that may be important to people's ideological outlooks. Indeed, the election surveys contained two such questions, one concerning attitudes towards women and the other, orientations to regional alienation. Both are potentially important ideological indicators, and these two dimensions are included in the following analysis.

Figure 4.1 summarizes a great deal of information about where supporters of the various parties are located on the standardized scales representing each of the eight dimensions considered. The mean scores of various party supporters on each scale is used to show the location of party supporters and the solid black sphere indicates the location of the median voter. Figure 4.1 reports these locations for voters outside Quebec in 1997.

There are a number of noteworthy findings. First, on the cynicism dimension, nearly all voters are distributed towards the right end of the scale, indicating that most voters in 1997 were quite cynical about the political classes and the responsiveness of government. Reform voters expressed the highest levels of cynicism and Liberal voters the least, but that finding comes as little surprise. Those supporting the party of government are usually somewhat more forgiving when it comes to evaluating the performance of the government of the day.

A second finding is important from a strategic point of view; there is evidence of a relatively consistent pattern. On seven out of the eight dimensions examined, supporters of the Reform party occupy an ideological position at one end of these ideological dimensions. The only exception to that pattern turns out to be the free-enterprise dimension, and in that instance, the locations of Reform and Conservative voters are almost indistinguishable from each other. But notice too that, on this dimension, the mean location of Liberal voters is also quite close to those of Reform and Conservative voters, and the location of the median voter is slightly to the left of the average Liberal voter.

Third, there is also something of a pattern at the opposite end of most of these same ideological dimensions. On six of the eight dimensions, New Democrats are the outliers at the other end. Together, New Democrats and Reformers occupy the opposite ends on five of the eight dimensions. In nearly every instance, the relative positions of Reformers and New Democrats correspond to what one would expect given conventional understandings about the left-right distributions of parties and supporters. Reformers are highest on moral traditionalism, regional alienation, and cynicism while being the least sympathetic to Quebec, outgroups, and women. New Democrats, by contrast, are the most critical of free enterprise and close relations with the United States while being the most sympathetic towards outgroups, Quebec, and women.

A fourth finding concerns the relative locations of Liberal and Conservative supporters. On seven of the eight dimensions, Liberal and Conservative supporters occupy contiguous positions on these dimensions. Indeed, on six of these dimensions—moral traditionalism, free enterprise, outgroups, Quebec, Canada/US, and women—the mean locations of supporters of these two parties are virtually identical. That finding, perhaps, reflects the fact that the two parties work from the principle that has guided brokerage parties, that is, to search for the ideological middle ground, with the result that two (or more) brokerage parties can end up occupying similar ideological terrain. Regardless

Figure 4.1: Party Location along Ideological Dimensions, Outside Quebec, 1997

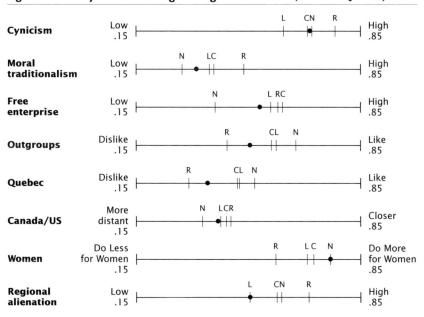

N = New Democrats   L = Liberals   C = Progressive Conservatives   R = Reform
● = Median Voter outside Quebec

of whether these parties consciously pursued these kinds of brokerage strategies, it turns out that supporters of the party of the old right, the Conservatives, appear to be ideologically closer to the Liberals than to their rivals on the right, Reform. As we shall see (Chapter 11), this finding shapes our understanding of what the future of the Canadian political right might be.

Figure 4.2 summarizes comparable results for Quebec voters, and there are two general pieces of evidence worth noting here. First, the ideological locations of Bloc voters are closest to the Quebec median voter on the majority of the dimensions considered. In fact, in three cases—free enterprise, outgroups, and Canada/US—the location of Bloc supporters is almost identical to that of the median voter. Furthermore, on a number of occasions where this is not the case, for example, moral traditionalism and women, there was almost an ideological consensus among supporters of all three parties.

But there are also two important exceptions to this general pattern, and each represents a different face of relations between Quebec and the rest of Canada. First, there was substantial disagreement between Liberal, Conservative, and Bloc supporters on the sovereignty dimension. Predictably, Bloc voters were

Figure 4.2: Party Location along Ideological Dimensions, Quebec, 1997

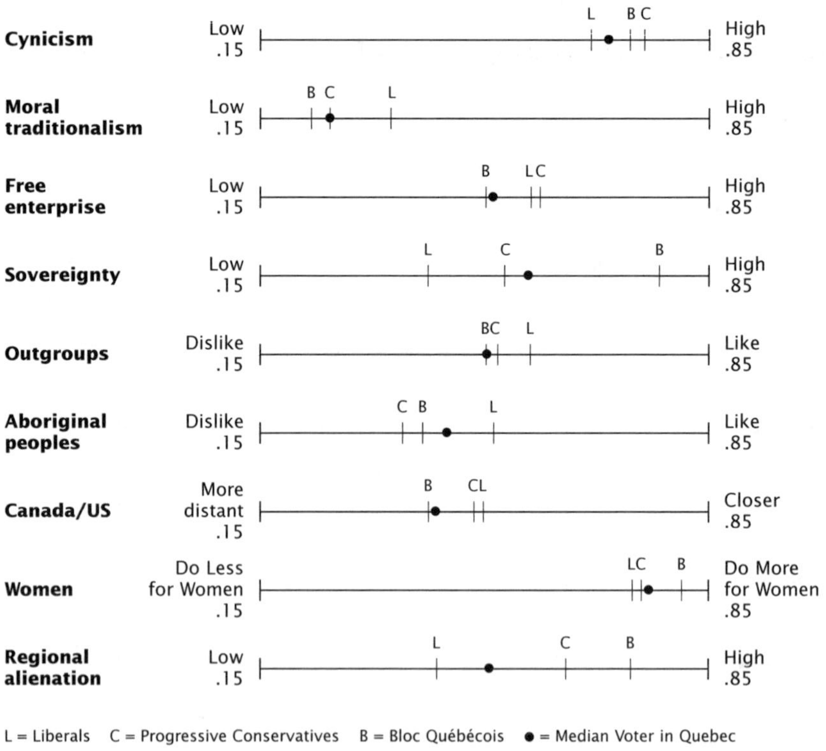

L = Liberals   C = Progressive Conservatives   B = Bloc Québécois   ● = Median Voter in Quebec

located towards the 'high' end of the polarity on the sovereignty dimension, Liberals occupied the opposite polarity, and Conservatives came closest to the median position. Second, a similarly diffuse set of beliefs is also evident when it comes to regional alienation. Bloc voters are located at the high end of the regional-alienation dimension; they were far more likely than their Liberal or Conservative counterparts to believe that Quebec gets worse treatment from the federal government than the other provinces.

The contrast between the relative consensus on most ideological dimensions and the absence of consensus on the two dimensions that reflect outlooks towards Quebec and Ottawa underscores a central point: namely, political parties in Quebec may have had little to gain by differentiating themselves from the others on most ideological dimensions, but they may have a great deal to gain and lose by differentiating themselves on sovereignty and regional alienation. And on the sovereignty dimension, Liberal and Conservative voters shared the federalist terrain whereas the Bloc voters were mostly the lone occupants of the sovereignist terrain.

These results suggest that the two preconditions for ideological voting were in place in 1997. First, voters both inside and outside of Quebec did exhibit a coherent structure to their ideological beliefs. Second, there was some resonance between ideological outlooks and partisan choice. Which particular outlooks may have mattered most to voter choices remains to be determined; that issue is taken up and placed in larger context in the second part of this book. The central point for now is that those ideological outlooks had the potential to shape partisan choices.

Ideological Change?

We began with the observation that ideological change might well help to account for the fluidity in Canada's partisan landscape between 1988 and 1997. Is there any evidence indicating that ideological change has taken place? Certainly, it is not difficult to cobble together qualitative indications suggesting that Canadian values have changed over the last 15 years or so. And this change might well be interpreted as some sort of 'move to the right'. For example, the strength of the Conservatives in the early 1980s grew in tandem with the emerging new rights associated with the Thatcher and Reagan years in Britain and the United States (Krieger 1986). By enthusiastically sharing the stage with the icons of the new right in the Anglo-American world, Prime Minister Mulroney seemed to be endorsing the same kind of political agenda. The successes of the Reform party in the 1993 and 1997 federal elections may similarly attest to the growing appeal of a more sharply defined new right. After all, Reform's rise coincided with the shift away from the ideals of the welfare state and towards those of the minimalist state, and the political rhetoric accompanying that shift has been repeatedly echoed by successful

Conservative parties in a number of provincial elections (Blizzard 1995). Then again, there are also indications that the Liberal party may have gained and retained power by moving to the right with its own policy platforms, for example, by cutting social spending and attacking deficits.

To those qualitative observations can be added some evidence from public-opinion polls. The data are somewhat sketchy, but they paint a plausible picture. One element common to new-right thinking is a declining sympathy towards minorities of various sorts. Another strand of new-right beliefs is a weakening support for a cluster of welfare issues. The 1988, 1993, and 1997 Canadian Election surveys contained identical, or very similar, questions about feelings towards a variety of groups, including people on welfare, aboriginal peoples, immigrants, and minorities. People on the 'left' are usually seen to be more sympathetic than those on the 'right' to these kinds of groups, and public opinion data suggest that sympathy for all four groups declined over the course of the decade. One conclusion that could be quickly drawn from these findings is that this dwindling of sympathy for different kinds of outgroups was precisely the kind of ideological shift that swelled the ranks of the Reform party. But when the evidence is sifted more carefully, a slightly more complicated picture emerges. Survey evidence does indicate, for example, that Reform party supporters are consistently the least likely to want more immigrants to come to the country. But the far more telling point is that the progressively toughening attitudes towards groups such as these were shared by voters from *all* of the political parties.

Together, the success of parties of the right, the changes in public political rhetoric, the Liberals' drift away from social supports and towards deficit cutting, and assorted public-opinion evidence all support the interpretation that Canadians' ideological orientations have moved to the right in recent years. But these strands of evidence are somewhat narrow in scope, the data are not always directly comparable, and this kind of evidence has to be interpreted very cautiously. It certainly falls short of conclusive proof. What is required is a more systematic probing of the available evidence, some assessment, using directly comparable evidence, of shifts, and a deeper exploration of whether, and how, any changes in ideological outlook are expressed in electoral choices.

It turns out that nearly all the items that make up six of the eight dimensions identified in the factor analysis are contained in both the 1997 and 1993 Canadian Election surveys (see Appendix B for the list of items in the modified ideological scales). This means that it is possible to create identical scales representing each of these dimensions for both 1993 and 1997. And from those scales it is also possible to determine whether there was any significant change in the voting public's ideological outlook between 1993 and 1997 on these central dimensions.

There are some key findings that come from the cross-time findings. Cynicism was extremely high in 1993 and fell somewhat by 1997. More Canadians expressed higher levels of moral traditionalism in 1997 than in 1993. There was also a significant increase in support for free enterprise while support for outgroups eroded somewhat. Sympathy towards Quebec fell quite sharply during the same period and attitudes towards the United States also became cooler. What is impressive about these findings is not so much the scale of the changes but that they are additional evidence consistent with the conclusion that Canadians did move to the right between 1993 and 1997. Demonstrating aggregate change is one thing. The more central question for the present purposes is whether, and how, any of these aggregate ideological shifts are reflected in the partisan landscape.

The ideological outlook of voters can be illustrated graphically by employing the very same scales and by determining where supporters of the various parties were located in ideological space in both 1993 and 1997. Figure 4.3 simultaneously locates respondents on two dimensions that are often associated with the new right—an enthusiasm for free enterprise combined with support for traditional family mores (Isaac 1990).

A diagonal line drawn from the lower left corner of the graph to the upper right corner would roughly capture conventional understandings of left-right orientations. The results reported in Figure 4.3 plainly show that party supporters

Figure 4.3: Location of Party Supporters: Moral Traditionalism by Free Enterprise, 1993–1997

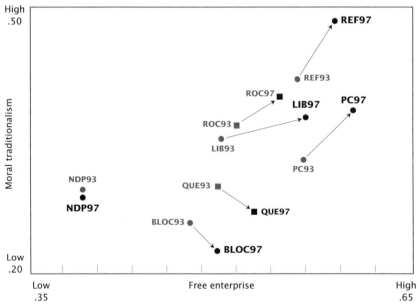

Note: The figure reports the mean scores of the standardized ideological scales by vote. Data for the NDP, Liberal Party, Progressive Conservative Party, and Reform Party are drawn from the non-Quebec sample. The aggregate mean scores for non-Quebec and Quebec in 1993 and 1997 are also reported. See Appendix B for the wording of the questions.

'moved' in value space between 1993 and 1997. The light grey dots with the '93' suffix show where party supporters were located in 1993, and the black dots show where they were located in 1997. The grey and black squares indicate the median location of all voters in Quebec and the rest of Canada in 1993 and 1997 respectively.

First, the data show that voters outside of Quebec moved on an upward and rightward trajectory between 1993 and 1997. Quebec voters became more favourable towards free enterprise, but also less traditional in their moral outlooks. Notice too that there are shifts in partisan locations. For instance, Reformers and Conservatives both moved to the right in 1997; both travelled along an upward and rightward trajectory. Significantly, so did supporters of the Liberal party. In fact, on the free-enterprise dimension, Liberal supporters in 1997 occupied virtually the same ideological space as Reformers and Conservatives had occupied in 1993. Bloc supporters also became slightly more pro-free enterprise between 1993 and 1997.

The other striking result is the stability of the ideological location of the New Democrats on these two dimensions, a finding that is consistent with the idea that the party is one of principle. In 1997 New Democrats staked out exactly the same value space as they did in 1993. One consequence of all of these shifts on these ideological dimensions is that the ideological gap between the traditional left and the traditional centre, the Liberals, widened between 1993 and 1997.

Two other ideological dimensions are illustrated in Figure 4.4: cynicism and attitudes towards outgroups. Recall that cynicism was the most powerful dimension structuring orientations of citizens outside of Quebec (Appendix B). However, it turns out that the presence or absence of cynicism has nothing to do with where people place themselves on the left-right ideological scale.[3] Orientations to outgroups, though, are connected to left-right ideological locations in the expected direction; that is, those on the left are more sympathetic to outgroups.[4]

Figure 4.4 provides a striking illustration of the uniqueness of Reform party supporters on these two dimensions. In 1997 Reform party supporters were clearly by far the most cynical about politics; they were also by far the most severe in their views towards outgroups. As it happens, these views also turned out to be remarkably stable. In these two respects, Reform supporters did not change one iota between 1993 and 1997. For the other voters, especially supporters of the Liberals, the Bloc, and the NDP, the most noteworthy changes have to do with falling levels of cynicism. Given the remarkably high levels of cynicism evident in 1993 and the declines in cynicism on the part of the Bloc and the NDP between 1993 and 1997, this downward shift might be construed as a return to normal. After all, the 1993 federal election was held at a time when Canadians had fresh memories of the troubled departure of former Prime Minister Brian Mulroney, the least popular political leader on record.

Two other findings are worth noting from Figure 4.4. The graphic plainly illustrates the size of the gap, indeed the chasm, separating the two parties of the right. On these two dimensions, it is the Liberals, the Bloc, and the Progressive Conservatives that occupy the middle ground. That middle ground might be characterized as somewhat fluid, but it is a middle ground none the less. What distinguishes the parties of the right is not their support for free enterprise, but rather, according to figures 4.3 and 4.4, cynicism, severe attitudes towards outgroups, and family values. Once again, Reform supporters sit at one extreme, and the New Democrats at the other.

Attitudes towards outgroups is one of the communal orientations that coherently structure Canadians' orientations. The other two are how Canadians outside of Quebec view Quebec, and opinions about Canada/US relations. Of these, it is views about Quebec that turn out to be the most powerful. The most significant finding reported in Figure 4.5 has to do with the 1993–7 changes in attitudes towards Quebec. The changes between 1993 and 1997 reflect both convergence and divergence. The Liberals moved towards the Conservative position on Quebec, while the Conservatives moved towards the Liberal position on Canada/US. Between 1993 and 1997 supporters of the Progressive Conservatives and the Liberals converged to occupy essentially the same

Figure 4.4: Location of Party Supporters: Cynicism by Outgroups, 1993–1997

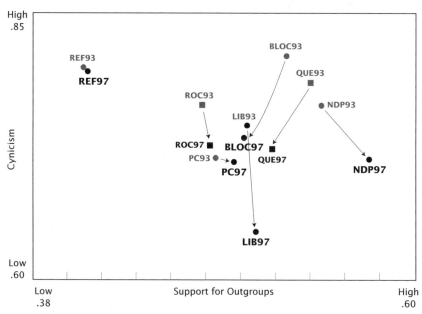

Note: The figure reports the mean scores of the standardized ideological scales by vote. Data for the NDP, Liberal Party, Progressive Conservative Party, and Reform Party are drawn from the sample outside Quebec. The 1997 ideological scales are modified to correspond to the variables in the 1993 scales. The aggregate mean scores for non-Quebec and Quebec in 1993 and 1997 are also reported. See Appendix B for the wording of the questions.

ideological space. But the differences between supporters of the parties on the right widened as Reform party supporters became significantly less sympathetic to Quebec.

Conclusion

There is a growing body of evidence indicating that in many advanced industrial states, ideological changes can have a profound impact on party systems and on the choices voters make. The extent to which ideology matters undoubtedly depends upon a variety of factors, including institutional conditions, the scope and scale of ideological change, how these factors jointly interact with socio-structural dynamics, and how political parties themselves respond to the shifts. Political parties can ride these shifts or they can resist or ignore them. The Canadian record of socio-structural and value change mirrors West European experiences, so it is plausible that value changes in Canada may have reverberated in similar ways and with comparable effect.

Figure 4.5: Location of Party Supporters: Canada/US by Quebec, 1993–1997, Outside Quebec

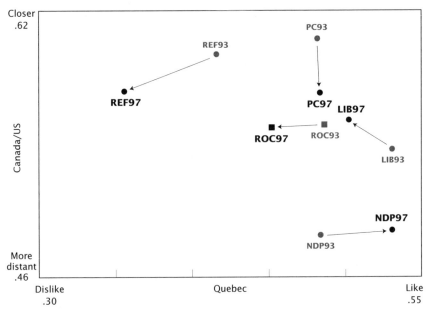

Note: The figure reports the mean scores of the standardized ideological scales by vote. The 1997 ideological scales are modified to correspond to the variables in the 1993 scales. The aggregate mean scores for the non-Quebec sample in 1993 and 1997 are also reported. See Appendix B for the wording of the questions.

This chapter has presented some evidence that the conditions for ideological considerations to matter in electoral choices seemed to be in place in 1997. To a significant extent, Canadians' attitudes towards their social, economic, and political worlds were organized in coherent ways and hence were available to appeals by political parties. Party supporters seemed to locate themselves in the kinds of ideological spaces that suggest that voters were responding to party appeals. Furthermore, there is evidence of ideological movement in directions that approximated the kinds of changes in policy and rhetoric of the political parties between 1993 and the campaign of 1997. Collectively, these findings add further weight to the interpretation that the Canadian ideological landscape experienced a shift to the right, at least in the areas that have been explored above. It is not always clear that Canadians themselves always interpret these shifts expressly through the ideological vocabulary of 'left' and 'right'.[5] One reason is that the content of left and right is sometimes vague and subject to change. Furthermore, it is not at all clear that every relevant ideological dimension can be readily folded into, or captured by, the single dimension 'left' and 'right'.[6] Added to this is the difficulty of clearly identifying the boundaries separating the 'new' and 'old' lefts as well as the 'new' and 'old' rights.[7]

Ideology, however, is but one element among many that could have affected voters in the 1997 election. The other questions to be addressed in the following chapters concern the importance of ideology in relation to such other factors as leadership, economic conditions, strategic considerations, and issues.

Chapter 5

Low Turnout:
A Sign of Disaffection?

In the 1997 federal election, just 67 per cent of eligible voters cast a ballot. In other words, one elector out of three decided not to vote, and that qualified as the lowest voter turnout at a federal election since the 66 per cent turnout in 1925. Why was turnout so low in 1997? Was it a reflection of the widespread political malaise that we have just documented? Perhaps turnout is declining because disaffection with politics and politicians is growing. Then again it just might be that voters felt the 1997 election did not raise any important issue. Why bother to vote if nothing much seems to be at stake? Another possibility is that citizens may have reasoned that there was little doubt that the Liberals would form the government and so whether one voted or not would not matter much in the end.

Certainly the 67 per cent turnout was the lowest since 1925, but how much lower than usual was it? Just how serious a problem was voter turnout in 1997? To answer those questions, we have to look at the 1997 turnout in relation to other Canadian federal elections. And from that vantage point the relevant question is what accounts for variations in turnout from one election to another. Another pertinent question is how voter turnout in Canada compares to that in other democracies. And does the evidence from these other cases provide useful clues that might explain the varying participation rates in Canada?

The third part of the chapter delves into the survey evidence more deeply to identify the characteristics of those who did not vote in 1997. Is non-voting evenly distributed within the population? Or are there some identifiable groups that are more likely than others to abstain? If abstainers are lodged in a part of society that is growing, that might explain a decline in voting levels. For example, it is entirely possible that the youngest generation feels the most alienated from traditional electoral politics and so turnout may have dropped the most in that generation.

How Low Is 67%?

Average turnout in Canadian federal elections since 1945 stands at about 74 per cent (see Figure 5.1).[1] That is slightly lower than in electoral democracies at large, which is 77 per cent (Blais and Dobrzynska 1998). But perhaps the most useful comparison is with other established democracies, excluding countries where voting is compulsory and the United States and Switzerland, where turnout is exceptionally low for very specific reasons that do not apply to Canada.[2] Among established 'voluntary-voting' democracies, average voter turnout stands at about 82 per cent (Black 1991). By that standard, then, voter turnout in Canada is eight points below the average. Why?

There are two main reasons. The first is the electoral system. In plurality electoral systems, like our own, turnout tends to be about three points lower than in systems that use proportional representation (Blais and Dobrzynska 1998). The second reason is that turnout tends to be higher in small, densely populated countries (Blais and Dobrzynska 1998), and Canada's population is thinly dispersed over a very large territory.

That said, it is clear that voter participation does not depend on just these two factors; turnout varies from one election to another, though not usually very widely. Of the 17 elections since 1945, turnout varied between 73 and 77 per cent in ten cases. The three highest turnout levels were in the three successive elections held between 1958 and 1963. The three lowest (leaving aside 1997) were in the only election held in the winter (in February 1980) and in the only two held in the summer (in August 1953 and July 1974).[3]

These variations from one election to another can be explained by two factors, the first of which is the season. That is, the evidence[4] indicates that voter turnout is six points lower when an election is held in the summer or winter. Average turnout in elections that took place in the spring or fall is 75 per cent. The second factor is the closeness of the race (see Blais and Dobrzynska 1998). The data show that Canadians are somewhat more prone to vote when the election is close, although the connection between the closeness of the race and levels of turnout is not as strong as some might suppose. Everything else being equal, turnout is three points higher when the election is extremely close (when the two leading parties have the same share of the vote) than when it is not close at all, as in 1997 (when there is a 19-point difference between the first and the second parties). All in all, our data indicate that if the election had been typical in terms of closeness (the median distance between the two leading parties is 10 points), turnout would have been 69 per cent instead of 67 per cent. In other words, the fact that the 1997 election did not qualify as a really close competitive electoral race explains only two of the eight-point gap between the 1997 turnout and mean turnout in spring or fall elections.[5]

Figure 5.1: Voter Turnout in Canada since 1945

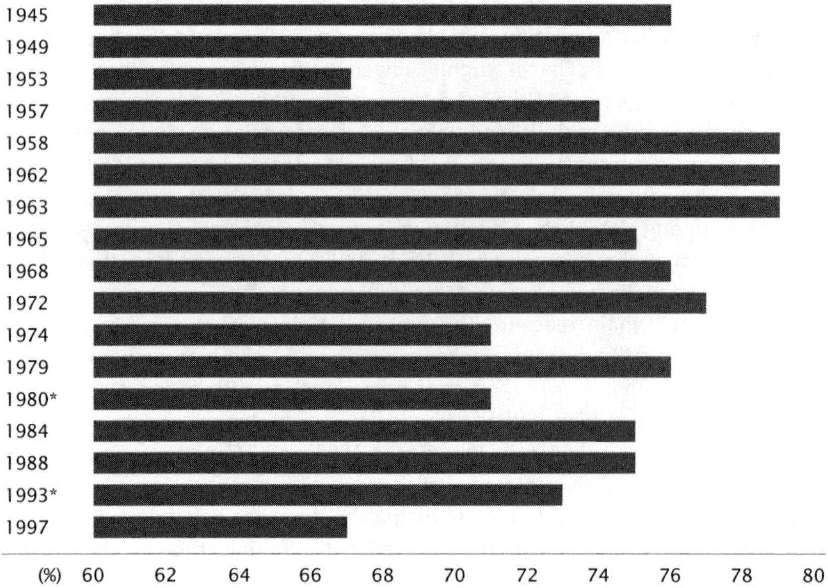

*Adjusted

What about interprovincial differences in voter turnout? In 1997 turnout was particularly low in Newfoundland (55 per cent) and Alberta (59 per cent), but reached 73 per cent in Prince Edward Island, New Brunswick, and Quebec. Newfoundland's voter turnout rate is usually about 10 points below the Canadian average. The fact that Newfoundland is the poorest province in the country and has the highest unemployment rate undoubtedly has something to do with the exceptionally low turnout in that province. Between 1993 and 1997 turnout decreased by about 10 points in Manitoba, Saskatchewan, and Alberta.

Turnout exceeded 70 per cent in both 1993 and 1997 in only three provinces: Prince Edward Island, New Brunswick, and Quebec. PEI is traditionally the province with the highest turnout, and those high turnout rates are usually attributed to the fact that the ridings there have a long tradition of being highly competitive and significantly smaller than average for the country. The situation is different in New Brunswick and Quebec, whose turnout has been more or less average in the recent past. It is striking that turnout hardly declined at all between 1993 and 1997 in New Brunswick and Nova Scotia, both of which experienced intense three-party contests in 1997. As for Quebec, turnout remained relatively stable in the 1990s while it declined in the rest of the country. The intensity of the fight between sovereignists and federalists in Quebec has probably prevented a drop in turnout. Furthermore, sovereignists who used to abstain in federal elections came back to the polls with the emergence of the Bloc (Johnston et al. 1996a).

There is no question that voter turnout in 1997 was unusually low. One reason is that there was no real race for who would form the government. But that explanation accounts for only two of the eight-point gap between the 1997 turnout and average Canadian turnout (for spring or fall elections). For a more complete account, we have to look for other explanations.

Who Did Not Vote?

Knowing who votes and who does not may provide useful clues about why some people choose not to vote. A growing body of research in other countries consistently indicates that there are two important socio-demographic determinants of non-voting: age and socio-economic status (see Blais 1998; Franklin 1996; Pammett 1991; Verba, Nie, and Kim 1978; Verba, Schlozman, and Brady 1995; Wolfinger and Rosenstone 1980). Turnout is lower among those with less education and lower income; this is usually attributed to the fact that people at the margins of society lack resources and interest in politics. Turnout is also lower among younger people, who are less integrated in society.

Table D.1 (in Appendix D) shows that the same relationships applied to Canada in 1997. Turnout was lower among the young, the less educated, and the poor. Age is the variable most closely correlated with voting. Reported turnout remained at a very high level in all age groups over 40, but it was much lower in the younger age groups. Education emerged as the second-most important variable. After age and income are taken into account, the gap between those with a university education and those who did not complete high school was a massive 18 percentage points.

Turnout is also related to some other background factors. People who are more religious are more inclined to vote, perhaps because they are more likely to believe that voting is a moral obligation (Blais 1998). On the other hand, recent and non-Christian immigrants are less likely to vote, perhaps because they are less integrated into Canadian society or they are less likely to be mobilized by the parties (Rosenstone and Hansen 1993). Marital status also counts for something. Married people are more likely to vote, probably because married people tend to be more integrated into their social milieu (Wolfinger and Rosenstone 1980; but see Stoker and Jennings 1995). At the same time, the effect of being married disappears when there are children in the household, since the presence of children leaves parents less time to follow political affairs. Finally, turnout remains higher in Quebec even after all these socio-demographic characteristics are controlled for, probably because of the intensity of the battle between federalists and sovereignists.

One implication of these findings is that the decline in voter turnout might be a consequence of socio-demographic changes in the Canadian population.

Are those groups that tend to abstain growing in size? The short answer is no. As we have seen, the two most important determinants of voting are age and education. It turns out that the proportion of young and less educated people in the electorate is shrinking, not expanding. In effect, turnout is declining in spite of socio-demographic changes that should cause it to rise.

There are at least two possible explanations for why age and levels of voter turnout are connected: age differences may reflect *life-cycle effects*, or they may indicate *generational effects*. In the case of life-cycle effects, the connection between age and various types of political behaviour reflects the individual's maturation process. For example, younger people are often ideologically less conservative and more idealistic, presumably because, having fewer responsibilities, they can afford to be more idealistic. People acquire a deeper stake in the status quo and become more conservative as they get older and take on responsibilities like a full-time job, a family, and a mortgage. When it comes to voter turnout, the life-cycle interpretation suggests that people are more likely to vote as they get older. The generational effect interpretation suggests that the connection between age and non-voting might be explained by the fact that the formative part of a specific age cohort was spent under a unique set of historical conditions that made voting less attractive or meaningful.

It is important to sort out whether the reason the young are less likely to vote is that they are young (life-cycle effects) or that they are a new generation (generation effects), because quite different practical implications flow from each interpretation. If the link between age and non-voting is attributable to life-cycle effects, the implication is that young abstainers will be more likely to vote as they mature. But if the link is due to generational effects, the implication is that voting will not increase in that particular cohort with the passage of time.

With data from a single time it is not possible to demonstrate conclusively that the link between age and low voting levels is due either to generational or to life-cycle effects. The only way to disentangle these two effects is to look at patterns of change over a number of elections. With cross-time data it is possible to see, for instance, whether turnout increases or decreases in a given cohort as it gets older. The analysis presented in Table D.2 of Appendix D, which takes a longer view, is based on a pooling of data from the Canadian Election Studies conducted in 1988, 1992 (the referendum on the Charlottetown Accord), 1993, and 1997, and includes more than 10,000 respondents.

In this case, life-cycle and cohort effects are separated by following the method proposed by Johnston (1989; 1992).[6] The results reported in Table D.2 show that differences between age groups mostly reflect a life-cycle effect, or in other words, that the propensity to vote increases as one grows older. Generational effects are detectable but modest; the generation born after 1970 is somewhat less likely to vote than previous generations were at the same age, but the difference is only six percentage points. These data suggest that generational replacement could account for only a one-point drop in turnout between 1988 and 1997. But there are indications that new generations of electors are less inclined to vote. As these new generations come to represent a larger share of the electorate, turnout may be heading downward in the long term. To determine why this new generation is less likely to vote entails probing the attitudes that lie behind citizens' decision to vote or not to vote.

Reasons for Not Voting

People may decide not to vote for a host of different reasons, at least three of which deserve detailed investigation. The first and perhaps most obvious one is *lack of interest in politics*. The second is *cynicism*. People who are disenchanted with their political world and who feel that politics is dirty and that politicians in general cannot be trusted may take the view that no one deserves their support. As the evidence presented in Chapter 4 demonstrates, there is widespread and growing cynicism in the Canadian electorate. Perhaps that was the driving force behind the low turnout observed in 1997. There is also the possibility that the crucial factor was not cynicism as such but the *lack of party attachment*. We would expect those who feel some attachment to a party to be more inclined to vote and, conversely, those with no party identification to abstain in greater numbers. Which of these three attitudes—lack of interest, lack of attachment, or cynicism—had the greatest influence on turnout in 1997?

Column 2 of Table D.1 shows that the decision not to vote was indeed related both to lack of interest in politics and to lack of party attachment. Surprisingly enough, cynicism did not seem to be related to abstention when the two other attitudes are taken into account, but that probably does not mean that the low turnout observed in 1997 was not a sign of disaffection with politics, because the low level of interest in politics is itself partly a result of cynicism. As a matter of fact, cynicism is related to abstention when we control for all socio-demographic variables but not for lack of interest or of party attachment (result not shown). All this suggests that the low turnout in 1997 was partly due to widespread cynicism.

None the less, cynicism clearly supplies only one part of the explanation. The average score on our cynicism scale (which runs from 0 to 1) is .7, an indication that Canadians tend to be quite cynical. Our results show, however, that if Canadians were only moderately cynical and the average score were .5 instead of .7, turnout would increase by only two points.[7]

Cynicism is on the rise in Canada, but it is not a new phenomenon. For instance, the proportion who said that the government does not care much what people think has increased from 59 to 70 per cent from 1974 to 1997. If cynicism has increased by 10 percentage points over the last 25 years, this would account for a one-point drop in turnout. Furthermore, there is no relationship between age and cynicism. It is *not* because they are more cynical that the generation born after 1970 is less prone to vote.

But even when these three factors—low interest in politics, cynicism, and weak party attachments—are considered together, the indications are that they still provide only a partial explanation for the low turnout in 1997.

The fact that voter turnout in 1997 was the lowest in more than 70 years suggests that the decision to vote or not to vote may also have hinged on more specific assessments of the 1997 election. Some elections may seem to matter less than others, so the rate of abstention might reflect the view that the 1997 election was not a highly charged one, that there was nothing vital at stake. Another possibility is that even if citizens believed there were important issues, they thought there were no meaningful choices for them.

Column 3 in Table D.1 of Appendix D shows that both of these perceptions did increase the likelihood that people would not vote. More than one in five (21 per cent) of our respondents could *not* name any issue that was most important to them personally in the election. Everything else being equal, the likelihood of voting was 14 points lower among that group. The percentage of respondents who were unable to name an important issue in the 1988 election was 13 per cent. If the percentage had been the same in 1997, turnout would have been one point higher.

Likewise, about one elector out of ten held the view that none of the parties were relatively close to their own views on the issues of how much to accommodate Quebec and on the difficult choice between cutting taxes and preserving social programs.[8] Not surprisingly, these people were also less likely to vote. But this can hardly account for the size of the drop in voter turnout in 1997.

Conclusion

Was the low turnout in 1997 the result of growing disaffection with politics? For the most part, the answer is no. Certainly, those who are cynical about politics are less prone to vote, and it is also true that cynicism is growing. But cynicism has always been present to some degree and cynicism happens to be only one of the many factors affecting turnout.

The specific and immediate context of an election also helps to explain variations in the levels of voter participation on election day. The fact of the matter is that voters did not see the 1997 federal election as a high-stake election. The perception that there was no real race for who would form the government did not help either.

Perhaps the most important finding presented in this chapter is the evidence that the generation born after 1970 does not vote as much as its predecessors. The implication of that finding is that turnout may be heading downward over the long term. But it is not because it is more cynical that members of the youngest generation are less likely to vote. It could be that it is just because they are less convinced of the view that voting is a moral obligation.[9]

Regional variations, election campaigns, the media, ideology, and turnout all qualify as system-wide contextual factors that shaped the opportunities and constraints facing each of the political parties in the 1997 election. The task now is to consider how these opportunities and constraints worked for each of the parties and to examine the more specific factors that drew voters to some parties rather than others.

Chapter 6

A Small Liberal Victory

In winning the 1997 election, the Liberals took twice as many votes as any other party, and in terms of both votes and seats, they finished first or second in eight out of ten provinces. Yet they attracted just 38 per cent of the total vote, a level that falls three percentage points short of their share of the vote in the 1993 election. Other evidence of fragility was the geographic distribution of electoral support across the country: in the Atlantic provinces, for example, the Liberal share of the vote slumped from 57 to 33 per cent. The outcome of the 1997 election raises two questions: Why did the Liberals win the election? And why was the victory so small?

There are several plausible explanations for the Liberals' victory. First, there is the possibility that the Liberals won almost by default, because they could count on a core of loyal supporters who identify with the party and who vote Liberal unless they have compelling reasons to do otherwise.

The state of the economy could also provide important clues to the Liberal victory, since incumbent governments usually reap political rewards from being in power when the economy is strong, and most indications are that the Canadian economy was fairly strong during the run-up to the election. The rate of unemployment, a key economic indicator explaining electoral outcomes in Canada (Nadeau and Blais 1993; 1995), fell from 11.2 to 9.6 per cent during the Liberal mandate. But the fact remains that the Liberals actually lost votes despite improvements in the economy. Does this declining support for the Liberals mean that the economy matters less than is sometimes alleged? Might the gains on the economic front have been offset by losses on other fronts? Or could it be that many Canadians did not think the economy had really improved?

A third plausible explanation concerns the other face of incumbency. Though the government can decide when an election will be called, it none the less has a governing record. Governing parties put the best face on that record while opposition parties like to criticize it. But at the end of the day it is elections that give people the opportunity to render their verdict on the performance of the government. Was the Liberal victory so small because many voters were dissatisfied with the Liberal performance?

No assessment of an election outcome for any party would be complete without giving serious consideration to the leadership. Was Jean Chrétien particularly popular or unpopular? How did he fare compared to his rivals? How was he perceived in his native province? Was he an asset or a liability for the Liberal party?

Is the Liberal Party the 'Natural' Party of Government?

In 13 elections out of 17 since 1945, the Liberal party has got more votes than any other party.[1] Three times out of four, it has out-polled all the other parties. And over the years the Liberals have built up a core of loyal supporters, more so than any other party. Can the Liberal victory be imputed to the presence of such a core of supporters?

This raises the issue whether (and how many) Canadians develop some kind of long-term attachment to specific parties, and how stable and strong are these attachments. Usually referred to as *party identification*, this attachment is thought of as a psychological identification; it involves 'a feeling of closeness to a political party; just as people identify with their religious group or their ethnic group they identify with a political party' (Gidengil 1992, 231).

According to one line of explanation, the Michigan school, voters who identify with a party are *predisposed* to vote for that party. This does not mean that those who are predisposed to vote for a particular party will always do so; specific considerations in a particular election might induce them to switch support to another party. But most people will vote for the party they identify with in most elections.

The exact meaning, strength, and stability of party identification—and how to best measure it—have been a matter of vigorous debate in Canada and elsewhere (for a review of the Canadian debate, see Gidengil 1992; Kam 1998). There is little doubt that some people have a relatively strong and stable attachment to a particular party. Clarke and his colleagues, whose work draws attention to the flexibility of party identification, suggest that somewhere between a quarter and a third of the Canadian electorate qualify as 'durable partisans'— voters who tend to support the same party from one election to the next (Clarke et al. 1979; 1991; 1996).

The 1997 Election Study used the following question to measure party identification: 'In federal politics, do you usually think of yourself as a Liberal, Conservative, NDP, Reform, Bloc Québécois, or none of these?' To minimize the risk that people might think this question was about which party they preferred and voted for, three precautionary steps were taken. First, the partisan identification question was asked in the campaign survey, when many voters had not quite made up their mind. Second, the question was asked towards the end of the questionnaire, a long time after the question about vote intention. The third precaution was to give respondents the option of saying, 'I do not identify with any party.'

Other research shows that people who identify weakly with a party tend to give relatively unstable answers (Blake 1982; Clarke and Stewart 1987). For that reason it is wise to be cautious about interpreting the data and assume that only those who say they have strong attachments to a party qualify as real 'partisans'. We asked the follow-up question to those who indicated an attachment to a particular party: 'How strongly (Liberal, Conservative, NDP, Reform, Bloc Québécois) do you feel: very strongly, fairly strongly, or not very strongly?'

Considering only those who said they identify very or fairly strongly with a party, we get the following distribution for the country as a whole: 23 per cent Liberal, 11 per cent Conservative, 6 per cent Reform and NDP, 5 per cent Bloc, and 48 per cent with no identification. This approach suggests that about half of Canadian electors have an attachment that predisposes them towards a particular party, a finding that corresponds very closely to the percentage (51 per cent) reported by Clarke and his colleagues as having a stable party identification from 1988 to 1993 (Clarke et al. 1996, 57).[2]

That evidence plainly shows that the Liberals enjoy a strong edge among those who qualify as partisans. It is also significant that the Conservatives have almost twice as many partisans as Reform.

As has already been indicated, predispositions do not mean that 'partisans' will always vote for 'their' party, but the expectation is that they will do so most of the time. As it turns out, in 1997 four partisans out of five voted for the party with which they identified. Furthermore, the likelihood of voting for 'their' party is about 25 percentage points higher among partisans than among non-partisans. That finding holds even after such factors as socio-demographic characteristics and ideological orientations are taken into account.

One finding that is absolutely clear is that the Liberals have a larger core of loyal supporters than the other parties. To illustrate the importance of the Liberal edge among partisans, we can examine the data to show what the results of the election would have been if the Liberals had had no such edge.

In Quebec, 48 per cent of those interviewed say they identify with a party. How different would the vote have been if this 48 per cent had been evenly distributed between the three main contesting parties, if 16 per cent had each identified with the Liberals, the Conservatives, and the Bloc? Under that scenario the Conservatives would have obtained six more points (28 per cent instead of 22 per cent), at the expense of both the Liberals and the Bloc. About half of the gap between the Liberals and the Conservatives can be attributed to the near-absence of traditional Conservative partisans in Quebec. So it turns out that the Liberals managed to retain their first position among Quebec federalists in large part because of the loyalty of their supporters.

Outside Quebec, 53 per cent of respondents identify with a party. Suppose again that party identification were evenly distributed between the main contending political parties. What would have happened if 13 per cent had each identified with the Liberals, the Conservatives, the NDP, and Reform? Under those circumstances, according to the evidence, the NDP and Reform would have each obtained three more points, at the expense of the Liberals. The Liberals would have had 33 per cent of the vote outside Quebec, instead of 39 per cent, and Reform 30 per cent instead of 27 per cent. As it happens, three-quarters of the Liberal-Reform gap can be attributed to the fact that the Liberals had many more traditional partisans than Reform.

It is important not to exaggerate the importance of traditional loyalties. After all, half of the electorate has no attachment to any political party. Moreover, such loyalties do not explain why Reform outpolled the Conservatives and the NDP outside Quebec. None the less, the point remains that the Liberals start with an edge in any election. For many voters, then, supporting the Liberals is the default position, and this helped the Liberals win the election in 1997.

Some of that Liberal edge comes from the party's strong support that the party enjoys among three particular groups: non-francophones in Quebec, Catholics, and Canadians of non-European ancestry outside Quebec. The first group is small but overwhelmingly Liberal. Catholics still make up about a third of the electorate outside Quebec, and most of the time a clear majority of this group votes Liberal. Canadians of non-European ancestry are a smaller but growing group; their support for the Liberals equals that of Catholics. Together, these three groups make up about one-third of the electorate. That is why the Liberal party is sometimes regarded as the 'natural' party of government; those traditional strongholds of partisan support mean that many Canadians feel predisposed to vote Liberal and will do so unless there are compelling reasons to do otherwise.

It could be argued that it is only in Ontario that the Liberals are the dominant party.[3] And indeed, as Table 6.1 illustrates, there are as many Reform as Liberal partisans in the West, as many Bloc as Liberal partisans in Quebec, and as many Conservative as Liberal partisans in the Atlantic provinces. But the Liberals are strong (though not necessarily dominant) everywhere, and, as shown in Chapter 2, they were the second choice of many voters. Furthermore, even outside Ontario the Liberals enjoyed a substantial lead in the vote: 32 per cent of the vote versus 19 per cent for both Reform and the Conservatives. What remains to be explained now is why the Liberal victory was so small.

The Economy and the Vote

One theory that comes close to qualifying as a 'law of electoral success' is that the electoral fortunes of incumbent governments hinge to a great extent on the state of the economy. That same finding has been repeatedly confirmed in

Table 6.1: Distribution of Party Identification, 1997

	West %	Ontario %	Quebec %	Atlantic %	Canada %
Liberals	16.0	31.4	20.9	17.6	23.1
Conservatives	11.6	13.2	5.8	19.4	11.3
NDP	9.6	6.5	1.1	5.2	5.9
Reform	16.1	3.5	—	2.4	6.2
Bloc	—	—	19.7	—	5.1
None	46.7	45.4	52.5	55.5	48.4

almost every democracy with competitive elections regardless of the particulars of the party system and of the variations in institutional arrangements (Norporth 1996, 303). Moreover, there is substantial evidence that the same relationship holds in Canada (Archer and Johnson 1988; Clarke and Kornberg 1992; Happy 1992; Nadeau and Blais 1993; 1995).

In general, the Canadian economy looked reasonably robust in the months preceding the 1997 election. Between the last quarter of 1993 and the first of 1997, the unemployment rate dropped from 11.2 to 9.6 per cent, the inflation rate remained under 2 per cent, and per capita GDP grew by 1 per cent annually on average. Although these gross indicators suggest that the economy was in good shape, the picture was not entirely rosy. Over the same period, Canadians' average disposable (that is, after-tax) income actually decreased by some 2.5 per cent. That said, the unemployment rate, the key economic indicator, had gone down and this improvement should have helped the Liberals.

Unfortunately for the Liberals, most of the improvement took place in the first half of their term. One possibility is that the Liberals did not benefit from the economic recovery because Canadians have short memories and react only to the state of the economy in the months immediately preceding the election. According to the Nadeau-Blais (1993) model, what really matters is where the unemployment rate stands in relation to where it used to be in the 30 months preceding the election. By that calculation, the Liberals should have received about 41 per cent of the vote.

In the final analysis, it is not the objective reality that necessarily counts. What matters is Canadians' perceptions of that reality. In order to discover what those were, we used a whole gamut of questions. Three aspects of peoples' views of the economy were explored particularly closely: personal finances, the provincial economy, and the Canadian economy. In the last case, the surveys examined general perceptions both of the economy and of the unemployment situation in particular. And for each dimension, we asked for both retrospective and prospective judgements. For instance, we inquired whether the respondents' personal financial situation had gotten better or worse during the previous year (retrospective) and whether they expected it to improve or worsen during the following year (prospective).

In each case most of the respondents thought that the economy was 'the same', that it had neither improved nor deteriorated. Nor did they think things would change substantially in the following year (see figures 6.1 and 6.2).

At the same time, there was a feeling that the national economy was in better shape than the individual's pocketbook. This is probably related to the view that the economic recovery had benefited mostly the wealthy: 71 per cent of our respondents said that the gap between the rich and the poor had widened over the last few years.

Prospective judgements were more positive than retrospective ones, a number of respondents being inclined to believe that economic conditions had not been very good lately but that they might improve slightly in the future.

People were particularly critical in their evaluations of the unemployment situation, and the findings in this regard are truly striking. Even though the unemployment rate had actually gone down since the Liberals won the 1993 election, some 37 per cent of respondents thought it had gone up. Only 17 per cent of respondents thought it had gone down.

It is not absolutely clear why so many Canadians got the facts wrong, but there is room for speculation. One possibility is that many felt that the unemployment rate was still unacceptably close to 10 per cent and that the decline was too slight to be significant. Perhaps what mattered was that there had not been any real decline since 1995. It is also possible that many had heard that the actual *number* of unemployed had not decreased. Yet another possibility is that the small rise in the jobless rate in April, from 9.3 per cent to 9.6 per cent, announced early in the campaign, drew people's attention away from the long-term trend. Whatever the reasons, it is clear that perceptions of the unemployment situation were much less positive than the 'objective' reality suggests.

The vital question then becomes what the impact of these perceptions was on the vote. The findings reported in Appendix C indicate that the economy had a greater effect on the vote outside of Quebec. Both retrospective and

Figure 6.1: Economic Perceptions: Retrospective

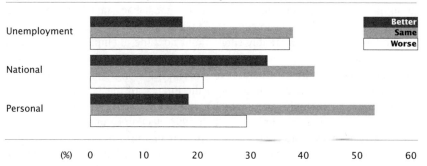

Figure 6.2: Economic Perceptions: Prospective

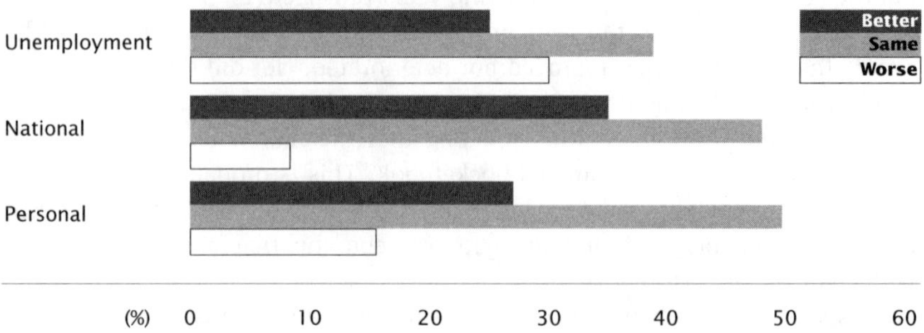

prospective judgements and both general evaluations of the economy and more specific perceptions of unemployment mattered. General views of the economy counted more than evaluations of one's personal situation, though the degree of optimism about one's future personal finances had some effect.

Overall, economic perceptions were mildly positive, and this helped the Liberals. According to estimates based on the survey data, the Liberal vote would have been two points lower if mean perceptions had been neutral.[4] The Liberals gained two or three points because of favourable judgements about the future of the Canadian economy and they lost one point because of the gloomy verdict about the unemployment situation.

The Liberals benefited the most from optimism about the future of the Canadian economy in Ontario. It was not that Ontarians were much more optimistic about the economy but rather that economic optimism was much more of a factor in their vote than in the West or the Atlantic provinces (Gidengil et al. 1999).

All in all, the Liberals benefited slightly from a slightly improving economy. They would have gained more if more voters had recognized that the unemployment rate had declined during the Liberal mandate. It could be argued that the decrease was so small that it was equally correct to say that unemployment had stayed the same or had gone down. More detailed analysis shows that if half the electorate had thought that unemployment had been going down and the other half had thought that it had stayed the same, the Liberal vote would have been some three points higher outside Quebec.

The Liberals were remarkably silent about how the unemployment rate had in fact improved during their mandate: the jobless figures, for instance, were not mentioned at all in the Liberal plan, *Securing Our Future Together*. How can this silence be explained? Was it not in the interest of the Liberals to remind voters that the unemployment rate had declined since 1993? One problem haunting the Liberals, certainly, was their 1993 election campaign cry of 'jobs, jobs, jobs'. That was the central plank in their platform of election promises. To try to take credit for a falling unemployment rate during the period 1993–7 would almost certainly have caused the opposition parties to emphasize the fact that the number of people out of work had actually risen. And how could a government whose first commitment was supposed to be jobs pretend to be satisfied with an unemployment rate of almost 10 per cent?

Given those constraints, the Liberals' main message in the 1997 campaign was that the economic future of the country was rosy. As Jean Chrétien put it in *Securing Our Future Together*, 'after four years of Liberal government . . . Canadians have good reasons for optimism and hope'. This was an easier message to sell, and it worked. As the data show, Canadians were optimistic about the future of the economy, and this optimism did help the Liberals.

In short, the Liberals gained about two points because the economy had slightly improved. Many Canadians failed to appreciate the small decrease in the unemployment rate that took place between 1993 and 1997, and this hurt the Liberals. But the party succeeded in convincing voters that better times were around the corner, and this conviction produced votes for the Liberals, especially in Ontario.

Assessing the Performance of the Liberal Government

During campaigns, opposition parties enjoy the luxury of being able to criticize a government's record. And the Liberals were vulnerable on a number of points that need to be considered one at a time. The place to start, perhaps, is with the deficit and social programs.

In the 1993 election, the Liberals rode into office voicing strong opposition to the Conservatives' and Reform's proposals to eliminate the deficit in three or five years. The Liberals argued strenuously that it was enough to reduce the deficit progressively to 3 per cent of the GDP, that spending needed to be maintained in order to preserve social programs. The campaign rhetoric echoed familiar Liberal themes. But once in power, the Liberal government then proceeded to eliminate the deficit in four years and to cut transfers to provincial governments, a policy that led to reductions in social-program spending. The Liberals also promised they would do away with the unpopular Goods and Services Tax (GST), a commitment they failed to keep.

On these two fronts the Liberals seem to have made a classic U-turn and done the opposite of what they said they would do. Did Canadians feel betrayed by the Liberals? Did they believe the government had good reasons to change its course of action? Or did they just forget about all this? Another possibility is that the Liberal government was simply bending with a new political wind. As has already been shown in Chapter 4, between 1993 and 1997 Canadian values seemed to have undergone a shift to the right and the Liberal policy changes could be seen as responses to newly emerging public priorities. The critical issue here, though, is whether the voters would make the Liberals pay a price for sudden policy U-turns and for their unfulfilled commitments.

Not surprisingly, the evidence suggests that Canadians believed the Liberals had done a better job on the deficit than on social programs.[5] More important, perhaps, is that opinions about the Liberal performance on deficit reduction had an independent effect on the vote but opinions about performance on social programs did not (Appendix C). On this issue the Liberals did not lose votes; in fact they may have won some.

There are two main reasons why the Liberals managed to avoid electoral punishment on this issue. First, although Liberal policies were hard to reconcile with their 1993 campaign positions, those policies were consistent with the views of a majority of Canadians. When asked (in 1993) which option came closest to their view, 'we must reduce the deficit even if it means cutting programs', or 'governments must maintain programs even if it means continuing to run a deficit', 56 per cent chose the first option and only 33 per cent the second. Furthermore, a majority of voters did not really see the trade-off between the deficit and social programs in terms of zero-sum alternatives: in 1997, 60 per cent of our sample agreed with the statement that 'to maintain our social programs we must eliminate the deficit'.[6] Second, the Liberal government managed to evade some of the responsibility for cuts to the most popular social program, health care: 42 per cent of respondents saw health care cuts as the prime responsibility of provincial governments. Only 33 per cent attributed the cuts to the federal government.

But the voters did remember the GST promise; 79 per cent of the people surveyed said that the Liberals had promised to abolish the GST. Furthermore, the great majority of those (82 per cent) thought that the Liberals had not really tried to keep their promise. In other words, a substantial number of Canadians, some 64 per cent, believed that the Liberal government had broken a promise.

For the cynical, breaking promises might be dismissed as part and parcel of political campaigns. The vital issue from the standpoint of election outcomes is whether voters are motivated to punish promise breakers on election day. We asked those who thought the Liberals had broken their promise whether they felt very angry, quite angry, or not very angry about this; 28 per cent said they were very angry, and 30 per cent quite angry. These results clearly indicate the potential for such punishment on this issue, and punishment there was. After taking into account a multitude of factors, including predispositions, party identification, and cynicism, the propensity to vote Liberal was six points lower among those who thought that the Liberals had broken their promise about the GST. In effect, outside Quebec, the Liberals lost four points because of this broken promise.[7]

The Liberals had also promised to give top priority to jobs, but a surprisingly large number of voters had forgotten about that promise. Respondents were asked the following question: 'What were the Liberals elected to do in 1993: Create jobs or fight the deficit?' By most accounts the heart of the Liberal 1993 campaign was the commitment to create 'jobs, jobs, jobs'. But only 36 per cent said 'create jobs', 28 per cent of respondents referred to the deficit, 23 per cent mentioned both, and 12 per cent said they did not know. The Liberals benefited from voters' short memory.[8]

Despite the fact that many voters had forgotten the 1993 campaign promises, the Liberals were given a low score on job creation: only 26 per cent of our respondents thought the Liberals had done a good job. Dissatisfaction was widespread but not very deep: only 15 per cent said they had not done a good job at all. When we controlled for everything else, the Liberal vote was five points lower among those who gave the Liberals a low score on job creation. According to our estimates, opinions about poor performance on jobs cost the Liberals about one point. Public evaluation of the Liberal performance on the job front was not inconsequential, but it did not matter as much as the GST.

Finally, perhaps the most dramatic domestic political crisis during the Liberal mandate was the 1995 Quebec referendum. Although the No side did win the referendum, the drama was provided by the narrowness of the victory—a tiny 50.6 per cent of the votes. The country came dangerously close to a break-up, and media commentary during the closing days of the campaign and in the immediate post-referendum analyses was widely critical of how the government had handled the whole affair. But did Canadians hold the Liberal government responsible for this near-defeat? What did they think about the actions taken by the government after the referendum? Or were public memories short on this matter as well as others?

On this particular issue, about equal numbers of respondents said the governing Liberals had done a good and a bad job, and few thought they had done a very good or bad job, but resistance to accommodating Quebec did hurt the Liberals in the West. The important point is that the overall effect on the vote was minimal.

In some respects, given the near-fiasco in the Quebec referendum on sovereignty, it is truly remarkable that so few Canadians were deeply dissatisfied with the Liberals about the national-unity issue. Outside Quebec, only one respondent out of four both thought that it was very or somewhat likely that Quebec would separate and expressed concern about the possibility of separation. And even within that particular group of respondents, more expressed satisfaction with the Liberal performance than dissatisfaction. The main reason for such satisfaction may well have been that most Canadians outside Quebec approved of the Liberal government's post-referendum strategy, especially the so-called plan B, a 'hard'-line strategy that questioned the legality of secession, claimed a federal government role in the formulation of any referendum question, served notice that a 50 per cent + 1 margin of victory in any referendum might not suffice, and argued that if Canada can be partitioned, then so can Quebec. The plan was intended to encourage Quebec to remain in Canada by drawing attention to the negative consequences of any secession (Trent 1996). A full 80 per cent of those surveyed outside Quebec disagreed with the statement that 'Quebec has the right to separate, no matter what the rest of Canada says.'

It comes as no surprise to discover that the unity question occupies a unique place in the vote decisions made by people in Quebec (see Chapter 4). In Quebec, the only specific type of performance that seems to have an independent impact on the Liberal vote concerns national unity. The issue, of course, concerns only federalists. A good number of them identify with the Liberals and may be prone to express satisfaction with their party on most matters. But what about federalists with no party identification? Did they think that the federal Liberals in general, and Jean Chrétien in particular, were to blame for the closeness of the referendum?

Relatively few, it would seem. Only one out of five non-partisan federalists thought that Quebec separation was very or somewhat likely and expressed worry about that possibility. And 43 per cent of these nervous federalists said that the Liberals had done a good job on national unity. A strong majority (73 per cent) of Quebec federalists said that in their view, Quebec does not have the right to secede unilaterally.[9] And among those who had strong views on this, 63 per cent thought that the Liberals had done a good job on national unity.

The Liberal record was open to sharp and critical scrutiny on a number of fronts and opposition parties tried to exploit these weaknesses during the campaign. But when all of the evidence is in it becomes clear that, for voters at least, the Liberal record held up reasonably well. Admittedly, the Liberals failed to capitalize on what might have given a strong boost for the party—the issue of unemployment. But then again to fix on the unemployment issue carried risks and in this respect the party was under significant strategic constraints. In two other areas, weaknesses turned into sources of support. First, the Liberals' policy shift to the right did not cost them votes; in fact, the evidence is that they gained ground from the shift. The Liberals were rewarded for lowering the deficit, and they escaped punishment for cutting transfers and, indirectly, social programs. Here, they seem to have read the shifting priorities of the public correctly. They also managed to escape blame for the closeness of the Quebec referendum. The tough plan B turned out to be quite popular both outside Quebec and among Quebec federalists. But the Liberals did feel the wrath of angry voters about the GST. That broken promise cost them about four points outside Quebec.

What about Jean Chrétien?

A large body of evidence shows that leaders can make or break the fortunes of political parties at election time. Some political parties are swept into office on the coattails of enormously popular leaders. Such was the case with the Liberals and Pierre Trudeau in the late 1960s, and John Diefenbaker undoubtedly helped the Progressive Conservatives achieve their historic election sweep in the 1958 federal election. But in other cases, leaders can be a liability. The defeat of the Conservative party in the 1993 federal election, for example, had a lot to do with the voters' aversion to one of the country's most unpopular leaders in recent political memory.

In 1997 a vote for the Liberal candidate was also a vote for Jean Chrétien as the Prime Minister of Canada. How much (or little) did Canadians like Jean Chrétien? Did they vote Liberal because of Jean Chrétien or in spite of him?

Figure 6.3 indicates the average rating given to the different leaders in and outside Quebec, on a scale from 0 to 100, in the last week of the campaign. Outside Quebec, the most popular leaders were Chrétien and Charest, whose ratings were about 10 points higher than those of McDonough and Manning.[10] In Quebec, however, Charest emerged as the most popular leader, and Chrétien's ratings are only slightly higher than those of Duceppe.

How much did the popularity of the leaders matter in the election?[11] One way to discover that is to look at the difference between the rating given to a leader and the highest rating given to another leader. For instance, if a respondent gave Chrétien a score of 50 and if the highest score among the other leaders was 40, the 'Chrétien' variable would equal + 10. According to that analysis, the probability of such a person voting Liberal, controlling for all other factors, was nine points higher than that of a respondent whose scores were reversed (40 for Chrétien and 50 for the preferred leader). Clearly, then, voters' feelings about Jean Chrétien did affect their vote.

One way to bring the effect of the leaders into focus is to look at the evidence in a slightly different way. Suppose all the leaders had been equally popular, what effect would that have on the election outcome? According to our estimates, Chrétien's popularity, relative to that of Manning and McDonough, gave the Liberals an additional five points outside Quebec, and his relative unpopularity in Quebec cost the party three points in that province.

In short, Chrétien was an important asset for the Liberal party outside Quebec. He was as popular as Charest and more popular than either Manning

Figure 6.3: Evaluations of Leaders (last week of campaign)

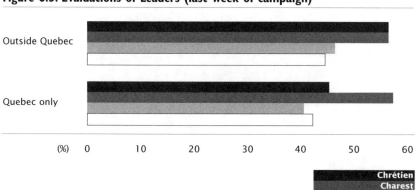

or McDonough. But in his native province, Chrétien was less popular than Charest and only slightly more popular than Gilles Duceppe.

Conclusion

The Liberals won the election for a combination of reasons. First, they could count on a larger core of loyal supporters; second, the voters were fairly optimistic about the future of the Canadian economy; third, the Liberals' decision to focus on the deficit was in keeping with public opinion; and fourth, their leader, Jean Chrétien, was more popular than the other leaders, at least outside Quebec. But the Liberal victory was small for two other reasons: quite a number of voters were angry about their broken promise on the GST, and they did not consider that the unemployment situation had improved during the Liberals' mandate.

Of course, the shape of the Liberal victory was also partly defined by the successes and failures of the other parties. As we will argue in the next two chapters, the continued success of the Liberal party depends largely on the future direction of the Conservative and Reform parties.

Chapter 7

The Progressive Conservatives: A One-Man Show

The magnitude of the Progressive Conservatives' defeat in 1993 is hard to overstate. Never before had a governing party been so decisively rejected by Canadian voters. The Conservatives plunged from 43 per cent of the popular vote in 1988 to 16 per cent in 1993 and saw their number of seats plummet from 170 to two. As a result, the Conservative party, one of the two parties that had dominated Canada's electoral life since Confederation, actually lost its status as a party in the House of Commons.

In the 1997 election, the goal for the Conservatives was to pick up the pieces and rebuild the party as a Canada-wide electoral force. But the 1997 election did not provide the hoped-for comeback. Though the Conservatives did increase their share of the vote by three points to draw almost even with the Reform party, their gains were concentrated in Quebec and Atlantic Canada. Outside of Quebec, they were decisively outpolled by Reform. And because of the first-past-the-post electoral system, they ended up fifth in number of seats.

The key to electoral success is to attract new voters while keeping long-time supporters in the fold. This suggests two possible explanations for the Conservatives' inability to rebound. The first possibility is that the remaining core of loyal partisans was just too small. This raises a series of questions. How many Canadians still identify with the Conservative party? Are there particular segments of Canadian society that are more likely to vote Conservative? And to what extent is Conservative support rooted in basic ideological outlooks? A second possibility is that the Conservatives simply failed to come up with winning appeals. The party chose to campaign on a promise of reducing personal income taxes by 10 per cent, but did that promise help them? How interested were Canadians in cutting taxes?

Even more than campaign promises, the Conservatives pinned their hopes for a comeback on their new leader, Jean Charest, but his performance was something of a paradox. Charest was the best-liked leader in Quebec, and his popularity outside Quebec was equal to that of Jean Chrétien (see Figure 6.3).

Though he was also widely considered to have 'won' the televised leaders' debates, as the analysis of campaign dynamics in Chapter 2 demonstrated, that did little to help the party on election day. What qualities in Jean Charest appealed to voters? And why did his personal popularity not translate into a larger share of the vote for his party? Was he hurt, like his predecessor Kim Campbell, by the belief that he was too close to Brian Mulroney?

A Shrunken Core

In the 1993 federal election, the Reform party had hollowed out the core of Conservative support (Johnston et al. 1996b). Those who had voted Conservative in the 1988 election were twice as likely to defect to Reform in 1993 as those who had voted for any other party. In fact, half the Reform voters in 1993 had been Conservative voters in 1988. It was a similar story with the Bloc Québécois: people who had voted Conservative in 1988 were more than four times as likely to defect to the Bloc as those who had voted Liberal in 1988. One-third of the Bloc vote in 1993 had come from former Conservatives.

As we saw in Chapter 2, the Conservatives were again the least successful of the five parties in holding on to their support in 1997 (though the defections were not nearly on the same scale as in 1993). They were moderately success-ful in winning over 1993 Bloc voters, but they failed to make substantial inroads into Reform support. The gains that the Conservatives did make in 1997 came primarily at the expense of the Liberal party. The flow of the vote across the three elections raises the fundamental question whether it is still meaningful to talk of the Conservative party as having a core of supporters.

One place to look for evidence of a loyal core of partisan support is to the socio-demographic characteristics of Conservative voters. Recall that the huge advantage enjoyed by the Liberals comes from that party's ability to count consistently on the disproportionate support of Catholic voters and those of non-European ancestry. The Conservatives do not enjoy any comparable pockets of support within the Canadian public. What stands out from the results of a detailed analysis of how socio-demographic factors affect the Conservative vote (see Appendix C) is the general weakness of the effects of social background characteristic on support for the party. This is especially striking in Quebec, where only a trivial proportion of the Conservative share of the vote is explained by voters' background characteristics. Francophones and those who are employed were somewhat more likely to vote Conservative than non-francophones and those outside the labour force. The problem, though, is that these groups were even more likely to vote Liberal or Bloc. Outside Quebec, the only strong effect is for residence in the Atlantic provinces, and this background factor is a new one for 1997; there is no evidence of it in 1988 or 1993 (Johnston et al. 1996b). For that reason, the sudden emergence of this Atlantic Canada factor is more likely to signify the region's new disaffection with the Liberals than a regionalized core of loyal support for the Conservatives.

Two established patterns of support do persist. The Conservative party continues to do significantly better among the more affluent and among Protestants. Both effects, however, are modest. Support for the Conservatives was less than five points higher among those with household incomes in the highest quintile, and the party's vote was only seven points higher among Protestants. And the Reform party was much more successful than the Conservatives in capturing the Protestant vote. Further evidence that a substantial part of the historic core of the Conservative party now resides within the Reform party lies in the pattern of effects for northern European ancestry. At one time, the Conservatives did rather better among this group, but they now do significantly worse. The voting intentions of this group have become decisively Reform. Fully half (51 per cent) of voters of northern European origin supported Reform in 1997, compared with only one in 10 (11 per cent) for the Conservatives.

The same pattern of weak effects holds for basic ideological outlook. Outside Quebec, only two such outlooks were associated with Conservative voting—views about women and beliefs about the capitalist system. Those who wanted to do more for women were more likely to vote Conservative than those who wanted to do the same or less. The pattern for Reform was exactly the reverse: the party was disproportionately attractive to those who wanted to do the same or less (see Appendix C). But even among those who wanted to do more for women, Reform (21 per cent) nosed out the Conservatives (19 per cent). Beliefs about free enterprise did help to motivate a Conservative vote, but Chapter 4 clearly shows that Conservative voters were barely distinguishable from Reform supporters when it comes to support for free enterprise. The Conservatives plainly do not occupy any ideological space that is distinctively theirs, at least in terms of their electoral base. Finally, there is an important non-finding. Views about accommodating Quebec had no significant effect on the Conservative vote outside the province. The Conservatives thus succeeded in neutralizing the national unity question, which is precisely what a party that aspires to win seats Canada-wide must do (Nevitte et al. 1995).

Ideological outlook has more effect on the Conservative vote in Quebec, but once again, there is no area of the ideological space that is distinctive to Conservative voters. To be sure, federalists were more likely than sovereignists to be attracted to the party, but federalists were even more likely to vote Liberal than Conservative. Belief in the virtues of free enterprise attracted Quebec voters to the Conservatives, but as in the rest of the country the Conservatives did not have this ideological space to themselves. In Quebec, this space was shared with the Liberals. Cynicism about politics and unfavourable views about aboriginal peoples were also associated with Conservative voting, but Conservative voters in Quebec were only slightly more cynical and slightly less sympathetic to aboriginal peoples than Bloquistes.

Probing the socio-demographic bases of Conservative support and the ideological preferences of their supporters brings the difficulties facing the Conservatives into focus. The Conservatives and the Liberals alike have been characterized as 'brokerage parties' (Clarke et al. 1996), and it is in the nature of brokerage parties that their support is fluid. Like their European cousins, the 'catch-all parties' (Kirchheimer 1966) or 'people's parties' (Smith 1990), Canada's brokerage parties have traditionally adjusted their positions to attract the median voter. This ideological flexibility is reflected in the weak relationship between fundamental ideological orientations and support for both parties. As we have seen, neither party's supporters in 1997 had a distinctive ideological profile. However, this emphasis on the fluidity of their appeals, risks missing a crucial characteristic of the successful brokerage party. The European literature plainly demonstrates that this type of party must also be able to count on what Smith (1990) terms the 'passive' support of core social groups, that is, voters who can be relied upon to continue supporting the party despite its shifting appeals. As we saw in Chapter 6, Catholics, Canadians of non-European ancestry, and non-francophone Quebeckers provide the Liberals with just such a core of loyal support. The Conservatives, on the other hand, lack strong ties with any social group, and for a brokerage party this is a critical weakness.

The contrast between the two parties is highlighted when we compare the number of loyal partisans. Counting only those who identified fairly or very strongly, the Conservatives can count on only 13 per cent of the electorate outside Quebec. As we saw in Chapter 6, the Liberal party can count on a much larger number of loyal supporters. The Conservatives, however, come out ahead of Reform, which could count on only 8 per cent. In any fight for the right, the Conservatives have the advantage in the number of solid partisans they can muster. Just what ties these supporters to the party, however, remains unclear. It may simply be a customary allegiance. The figures for Quebec offer the party less encouragement. Only 6 per cent of Quebeckers identified fairly or very strongly with the Conservatives. Both the Liberals (21 per cent) and the Bloc (20 per cent) have up to three and a half times as many core supporters.

In Search of a Winning Issue

With so few loyal supporters even outside Quebec, the Conservatives were all the more in need of a winning issue. Traditionally, the party had enjoyed a good deal of latitude in crafting its appeals. Before 1993 the Conservatives' strategic calculations were less complicated than the Liberals'. If the Liberals moved too far to the centre, they risked defections to the NDP on their left flank. The Conservatives, on the other hand, only had to be concerned about possible defections to their major party rival; there was no viable party to their right. With the emergence of the Reform party, the Conservatives lost this important strategic advantage, and in 1997 the task of finding a winning issue was further complicated by the legacy of 1993. As the party that had introduced the unpopular tax, the Conservatives could hardly campaign against the GST, and their credibility on the jobs issue required voters to forget their record of double-digit unemployment. As for national unity, the success of brokerage politics has been predicated on bridging, not exploiting, the cultural divide. With the median voter in Quebec and the median voter in the rest of the country occupying such different locations on the national-unity question, brokerage parties have had strong incentives to avoid politicizing this issue (Johnston et al. 1992).

The issue that the Conservatives tried to make their own was taxation and the centrepiece of their platform was a promise to cut taxes. Opinions about tax cuts, however, did little to motivate a vote for the party. Tax cuts were not among the few issues that had a significant effect on Conservative voting (see Appendix C), either in Quebec or in Canada at large.

The Conservatives were outflanked on the right by Reform, which came out in support of tax cuts as well. More to the point, Reform did much better than the Conservatives in attracting the votes of those who wanted tax cuts, getting 38 per cent (outside Quebec) to the Conservatives' 22 per cent. This competition from the right, however, turns out not to be the explanation. Tax cuts were just not a very important issue to most Canadians, and so views on the issue could do little to differentiate support for the parties. Thus, the Liberals did almost as well (35 per cent) as Reform among those who wanted to see taxes cut.

But those who wanted taxes cut were clearly in the minority. Only 27 per cent opted for cutting taxes when faced with the difficult choice between tax cuts and maintaining social programs. This figure varied little between Quebec (28 per cent) and the rest of the country (26 per cent). A majority of voters wanted the status quo.[1] On neither side of the national divide were taxes an issue. At the beginning of the interview, respondents were asked to name the issue that was most important to them in the election. Outside Quebec, only 7 per cent spontaneously mentioned taxes. In Quebec, this figure was only 1 per cent.

When respondents were asked to rate the personal importance of a number of issues, cutting taxes ranked last. Figure 7.1 shows the percentage of people who responded that a given issue was 'very important' to them personally. The three most important issues, to Quebeckers and non-Quebeckers alike, were creating jobs, keeping election promises, and fighting crime. Creating jobs was described as 'very important' twice as often as cutting taxes.

Obviously the Conservatives had failed to find a winning issue. They did manage, though, to get some electoral mileage out of two of the three issues that were most important to Canadians, at least outside Quebec. Those who were anxious about losing their jobs were significantly more likely to vote Conservative than those who were not (see Appendix C). Although the effect of this factor was largely confined to the Atlantic provinces, it is worth emphasizing that it was the Conservatives, and not the NDP, that benefited from employment insecurity. Of those Atlantic Canadians who said they were at least somewhat worried about losing their job in the near future, 43 per cent voted Conservative, compared with only 33 per cent for the NDP. The Conservatives

Figure 7.I: Issues That Were Important to Voters
(% saying the issue was personally very important)

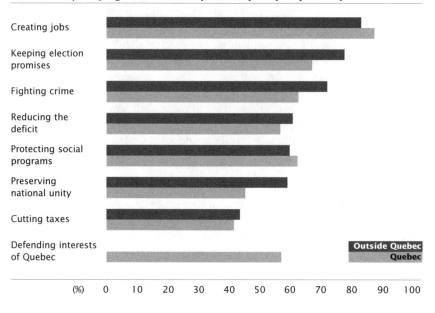

also fared better among voters who wanted to see the government take an active part in solving the unemployment problem. So, too, did the NDP, but they were outpolled by the Conservatives. The other issue that helped the Conservatives, albeit modestly, was broken promises. Those who believed that the Liberals had broken a promise to eliminate the GST were significantly more likely to vote Conservative. But once again, these voters were even more likely to choose Reform. The desire to get tough on crime did nothing to motivate a Conservative vote; indeed, the party attracted more support from those who favoured rehabilitation, but on this side of the issue, they were outpolled by the NDP.

On balance, then, it seems that issues did little to help the Conservatives. Tax cuts turned out to be a non-issue, and the party lost out to Reform in the competition to exploit the issue of broken promises. The one issue that did help them, namely jobs, is something of a surprise. The Conservative's success on this front may owe something to the NDP's (see Chapter 9) lack of visibility and its low standing in the polls.

The Charest Paradox

With their policies doing so little for the Conservatives, leadership became a critical factor. The party had high hopes for Jean Charest, a leader as comfortable in English as in French, who projected an image of freshness and relative youthfulness. Charest did prove to be popular with voters, tying with Chrétien as the most popular leader outside Quebec and far surpassing Chrétien and Bloc leader Gilles Duceppe in popularity in his home province. But if Charest was viewed so favourably, why did his party not do better? The analysis in Chapter 2, which illustrates the influence of the televised leaders' debates, underscores the paradox. Outside Quebec, voters were three times more likely (36 per cent) to name him as the winner of the English debate than any other leader. And inside Quebec, voters were over five times more likely (41 per cent) to name him as the winner of the French debate than his closest rival. Even so Charest was unable to translate these winning performances into more votes.[2]

The phenomenon of winning the debate but losing the election is not unusual in Canada. In 1988 John Turner was widely judged to have won the televised campaign debate, but Mulroney's Conservatives went on to win that election (Johnston et al. 1992). A weak leader can hurt a party, but a popular leader does not necessarily help very much. This was certainly true of Charest outside Quebec. One way to assess Charest's influence on the vote is to examine the difference between his rating and the highest rating given to any other leader. What would have happened to the Conservative vote if the average difference for Charest as the campaign drew to a close had been no higher than the average difference for his three rivals? According to our calculations, the Conservatives would have ended up with two points less outside Quebec (assuming, of course, that other factors affecting the vote remained constant). Now, two points is not a negligible boost, given the Conservatives' vote share (18 per cent) outside Quebec, but it pales in comparison with the boost Charest gave his party in Quebec. A similar calculation for Quebec shows that Conservative support could have been as much as 12 points lower without Charest's popularity. The Charest effect overwhelms all other effects on the Conservative vote in Quebec (see Appendix C), over half of which can be attributed to Charest's personal appeal.

What was it about Charest that made him so attractive to Quebec voters? One way to analyse leaders' appeal is to examine voters' evaluations of their personality traits (Johnston et al. 1992). These evaluations are obtained by asking voters to say how well various words and phrases describe each of the leaders. Figure 7.2 shows the percentage of Quebeckers during the final week of the campaign who responded that various traits described each leader very well. It turns out that Charest's personality traits were not viewed particularly positively. This becomes more apparent when opinions in Quebec are compared with those outside the province (see Figure 7.3). Compared with his two rivals in Quebec, though, Charest looked good. On four of the five traits measured, there were more highly favourable evaluations for Charest than for Chrétien and Duceppe combined. His most positively rated trait was providing strong leadership. The only trait on which he had to take second place, just behind Duceppe, was lack of arrogance. This was the one trait on which opinions of the Bloc leader actually improved across the campaign. At the beginning of the campaign, one in four Quebeckers (26 per cent) had said that arrogant described Duceppe very well.

Figure 7.2: Opinions of Leaders, Quebec (% saying phrase describes leader 'very well', final week of the campaign)

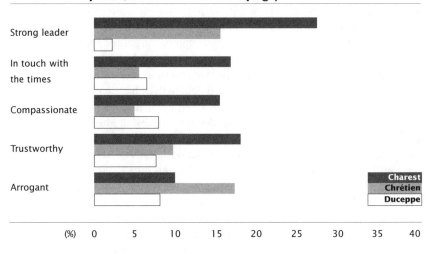

Charest's most highly rated traits were providing strong leadership and being in touch with the times outside Quebec, (see Figure 7.3). Note, though, that there were close contenders on both traits. Charest just edged out Chrétien on the leadership characteristic and came out only slightly ahead of NDP leader Alexa McDonough on being in touch with the times. And when it came to being compassionate, he placed a distant second to McDonough. On trustworthiness, Charest ranked behind both McDonough and Reform party leader Preston Manning, though none of the leaders was considered to be particularly trustworthy.

The fact that McDonough rivalled or surpassed Charest on four of the five traits and yet ended up well behind the Conservative leader in overall popularity (see Chapter 6) raises a question whether some traits matter more than others. That question can be answered by examining how much effect each trait had on overall popularity during the last week of the campaign.[3]

It turns out that the view that Charest was in touch with the times had no significant effect whatsoever on his overall ratings either inside or outside Quebec. The 'in touch with the times' trait was irrelevant to overall ratings for all three leaders in Quebec, but outside Quebec it was associated with higher ratings for every leader except Charest. Similarly, being considered compassionate did nothing to enhance Charest's popularity (or McDonough's) outside Quebec. Significantly, however, this compassion trait was associated with the overall ratings of Chrétien and Manning. In fact, all five traits had an independent effect for both Chrétien and Manning. The trait that had the strongest effect by far on Charest's overall ratings (and McDonough's and Duceppe's) was trustworthiness. This was the case both outside Quebec and within the province.

It is important not to overstate Charest's appeal. First, there was an awareness problem. Outside Quebec, Charest was hampered by the fact that many voters seemed to know little or nothing about him. During the first week of the campaign, as many as 40 per cent of those surveyed had said they knew nothing at all about him, and even during the final week of the campaign, almost 30 per cent of those interviewed were still saying that they knew nothing at all about him (see Figure 7.4). This lack of familiarity does not approach the figure for McDonough, but it was a serious handicap none the less.

Secondly, Charest's popularity in Quebec in 1997 paled beside that of Lucien Bouchard in 1993 (see Chapter 9) and significant numbers of voters shared some rather negative opinions of Charest. Two-thirds of Quebeckers (66 per cent) agreed that Charest was 'a one-man show'.[4] This opinion, however, reflected more on the party than on the leader. These voters believed that Charest simply did not have a strong team of candidates to back him up. This did not make them more reluctant to vote for the party, though. A much more detailed analysis of the data shows that this factor did not significantly affect the vote. What really hurt Charest right across the country was the impression that he was all style and little substance. Well over half of those interviewed outside Quebec (57 per cent) agreed that Charest had lots of style but really did not have much to say, and fewer than one in three (30 per cent) disagreed. The level of agreement in Quebec was remarkably similar (59 per cent). In Quebec,

Figure 7.3: Opinions of Leaders, Outside Quebec (% saying phrase describes leader 'very well', final week of the campaign)

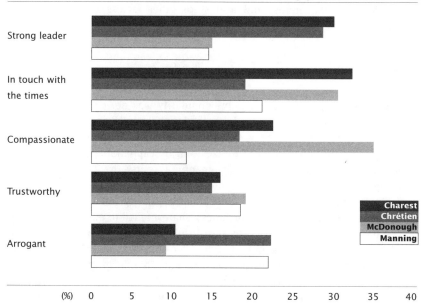

Figure 7.4: Knowledge of Leaders (% saying they knew nothing at all about the leader during the final week of the campaign)

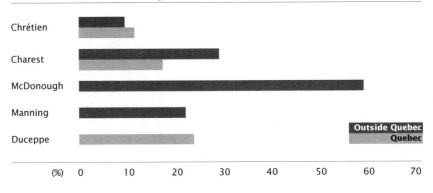

though, a mere 17 per cent rejected this unflattering characterization of the Conservative leader. The data demonstrate that this perception cost the Conservatives almost two points, a figure that was again very similar in both parts of the country.

Charest also suffered from having been a minister in Mulroney's cabinet. One voter in two (52 per cent) outside Quebec thought that Charest was too close to Brian Mulroney, and so did almost two in five Quebeckers (39 per cent). This view not only affected his personal popularity but also hurt the party, especially outside Quebec.[5] Those who shared this perception were significantly less likely to vote Conservative, even when party identification, relative leader evaluations, and a host of other factors that affected the Conservative vote were controlled for.

Conclusion

Charest was a popular leader, but his popularity was not enough to pull the Conservative party out from the long shadow cast by Brian Mulroney. The party had hoped to re-emerge as the logical alternative to the Liberal party by promising cuts in personal income taxes and by capitalizing on the personal appeal of their leader. But in focusing on tax cuts, the party hitched its campaign to an issue that too few voters cared about. Jobs topped the list of voters' concerns. Keeping promises was also a priority for many voters, and when it came to perceived trustworthiness Charest failed to outshine his rivals.

The party was also hampered by the shrinking of its core of loyal supporters. With Liberal identifiers outnumbering Conservative identifiers by close to two to one, the Conservatives had a formidable handicap in returning to a position of competitiveness. And they remain vulnerable to a loss of support. The Conservative vote in 1997 was only weakly rooted in social-background characteristics or basic ideological orientations that might tie voters to the party. And the party has lost its greatest asset in Quebec with the departure of Jean Charest to lead the provincial Liberal party. Joe Clark cannot hope to match his predecessor's personal appeal to Quebeckers, and on that appeal hinged much of the Conservatives' comeback in 1997.

The Conservatives may none the less pose the biggest threat to the Liberals. First, despite being decisively outpolled outside Quebec by the Reform party, the Conservative party retained a clear advantage over Reform in terms of party identifiers. With relatively few strong partisans, Reform is vulnerable to an erosion of support. Secondly, as we saw in Chapter 2, the Conservatives were the most popular second choice for Liberal voters, just as the Liberals were the most popular second choice for Conservative voters. Thirdly, and crucially, as we shall see in Chapter 8, Conservative voters are much closer to Liberal voters than they are to Reform voters on issues like accommodating diversity, law and order, and moral traditionalism. Arguably, Charest and his advisers made the wrong strategic calculation in the 1997 election. Instead of targeting Reform, they might have done better to focus on disgruntled Liberal supporters. There were many more Liberals than Reformers to be courted, and the similarities in the policy preferences of Conservative and Liberal voters suggest that they might have been wooed without inducing massive defections to the right.

Joe Clark's brand of red Toryism adds credibility to the Conservatives' move towards the middle. And his party faces relatively few constraints if it should choose to position itself closer to the Liberal party in the next election. The very lack of a distinctive ideological or social support base gives the Conservatives greater flexibility in moving around the ideological spectrum. It also means, thought, that the party lacks a critical ingredient of successful brokerage politics, namely a core of loyal supporters.

When all the other players were willing to play by the rules, brokerage politics kept the Conservative party a major contender. But the emergence of two parties intent on exploiting, rather than bridging, the national divide has fundamentally changed the nature of federal elections. The Reform party and the Bloc Québécois smashed through the brokerage system. The future of the Conservative party hinges very much on the future of these two new players. Will the Reform party succumb to the temptations of brokerage politics, or will it resist the electoral incentives to moderate its stands? And do Quebeckers still believe that they need a sovereignist party in Ottawa to defend the interests of Quebec? Some light can be shed on the first of these questions by taking a closer look at the challenges and opportunities facing the Reform party.

Chapter 8

The Reform Party and the Limits to Growth

The Reform party achieved its momentous electoral breakthrough in the 1993 federal election by following a textbook strategy for a new political party: find an area in the issue space that had plenty of voters but no competing parties and stake out a platform based on those issues.[1] The issue was Quebec, and the space left unoccupied by the three established parties was to take a harder line on accommodating Quebec (Johnston et al. 1992, 102–11). In pursuing this strategy, Reform, along with the Bloc Québécois, had shattered the old brokerage-style system, which had been predicated on bridging the national divide and neutralizing the national question, a strategic necessity for any political party that aspired to be a truly national party.

In politicizing the Quebec cleavage, Reform's strategy in 1993 may well have been optimal for a new political party, but it is a strategy that can be risky because it may encourage new parties to position themselves too far to one side or the other of an issue. If parties are not considered reasonable by the electorate, they will lose support. According to this view, voters have in their minds an idea about a 'region of acceptability' within which parties should operate, and any party that crosses this threshold of acceptability will be penalized (Rabinowitz and Macdonald 1989).

In the 1997 election, the Reform party received more or less the same share of the vote as in 1993. Does that mean that Reform had reached the limit to its potential growth? And, specifically, was its position on Quebec a limit to further growth? After all, only 29 per cent of voters outside Quebec wanted to do somewhat less or much less for Quebec. The bulk of the voting public clearly was satisfied with the status quo; nearly half of all voters (48 per cent) said they wanted to continue doing the same as now. Do voters think that the Reform party is too extreme, that it has crossed the threshold of acceptability?

By urging a harder line on Quebec in the 1993 election, the Reform party was able to destroy the fragile electoral coalition that the Conservatives under Brian Mulroney had built between the West and Quebec. Reform's game plan for the

1997 election was to forge an alliance between the West and Ontario, because no party can aspire to be a plausible alternative to the Liberals unless it has seats in Ontario. For that reason Reform's election campaign paid special attention to Ontario, especially the rural parts of the province. But the party failed to win a single seat in that province and its share of the Ontario vote stalled at its 1993 level. Why was Reform unable to win any seats in Ontario? Did Reform's brand of fiscal conservatism have less appeal to voters in central Canada? Or is Reform simply considered too extreme? Could it be that the party is seen as only speaking for the West? Or is it just that Ontarians like Preston Manning less than Westerners do?

The final question for Reform concerns the future. In 1993 the party attracted a huge number of defections from the Conservatives, but in 1997 the Conservatives were able to stem the haemorrhaging of support, dashing Reform's hopes of supplanting the party. Having failed to outpoll their rivals, Reformers have turned their attention to the so-called 'united alternative'. What does a comparison of the political preferences of Reform and Conservative voters tell us about the potential support base for this alternative?

The Bases of Reform Support

The puzzle for Reform is why it was unable to enlarge its share of the vote in the 1997 federal election. But before turning to that puzzle, we need to establish briefly why the party was able to match its 1993 vote. As was shown in Chapter 2, Reform was the most successful of all the parties in retaining the support of those who had voted for it in the previous federal election. A detailed analysis of the bases of Reform support (see Appendix C) provides important clues about why the party was successful at retaining its 1993 support base.

First, the Reform vote was more strongly rooted in social-background characteristics than the vote of any other party outside Quebec. This can be seen in the higher proportion of variance explained by social-background characteristics for the Reform vote (an adjusted R square of .15). Sex emerges as strongly associated with Reform voting: the Reform vote was 11 points higher among men (35 per cent) than among women (24 per cent) outside Quebec. Similarly, on the left, men were less likely than women to vote NDP by a margin of almost eight points. The role of sex at both ends of the party spectrum is considered in greater detail in Chapter 9.

More important however, were such other factors as region, ethnicity, and religion. Voters of European origin were twice as likely (31 per cent) to vote Reform as those of non-European background (15 per cent). Support was particularly high among voters of northern-European origin, fully half of whom (51 per cent) opted for Reform. Similarly, Protestants were almost twice as likely (35 per cent) as Catholics (19 per cent) to vote Reform. Ancestry and religion are related, but each factor has an effect that is independent of the other. The same applies to region, which will be examined in greater detail later in this chapter.

Given the role of these ethnocultural characteristics, it comes as no great surprise to discover that the Reform vote is also more strongly rooted in basic ideological and communal outlooks than is the case for any of the other parties outside Quebec. When these factors are included as predictors, they double the proportion of explained variation in Reform vote. Reform attracts the support of moral traditionalists and of voters who are opposed to doing more for women. It also appeals to those who are less sympathetic towards outgroups, regardless of whether those outgroups are defined as racial minorities or as aboriginal peoples. The two orientations that clearly have the most significant impact on Reform voting, however, are feelings about accommodating Quebec and political cynicism. The Reform vote is a powerful lightning rod for both anti-Quebec sentiment and generalized political disaffection as well as a feeling that the voter's province is treated unfairly. In these respects, especially, it echoes the profile of the radical populist right in Western Europe (Betz 1993; Betz and Immerfall 1998; Kitschelt 1995; Nevitte et al. 1998). As Betz (1993, 420) notes, these parties have enjoyed their greatest success when they have fused frustration with politics and politicians with resentment of regions that are seen as draining the country's resources.

The Reform party was also the main beneficiary of dissatisfaction with the Liberal record in government. At least three aspects of the Liberal party's performance in government helped to increase support for the Reform party— the deficit, crime, and national unity. Anger over the GST, however, helped the Conservatives as well as Reform.

Part of the frustration that Reform taps into is economic, though there were good reasons to suppose that the NDP would have been in the best position to reap the electoral benefits of economic discontent, not least because the NDP made the Liberal government's economic performance on jobs the centrepiece of its campaign (see Chapter 9). But it was Reform, not the NDP, that was best able to capitalize on this front. Voters who thought that Canada's economy had deteriorated and who saw no improvement in the unemployment situation were attracted to Reform. To be sure, the party got hardly any support from those who wanted to see the government play an active role in job creation. Quite the reverse. Rather, it was those who were sceptical of government intervention in the economy who turned to Reform.

Reform's 1993 election platform was based on a commitment to eliminate the federal deficit within three years. In 1997 the party tried to increase its support by adding the promise of tax cuts to this fiscally conservative platform. Our analysis of the Conservative vote in 1997 has already shown that campaigning on tax cuts may well have been a strategic miscalculation (see Chapter 7), since the desire for tax cuts was very much a minority position and the issue made only a very modest contribution to the Reform vote. When faced with the difficult choice between cutting taxes and maintaining social programs, barely one Reform voter in three (31 per cent) actually favoured tax cuts. The same conclusion applies to other issues, including the desire to get tougher on crime and opposition to gun control. Both positions helped Reform, but not much.

Why Is the Reform Party Considered Extreme?

In pressing for a harder line on Quebec, the Reform party seems to have distanced itself from the average voter, even outside Quebec. Doing less for Quebec is a minority position, and even among Reform's own supporters, only a small majority (57 per cent) favours a harder line towards Quebec. Has the party's position on Quebec contributed to a feeling that Reform is too extreme?

Outside Quebec, almost one voter in four (24 per cent) spontaneously named Reform when asked if there was any political party that is just too extreme. When those who voted Reform are taken out of the picture, the figure rises to 30 per cent. More important, these perceptions about Reform being 'too extreme' had a significant negative effect on Reform voting, even after a host of other relevant explanatory factors are taken into account. One of the reasons that the Reform party did not attract more support in 1997, then, is that a significant proportion of the electorate considered it to be too extreme. One way to find out why Reform is considered too extreme is to probe the data more deeply to see what attitudes are most strongly associated with this perception.

Those who wanted to do more for Quebec were more than twice as likely (50 per cent) as those who wanted to do less (22 per cent) to name Reform as a party they consider too extreme. But the fact is that fewer than 10 per cent of respondents actually wanted to do more for Quebec. Similarly, 51 per cent of those who wanted to admit more immigrants and 44 per cent of those who wanted to do more for racial minorities considered the Reform party to be too extreme. But once again, the proportion of the voting public taking either of these positions was modest—only 9 per cent and 25 per cent respectively. And only about 40 per cent of those who strongly disagreed with the idea that only married people should have children and that we would all be better off if more women stayed home with their children named Reform as too extreme. Respondents with these socially conservative views, though, made up almost one-third (32 per cent) of the total sample of respondents in the election surveys.

All of these factors clearly do contribute to the impression that the Reform party is too extreme, but they pale in importance when compared with two other considerations. Two-thirds (66 per cent) of those who strongly agreed that the Reform party speaks only for the West and almost three-quarters (73 per cent) of those who strongly agreed that Preston Manning is a threat to Canadian unity named Reform when asked whether there was any party that was just too extreme. Almost one-quarter (23 per cent) of the voting public shares these views. Two findings are central here. First, each of these two beliefs significantly reduces the likelihood of a Reform vote. Second, and more important for interpretive purposes, when these two items are included in the analysis, the view that Reform is too extreme no longer has any impact on the vote. This means that people's views about Reform being too extreme are almost entirely attributable to the twin perceptions that the party is only a mouthpiece for the West and that its leader threatens national unity.

Ontario: The Failure to Break Through

Although those impressions may have been particularly damaging to the party's chances in Ontario, there are other plausible explanations for why Reform failed to break through in that province. One possibility is that its policies simply had less appeal outside Western Canada, perhaps because support for fiscal conservatism has ebbed in Ontario or because fewer Ontarians want to get tough with Quebec. Then again, Reform's fiscal policy, or its approach to Quebec, may simply have mattered less to voters in Ontario.[2]

An examination of the data shows that Westerners and Ontarians are essentially indistinguishable in their views on deficit reduction and tax cuts.[3] In the West and Ontario alike, a clear majority supported deficit reduction and only a minority favoured tax cuts, but where the two regions do differ is in the importance of these issues to voters' choice of party. In contrast to the West, neither deficit reduction nor tax cuts had a significant effect on the vote in Ontario. This was also true of the party's calls for more severe policies on crime and its opposition to gun control. In fact, in Ontario a majority of our respondents (59 per cent) thought that only the police and the military should be allowed to have guns.

It turns out that the issue that kept more Ontarians from voting Reform was the government's role in job creation. In both regions, strong majorities believed that governments can and should do something to reduce unemployment.[4] The difference lay in the fact that job creation was simply not an issue in Reform voting in the West and therefore did not hurt the party whereas in Ontario this was the only issue that had a significant effect on the Reform vote. The more a person favoured government involvement in job creation, the less likely he or she was to vote for Reform.

The differences between the West and Ontario on the issues in the 1997 vote become even more striking on the matter of Quebec. Ontario residents are readier than Westerners to accommodate Quebec, though the gap is surprisingly small. In both parts of the country, clear majorities oppose recognizing Quebec as a distinct society, but the majority is smaller in Ontario (58 per cent) than in the West (65 per cent). Similarly, 40 per cent of Westerners would actually favour doing less for Quebec, but so would 34 per cent of Ontarians. Where Westerners and Ontarians really part company is in the importance of the Quebec question. In Ontario opinions on accommodating Quebec simply do not affect the Reform vote. The contrast with the West could hardly be sharper. In the West, opinions about Quebec are one of the prime factors motivating a vote for the party.

Two other factors differentiate the voting of Westerners and Ontarians. Moral traditionalists gravitated towards the Reform party in Western Canada, but not in Ontario. There was nothing to indicate, though, that Westerners were any more morally traditional on average than Ontarians.[5] The second difference is that Westerners were a little less sympathetic to outgroups than voters in Ontario and it was only in the West that voters who were less sympathetic towards outgroups were attracted to Reform.[6]

In short, Reform's inability to break out of the West cannot be attributed to ideological differences between Ontario and the West. Westerners are not more fiscally conservative, less willing to accommodate Quebec, or more socially conservative than their Ontario counterparts. On average, voters in the two regions are ideologically indistinguishable on these dimensions,[7] but what does differentiate them is the way that ideology plays into the Reform vote. A westerner's vote for Reform is more ideological in the sense that it owes more to underlying values. The one exception to that finding is that in both the West and Ontario the party had greater appeal to those who were opposed to doing more for women.

The fact that there are demonstrable differences in the ways that basic ideological outlooks and opinions on issues affect the vote in the two regions underlines a basic strategic challenge. How can one party successfully appeal to two quite different sets of concerns in the two regions? This, of course, has large strategic implications for any party aiming to cobble together cross-country support.

Reform's difficulties in Ontario are compounded by the fact that Preston Manning is less popular in Ontario than in the West. Not only did Manning score seven points lower (on a 100-point scale) in Ontario, but he ranked last, five points behind NDP leader Alexa McDonough (see Figure 8.1). Our calculations show that six points of the difference in Reform voting between Ontario and the West are directly attributable to the fact that Ontarians liked Manning less (Gidengil et al. 1999).[8] Even in the West, Manning ranked only slightly ahead of Alexa McDonough (though many more voters knew enough about him to provide a rating). In both regions, Manning was hurt by his stand on Quebec. In Ontario, one voter in two (50 per cent) agreed with the statement that Manning is a threat to Canadian unity. This is a strong statement, and yet it was also endorsed by almost two Westerners in five (38 per cent).

These findings bring into sharp focus the larger question whether Ontarians were more likely to consider the Reform party to be too extreme and, if they did, whether this hurt Reform's chances in that province. When respondents were asked whether there was any party that was just too extreme, 28 per cent of Ontarians spontaneously named the Reform party. Only the Bloc Québécois, a party committed to taking Quebec out of Canada, was mentioned more often

Figure 8.1: Average Ratings of Leaders, West and Ontario

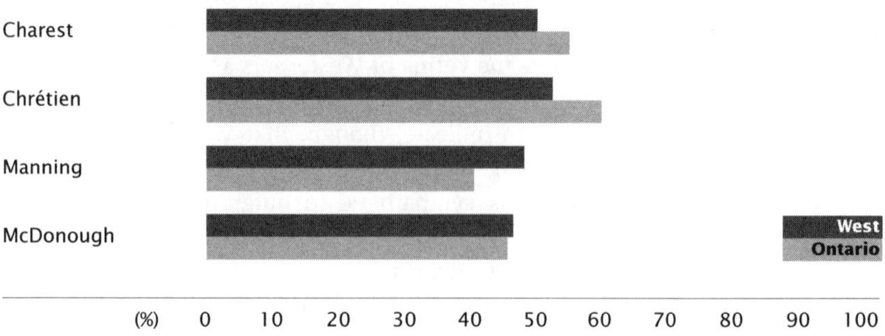

than Reform. No other party came close to being named so frequently. Reform received four times as many mentions as the NDP, the party mentioned the next most often in Ontario (7 per cent of mentions). If only those who actually named a party (one in four responded 'none') are considered and Reform voters are excluded, the results are even more dramatic. Over half (55 per cent) of those who named a party named Reform. What is truly surprising is that the figure for the West was exactly the same: after Reform voters are excluded, 55 per cent of Westerners naming a party as too extreme named Reform. In effect, the impression that Reform was too extreme not only hurt the party's chances of achieving a breakthrough in Ontario, but they also limited its capacity to expand its electoral base in the West.

The Reform party is also hurt by the impression that it speaks only for the West, a view that is shared by half of Ontarians (53 per cent). Even in its Western heartland, however, close to half (46 per cent) agree. The difference between the two regions lies in the fact that this judgement has a much stronger influence on vote choice in Ontario. Even in the West, though, it makes a Reform vote significantly less likely.

Those who consider Manning a threat to national unity, those who think the party is too extreme, and those who believe that the party speaks only for the West are all significantly less likely to vote Reform. And each of those opinions has an effect independent of the others. These findings apply both in the West and in Ontario. In Ontario, however, the view that Reform is too extreme has a significant effect only when the other two views are omitted. With the latter added, opinions about Reform's extremeness cease to have any effect whatsoever. This means that in Ontario the impression that the Reform party is too extreme is very much a function of the twin judgements that Manning jeopardizes Canadian unity and that his party speaks only for one region of the country.

Collectively, these findings point to the conclusion that there are real limits to how much the Reform vote can grow, even in the West, a conclusion that is reinforced by other findings. In the post-election survey, after the respondents were asked how they had voted, they were asked if they had a second-choice party. In Ontario and the West alike, Reform received fewer second-choice mentions than any of the other contending parties (see Figure 8.2). Only one voter in 10 (11 per cent) named Reform as their second choice. In Ontario, the Conservatives were the second choice of the largest number of voters (30 per cent), while in the West it was the Liberals (26 per cent).

One telling result reported in Figure 8.2 is the high proportion of voters in the West (27 per cent) who did not name a second choice. Among Reform voters, this figure rises to almost one-third (32 per cent). This percentage, which is much higher than the Ontario figure (17 per cent), draws attention to the role that disaffection may have played in Reform's success in the West. Does Reform do better in the West because Westerners are so disenchanted with the political process?

Though Westerners have become quite cynical about the political process, so, too, have residents of Ontario.[9] Moreover, the effect of cynicism on Reform voting is as strong in Ontario as in the West. The more sceptical the voters are about politics, the more likely they are to opt for Reform. This is one of the few parallel findings. Where the two regions differ is in the nature of their disaffection. In the West, generalized cynicism about politics is compounded by the belief that the region is not treated fairly. Westerners are twice as likely (36 per cent) as residents of Ontario (18 per cent) to believe that the federal government treats their province worse than other provinces. In Ontario, in fact, the people who think their province is actually treated better are more numerous (22 per cent) than those who believe the reverse. And that is a further limitation on Reform's appeal in Ontario. According to our estimates, these differences contribute almost three percentage points to the gap in Reform voting between the two regions.

The Reform party is clearly a vehicle for Western alienation. That disaffection gives the party a strong base of support, but it also limits its ability to

Figure 8.2: Second-Choice Party, West and Ontario (% naming each party)

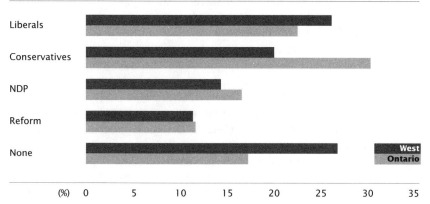

break out of the West. One important way that it does this is by fuelling the damaging impression in Ontario that it is just too extreme. The Reform party's problems in Ontario are compounded by the combined effect of two other factors: the difficulty of appealing to a quite different political agenda and the unpopularity of its leader. It may be that Reform could counter the impression that it only speaks for the West by having a leader from Ontario, but that could also erode its appeal to Westerners.

The Prospects for a United Alternative

Unless the Reform party can shed its image of being too extreme and too focused on the West, its prospects for growth do not look very bright. But what about the prospects for a consolidation of the right? Since the presence of two political parties occupying the right part of the political spectrum undoubtedly helps the Liberals, perhaps the best way for the parties of the right to defeat the Liberals is to consider some form of merger. But again, our results suggest that the prospects are dim for a Reform-Conservative merger.

Almost two-thirds (65 per cent) of Conservative voters agreed that the Reform party speaks only for the West, and almost as many (61 per cent) considered Preston Manning to be a threat to Canadian unity. And fully one-third (34 per cent) of Conservative voters mentioned the Reform party when asked if there was any federal political party that was too extreme. The results for second-choice votes offer even less encouragement to Reform strategists (see Chapter 2). Conservative voters were as likely to name the NDP (20 per cent) as their second choice as they were to name Reform (18 per cent). In fact, if second choices are any guide, Conservative voters would be almost two and a half times as likely to migrate to the centre as to the right: 44 per cent of Conservative voters named the Liberals as their second choice. Strategically, the Conservative party has little incentive to move to the right. There are more potential votes to be picked up from the centre than from the right: 38 per cent of Liberal voters named the Conservatives as their party of second choice, compared with only 27 per cent of Reformers (and there were, of course, more Liberal voters).

The difficulties facing a unite-the-right plan become even clearer when issues are considered. The three sets of issues that stand out as separating Conservative voters from Reform supporters are law and order, moral traditionalism, and accommodating diversity. These are precisely the issues that separate supporters of radical right parties from supporters of the older conservative parties in western Europe (Betz 1993; Ignazi 1992; Kitschelt 1995). Where Canada's new right party differs from its European relatives is on the economic dimension. In contrast to supporters of the European new right, Reform voters are very close to Conservative voters when it comes to issues like the deficit and government spending. But so, too, are Liberal voters, making this a very crowded part of the issue space.[10] And on the issues that define the new right, Conservative voters are as close to the Liberals—or closer—than they are to Reform voters.

Reform and Conservative voters do agree on the importance of fighting crime, an issue that was rated personally very important by 72 per cent of Reformers and 68 per cent of Conservatives. The differences emerge on the matter of how to go about accomplishing the goal (see Figure 8.3). Reform voters were more opposed to strict gun control laws than Conservative voters, they were more likely to favour the death sentence, and they were much likelier to see tougher sentences as the best way to deal with young offenders who commit violent crimes.

Reform voters were also more likely than Conservative voters to favour so-called traditional values. That is, they were much more likely to believe that we would all be better off if more women stayed home to raise their children and they were much less likely to want to do anything more for women. On both these questions, Conservative voters were actually closer to NDP supporters than they were to Reformers. Similarly, Conservative voters were less likely than Reform voters to agree that only married couples should have children.

Figure 8.3: Social Conservatism, by Vote, Outside Quebec (% giving socially conservative response)

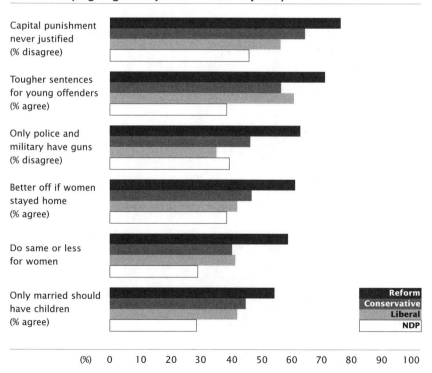

Reform voters were also less willing to accommodate diversity in the racial and ethnic domain (see Figure 8.4). This is evident when it comes to reducing federal spending on aboriginal peoples and doing less for racial minorities. It should be noted, though, that even among Reformers these are minority positions. The data do not warrant the sweeping charges of racism or ethnocentrism that have been levelled against Reform supporters. And on immigration, Reform supporters were not particularly distinct in wanting to admit fewer immigrants. Both of these findings suggest further need for caution in drawing parallels with the radical right in Europe.

The sharpest differences between supporters of the two right parties appear on the Quebec question. Fully three-quarters of Reform voters were opposed to recognizing Quebec as a distinct society, and well over half wanted to do less to accommodate Quebec. The degree of opposition to recognizing Quebec as a distinct society, even among non-Reform voters, suggests just how difficult a task it would be to achieve such recognition.[11] None the less, it is clear that Reform voters take a much harder line on Quebec than Conservative voters.

A final stumbling block for the Reform party in attracting the support of Conservative voters turns on the matter of leadership, for Conservative voters liked Preston Manning even less than Reform voters liked the then Conservative leader Jean Charest. While Reform voters gave Charest an average rating of 45

Figure 8.4: Views on Accommodating Diversity, by Vote, Outside Quebec (% taking the position)

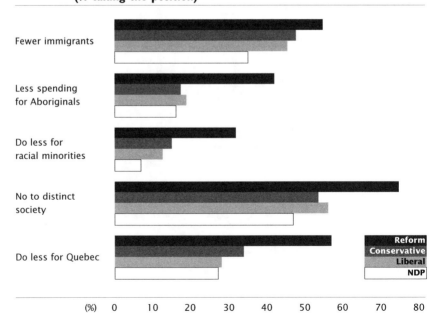

on a 100-point scale, Conservative voters gave Manning only 37. Indeed, excluding his own supporters, no other leader was liked so little by so many voters across the entire partisan spectrum. Manning was judged to be the least compassionate of the leaders, and he tied with Jean Chrétien as the most arrogant (see Figure 7.3). Manning *was* rated ahead of Charest and Chrétien on trustworthiness, but none of the leaders, Manning included, was judged to be particularly trustworthy. And perceptions of trustworthiness had less influence on his overall rating than on either Charest's or McDonough's.[12]

It is obvious that if the Reform party wants to engineer a united alternative on the right, it will have to soften its policy on Quebec. It will also have to work harder to shed its image of ethnocentrism and become more open to changing social values. It may even have to change its leader. Certainly, it will have to dispel the widespread impression that it only speaks for the West.

Conclusion

The Reform party had two objectives in the election: to displace the Bloc Québécois as the official Opposition and to gain seats in Ontario. It succeeded in the former (though aided by the Bloc's weaker showing in Quebec), but it failed to achieve the hoped-for breakthrough in Ontario. The preceding analyses show that for the most part appeals that worked in the West simply failed to help the party in Ontario. They also reveal significant differences between the regions in how the voters make their choice and testify to how regionalized Canadian voting has become.

The widespread view that the Reform party is too extreme points to the limits on its ability to grow. This view is closely associated with the twin beliefs that the party speaks only for the West and that Preston Manning is a threat to national unity. The extent of agreement with the latter proposition suggests that for many voters the Reform party has passed out of the region of acceptability. Perhaps one of the most surprising findings is that this lesson applies equally to Reform's Western heartland. This same constellation of beliefs also constitutes a formidable barrier to any consolidation of the two parties of the right, at least under Reform stewardship.

It is hardly surprising, then, that the first preference to emerge from the United-Alternative Conference in February 1999 was the creation of a new national conservative party. As we write, Reform members have yet to vote on whether to pursue this idea. Whichever way this vote goes, our analyses suggest that the prospects for success of such a party are doubtful. First, there are the differences in the issue preferences of the target voters. Regardless of whether the issue is race, gender roles, moral traditionalism, law and order, or Quebec, Conservative voters are closer to Liberal voters than they are to Reform voters. Second, it is one thing to urge Reformers to moderate their stands on issues like Quebec and private morality, as Alberta Premier Ralph

Klein did at the United-Alternative Conference, but quite another to induce them to comply. As we have seen, more than the vote of the other parties, the Reform vote is driven by fundamental values, and resistance to accommodating Quebec and moral traditionalism figure prominently among those value commitments. Fiscal conservatism, the proposed glue for the United-Alternative, exerts much less pull.

The prognosis, of course, depends upon which strategic options are eventually taken up. Preston Manning, at least, seems determined to develop flexible options to respond to electoral incentives. Flexibility, though, has its price. One of the few factors that cuts across regions to motivate a Reform vote was generalized political discontent. The Reform party is a political home for those who are deeply dissatisfied with the political process. The optimistic scenario is that incorporation into the political mainstream would serve to defuse some of that frustration with politics and politicians. The more pessimistic scenario is that disappointment with Reform's performance would persuade the disaffected that they simply have no political home and their disaffection could become profound. This is especially likely if Reform—or its successor—begins to look more and more like a traditional brokerage party. There is perhaps no more striking testimony to the compelling logic of brokerage politics than Preston Manning's attempts, however unsuccessful to date, to reach out to Quebec nationalists.[13]

Chapter 9

The NDP: Off the Radar Screen

Compared with the fiasco of the 1993 federal election, the NDP could count the 1997 outcome a success. The party regained official status in the House of Commons and with it the benefits that official status brings. It increased the number of ridings in which it qualified for financial reimbursement by over 80 per cent, and it achieved a historic breakthrough in Atlantic Canada. None the less, its 11 per cent share of the vote was surely a disappointment to the party. At the beginning of the campaign, party strategists had every reason to believe they would do better.[1] The Liberals appeared to be vulnerable on their left flank. They had barely succeeded in bringing the unemployment rate below double digits; they had reneged on their apparent commitment to do away with the regressive GST; and once returned to power they made deficit reduction their priority rather than protecting social programs. The Liberals' vulnerability was underlined by the fact that four out of every five (82 per cent) Canadians outside Quebec said that creating jobs was very important to them personally, three out of every four (77 per cent) said the same about keeping election promises, and three out of every five (59 per cent) felt the same way about protecting social programs.

A striking illustration of how far short the NDP fell in capitalizing on the Liberals' record is the fact that evaluations of Liberal performance failed to have any significant effect on the NDP vote (see Appendix C). Voters who were dissatisfied with the Liberals' performance in office were no more likely to turn to the NDP than those who were satisfied. This was true even when it came to creating jobs, keeping their word on the GST, and protecting social programs. It was the same for economic opinions. Remarkably, none of these factors had a significant effect on NDP support. Not even retrospective judgements of the unemployment rate helped the NDP. A majority of voters believed that the unemployment rate had not improved under the Liberals, but that did nothing to motivate a vote for the NDP. If the NDP had identified correctly what concerned the voters—and our polling certainly suggests they did—why did they not do better? Have traditional social democratic prescriptions simply lost their relevance to voters in an increasingly post-industrial society?

The NDP did, of course, fare much better in the Atlantic provinces, where it received almost one vote in four (24 per cent), won six of Nova Scotia's 11 seats, and unseated two Liberal cabinet ministers. Meanwhile the Liberals saw their popular vote share slashed by 24 percentage points, plummeting from 57 per cent in 1993 to only 33 per cent. In Canada's poorest region, the Liberals' deficit reduction strategy had taken its toll, particularly the cuts to unemployment insurance, and these cuts had not been offset by any marked improvement in the region's jobless rate. The major beneficiary of the Liberals' decline in that region was the NDP.[2] For that reason it would seem that the NDP succeeded in taking advantage of the frustrations of a region with chronically high unemployment and a long-standing dependence on federal transfers. But is it possible that much of this surge in the Atlantic provinces was attributable less to the NDP's platform than to its leader, Alexa McDonough, who has deep roots in the region? Indeed, her family's links with the left date back to the early years of the CCF and she is a former leader of the provincial NDP in Nova Scotia.

Although McDonough was the very first NDP leader from the Atlantic provinces, she was not the first woman to lead the party. The first was Audrey McLaughlin. In fact, in the 1993 federal election both the NDP and the Progressive Conservatives were led by women. For that reason and because a record number of women were running for Parliament, that election was supposed to mark women's 'historic breakthrough' in Canadian politics. On election day, however, both parties led by women suffered humiliating defeats. There is no shortage of explanations for these débâcles. Both women may have been the ultimate 'sacrificial lambs', drafted to fight elections they had little chance of winning.[3] The Conservative leader, Kim Campbell, was dogged by the legacy of Brian Mulroney, while the NDP's Audrey McLaughlin had to contend with the enormous unpopularity of the NDP government in Ontario (and, to a lesser extent, British Columbia). None the less, the suspicion persisted that Canadians may simply not be ready to accept a women leader (O'Neill 1998). Was McDonough's sex a factor in the voters' decision whether or not to vote for her party? And did it hurt or help? As we saw in Chapter 8, women were significantly more likely than men to vote NDP, while the Reform party proved disproportionately attractive to men. Is leadership the key to explaining these gender gaps or do the roots of the gender gaps lie in the realm of fundamental values and policy preferences?

The effect of leadership on the NDP vote was likely diluted by low visibility because so few voters knew anything about the party's new leader (see Figure 7.4). This lack of awareness may point to a deeper problem for the NDP. The party faced considerable handicaps going into the 1997 election. It had lacked official status in the House of Commons since the 1993 election, and it had to wage the 1997 federal election campaign on a skimpy budget of only $6 million, which was $1.5 million less than the party had in its campaign coffers in 1993 (Whitehorn 1997). Given those constraints, the only rational way to proceed perhaps was to target the limited funds (and the leader's time) on those ridings that appeared to be winnable. That strategy may help win some precious marginal seats, but it is of little help when it comes to building a country-wide profile. Perhaps the NDP was hampered by its inability to get its message across to the voters.

Out of Touch or Out of Sight?

The NDP is as close as Canada comes to having a traditional 'class party', but unlike its West European cousins the NDP has always lacked a strong basis of support among the working classes. Indeed, Canada is noted for the virtual absence of any country-wide class cleavage. Over 35 years ago, Alford (1963) characterized Canada as a case of 'pure nonclass voting'. In the intervening years there has been little evidence of any surge in class-based voting (Pammett 1987).[4] Any class effects have consistently been overwhelmed by religious, regional, and linguistic differences. But that was before the advent of the politics of deficit reduction.

Have the cuts to social programs since the last election done anything to strengthen the NDP's class base? When class is conceived in traditional terms of occupational status, the answer is a straightforward 'no'. Canadians employed in manual occupations were no more likely than others to vote NDP. In fact, if they were more likely to vote for any party, it was Reform (37 per cent). This lack of support for the class party may not be altogether surprising, given that the cleavage between the haves and the have nots cuts through traditional class categories, and that even the parties of the European left have experienced an erosion in their bases.

All this does not mean, however, that occupation or material circumstances more generally were completely irrelevant to the NDP vote. What did matter, though modestly, to NDP voting are production sector and household income. Continuing a pattern that was already emerging in the 1980s (Blais, Blake, and Dion 1990), public sector workers were significantly more likely to vote NDP than private sector workers. It would seem almost self-evident that those who are dependent on the state for their employment would be drawn to the one party that has opposed reduction in the size of government. By the same token, it is striking that even public sector workers were more likely to vote Reform (23 per cent) than NDP (18 per cent). The same kind of finding emerges for those who are most in need of the shelter of the welfare state. People with household incomes in the lowest quintile, that is, the bottom 20 per cent, were more likely to vote NDP than those in the highest quintile.[5] But even within this economically marginalized group only 17 per cent of the vote went to the NDP.

The weakness of any class effects is underscored by the further finding that people's assessments of economic conditions had no significant effect on the NDP vote. The same holds for evaluations of Liberal performance. Collectively, these results suggest that the 1997 NDP vote cannot be interpreted as a protest vote. What then did motivate people to vote for the party? The answer lies primarily in fundamental ideological outlooks and election issues.

One of the thorniest strategic problems for parties of the left has been how to reconcile the traditional working-class left with the new post-materialist left. This is what Przeworski and Sprague (1986) have termed 'the dilemma of electoral socialism'. To the extent that working-class voters tend to be socially conservative,[6] it can prove difficult to fit the old and new lefts together. In fact, the very lack of a working-class base may have facilitated the task for the NDP, for, as the evidence presented in Chapter 4 clearly shows, NDP supporters are the most sceptical of the capitalist system and the least morally traditional.

The party's non-traditional stance on issues of contemporary morality is seen in its greater appeal to secular voters and its lesser appeal to voters in traditional marriages (see Appendix C). The less morally traditional voters are, the more likely they are to vote NDP. On the economic dimension, the less voters are persuaded of the virtues of free enterprise and the more resistant they are to closer ties with the United States, the more likely their votes are to go to the NDP. The party also picks up more votes from those who are readier to accommodate Quebec. Finally, an important non-finding deserves emphasis. Cynicism about the political process does nothing to motivate a vote for the NDP, a finding which again suggests that this was no protest vote.

It was specific issues, not a general feeling of malaise, that attracted voters to the NDP. First, however, there is an intriguing non-finding. Gun control was a tricky issue for a party that simultaneously targets ridings in rural Saskatchewan and in the cities of southern Ontario. The fact that views about gun control had no significant effect on NDP voting suggests that the party succeeded in neutralizing the effects of this issue. The party fared worse, though, among those who would like to get tougher on crime.

The issues that did count as significant to the NDP vote are the predictable ones, namely, the deficit, jobs, spending cuts, and taxes. Those who were the least concerned about the deficit, who favoured government intervention in job creation, and who opposed both spending cuts and tax cuts, were significantly more likely to vote NDP. This comes as no surprise. After all, the NDP is Canada's social democratic alternative and the party campaigned on these very issues. More surprising is just how modest the influence of these issue positions turned out to be (see Appendix C). The jobs issue illustrates the central point. Jobs were the centrepiece of the NDP's campaign, but the effect of the jobs issue on voter support for the NDP was downright weak. Being unemployed or laid-off made no difference to the likelihood of voting NDP, and neither did concern about becoming unemployed or perceptions of the unemployment rate (either retrospective or prospective).

The problem was not that the NDP took a position on job creation that was wildly at odds with Canadians' preferences. Indeed, three out of five (60 per cent) Canadians outside Quebec shared the NDP's position that the government has a legitimate role to play in creating jobs. Most believed that job creation should not be left entirely to the private sector, and 70 per cent rejected the suggestion that there is not much any government can do to solve the unemployment problem. So the puzzle is why the NDP did not get more votes from these people. Part of the answer may have to do with the NDP's lack of credibility. When asked which party would be best at creating jobs, only 15 per cent of those surveyed (outside Quebec) named the NDP. Even among the party's own voters, barely half (51 per cent) named the NDP. The problem was compounded by lack of information. Few voters were even aware of the NDP's campaign promise to cut unemployment in half by the year 2000. When asked which party had made this promise, only 13 per cent were able to name the NDP.

The party fared better when it came to protecting social programs. One respondent in three (34 per cent) thought the NDP would do the best job of protecting social programs, and that figure rose to three in four (74 per cent) among its own supporters. But on this issue, the NDP was definitely taking a minority position. Only one Canadian in three (32 per cent) shared its rejection of the Liberal argument that the only way to maintain social programs was to eliminate the deficit.

More generally, there was a sense that the NDP is out of touch with the times. This opinion was shared by half (53 per cent) of those interviewed (a further 12 per cent could not give an opinion). Even among those who voted for the party, one in five (22 per cent) accepted this verdict. Focusing just on NDP voters provides some clues. For all their scepticism (82 per cent) of the notion that everyone benefits, even the poor, when businesses make a lot of money, barely more than one NDP voter in three would actually favour doing less for business (see Figure 9.1). More telling, perhaps, is the evidence that even fewer wanted to see labour unions have more power. The NDP's long-standing relationship with the unions turns out to be a very mixed blessing for the party. Unquestionably, people from union households are more likely to vote NDP (Archer 1985), but by a margin of only eight percentage points in 1997. In fact, the Reform party received more votes from union households than the NDP did. And beliefs about how much power unions should have kept more people from voting NDP. Even after an array of background characteristics and political preferences are taken into account, those who did not want to see unions have more power were significantly less likely to vote NDP. With almost one voter in two (48 per cent) actually wanting to see unions have less power, views about unions cost the NDP almost two points. Clearly, the party needs to weigh the organizational advantages of its ties with organized labour against the electoral costs.

Even when it comes to social spending, NDP voters are far from being whole-heartedly committed to traditional social democratic principles (see Figure 9.1). For all their scepticism about free enterprise, fewer than half rejected the argument that people who do not get ahead have only themselves to blame. Only a bare majority resisted cuts to spending on welfare, and fewer still

Figure 9.1: Opinions on Free Enterprise and Spending Cuts, Outside Quebec (% taking position indicated)

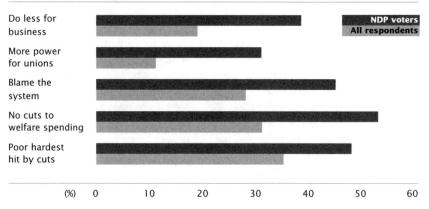

believed that the poor had been hit hardest by the Liberals' spending cuts. Finally, one NDP voter in three (32 per cent) accepted the argument that the deficit had to be eliminated in order to maintain social programs. Faced with the hard choices of the 1990s, many NDP voters seemed to be lukewarm social democrats at best.

The Atlantic Breakthrough

If the NDP message was going to hit home anywhere in 1997, it would surely be in the Atlantic provinces. In 1993 the region had given the Liberals their highest vote share (57 per cent), ahead even of Ontario's (53 per cent). In 1993 the expectation was that the Liberals would make jobs their priority and would protect social programs. Instead, the priority became deficit reduction, even at the expense of social spending. Faced with chronically high unemployment and cuts to federal transfers, Atlantic Canadians who had voted Liberal in the last federal election had reason to be angry in 1997. Did this anger fuel the NDP breakthrough in the region?

The evidence is surprising. People's evaluations of the Liberal performance had no significant effect at all on the NDP vote in the Atlantic provinces. Nor did their opinions about economic conditions. These striking non-findings are no less puzzling because they simply mirror the results for the country (outside Quebec) as a whole. In Atlantic Canada, if anywhere, dissatisfaction with Liberal performance should have translated into a higher vote for the NDP and yet this was not the case. The 72 per cent of Atlantic Canadians who believed that the Liberals had done poorly at job creation were no more likely to vote NDP than those who were satisfied. The same is true of the 59 per cent who thought the Liberals had done a poor job of protecting social programs. Atlantic

Canadians were more likely (46 per cent) than others to believe that the unemployment rate had actually gone up since the Liberals came to power—and to believe that it would continue to rise (36 per cent)—and yet these negative perceptions failed to motivate an NDP vote. The same is true of the 30 per cent who believed that the Canadian economy had deteriorated, along with the 37 per cent who said the same of their personal finances.

Material circumstances, however, did have some bearing on the NDP's success in the Atlantic provinces. Those who were unemployed or laid-off were significantly more likely to vote NDP, and those with family incomes in the highest income quintile were significantly less likely to. Moreover, the issues that counted when it came to voting NDP were jobs and the deficit. At the same time, barely one Atlantic Canadian in five (19 per cent) named the NDP as the party that would do best at creating jobs.

Views on spending cuts also failed to have any significant effect; there is no indication that these mobilized people to vote NDP. Those who were reluctant to countenance further spending cuts—and they were significantly more numerous in the Atlantic provinces[7]—were no more likely to vote NDP than those who favoured cuts. Again, this is a surprising finding, given the region's long-standing dependence on federal transfers and the fact that 60 per cent of the region's residents believed that the federal spending cuts had been unfair. Why did this issue not help the NDP? A combination of factors was at work. First, Atlantic Canadians were only slightly less likely (57 per cent) than other Canadians to believe that it was necessary to eliminate the deficit in order to maintain social programs. Second, they were more likely (49 per cent) than other Canadians to believe that the best way to fight unemployment was to reduce taxes, and when confronted with the difficult choice between maintaining social programs and cutting taxes, they were more likely (31 per cent) to favour tax cuts. Finally, they were no more likely (34 per cent) than other Canadians to name the NDP as the party that would be best at protecting social programs.

What really mattered when it came to voting NDP were basic ideological beliefs. Scepticism about the workings of the capitalist system had a much more powerful impact on the NDP vote in Atlantic Canada than anywhere else in the country. The same applied to views about continental integration, though the effect is weaker.[8] The appeal of the NDP to Atlantic Canadians, in other words, lay very much in the realm of fundamental principles, which may be why the region's residents were much less likely (32 per cent) than other Canadians to believe that the NDP is out of touch with the times. Where Atlantic Canadians seem to be sceptical is about the party's ability to put its principles into effective practice.

Another factor contributing to NDP support in Atlantic Canada was cynicism about the political process.[9] In contrast to other parts of the country, the NDP was more attractive to voters who subscribed to a cluster of negative beliefs about politicians and about the unresponsiveness of government. If Atlantic Canadians thought that politicians are ready to lie to get elected, that they hardly ever keep their election promises, that members of Parliament lose touch with their constituents, and that the government does not care what they think, they were more likely to vote NDP. To the extent that the NDP vote in the Atlantic provinces did entail any elements of protest, it was manifested in this expression of general political malaise.

This leaves the role of Alexa McDonough. Feelings about McDonough did have a significant effect on Atlantic Canadians' vote. NDP voters in the region rated McDonough, on average, 10 points higher than their second-ranked leader. This is not an inconsequential amount, but why could she do no better among Atlantic voters at large than a tie in the popularity stakes with the Liberal and Conservative leaders? As the party's first leader from the region, she might well have hoped for more. McDonough's problem in the Atlantic region, as elsewhere in the country, was that many voters seemed to know little about her. Certainly, she was more familiar there than elsewhere, but even so, two in five (39 per cent) Atlantic Canadians said that they knew nothing at all about her. The problem was that those who knew about her were concentrated very much in her home province of Nova Scotia. Only 14 per cent of Nova Scotians said that they knew nothing at all about McDonough. Elsewhere in the region, the figures ranged from 48 per cent in Prince Edward Island to 61 per cent in Newfoundland.[10] Feelings about McDonough followed a similar provincial gradient. Nova Scotia was the only province to give her a favourable average rating (57 points on a 100-point scale). In Newfoundland she averaged only 40 points.[11] It is clear that outside her home province, visibility was again the problem for McDonough.

The Gender Gap

We have already seen (Chapter 8) that women were significantly more likely than men to vote NDP. In fact, at almost eight percentage points, the so-called gender gap in NDP voting rivalled the gap between union and non-union households. Though it might be thought that the presence of Alexa McDonough can explain the NDP's greater appeal to women, it turns out that ideological outlook is more important than leadership, suggesting that the gender gap in NDP voting may have staying power.

Leadership was certainly a factor in the gender gap. Women not only liked McDonough more than men did (see Figure 9.2), but relative ratings of McDonough had a greater impact on their vote.[12] And when leadership is added to the vote model, the sex difference in NDP voting shrinks to insignificance (see Appendix C). This is an indication that feelings about McDonough help explain why women were more likely to vote NDP.

It is important not to overstate women's liking for McDonough, though. First, many women felt that they knew very little, if anything, about her. The percentage of women interviewed during the campaign who reported that they

Figure 9.2: Sex Differences in Ratings of Leaders, Outside Quebec (average ratings on a 100-point scale)

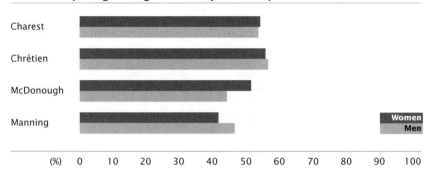

knew 'nothing at all' about McDonough was almost as high (59 per cent) in the last week of the campaign as it was in the opening week (61 per cent).[13] And among those who said they knew something about her, 10 per cent felt unable to rate her. Secondly, women's feelings towards McDonough were on average fairly neutral, though they did react to her more favourably than men. While women ranked her third, behind Chrétien and Charest, she was in fourth place among men, behind Manning. And McDonough's average rating among men was clearly negative. This sex difference in feelings about McDonough (and Manning) stands in marked contrast to the almost complete absence of sex differences in feelings about Chrétien and Charest.

Among those who knew at least something about McDonough, women and men alike thought her the most compassionate of the party leaders and the least arrogant (see Figure 9.3).[14] Women also found McDonough to be the most trustworthy and the most in touch with the times. Men, on the other hand, considered both Charest (31 per cent) and Manning (26 per cent) to be more in touch with the times than McDonough, and they considered both leaders (21 per cent and 19 per cent) to be at least as trustworthy as McDonough. Being compassionate and lacking arrogance may be worthy character traits, but they do not apparently go with an image of strong leadership. 'Providing strong leadership' was judged to be McDonough's weakest attribute. This was true for women as well as for men, though women were less harsh in their judgements.

Providing strong leadership is a stereotypically masculine trait, just as being compassionate is a stereotypically feminine trait (Huddy and Terkildsen 1993). But there are reasons to be cautious about jumping to conclusions that Canadian voters were stereotyping the sole female leader. After all, the evaluation that she was 'compassionate' could just as well have been a reflection of her policy stands or her party label. Similarly, women may have been attracted to her party as much for what she stood for as for any particular personality traits or, still less, simply because she was a woman.

Figure 9.3: Sex Differences in Opinions of McDonough, Outside Quebec (% saying phrase describes the leader very well)

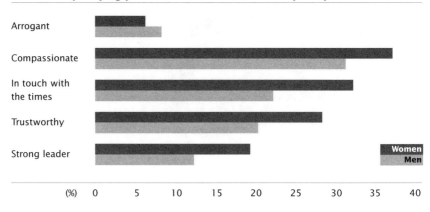

There was indeed much more to the gender gap than McDonough's greater appeal to women. After all, the gap on the left had its mirror image in a gap on the right, where women were significantly less likely than men to vote Reform (see Chapter 8). And both gender gaps are reflected by sex differences on some of the main issues of the campaign. First, there were differences in priorities (see Figure 9.4). Men put reducing the deficit ahead of protecting

Figure 9.4: Sex Differences in Personal Importance of Issues, Outside Quebec (% saying issue is personally very important)

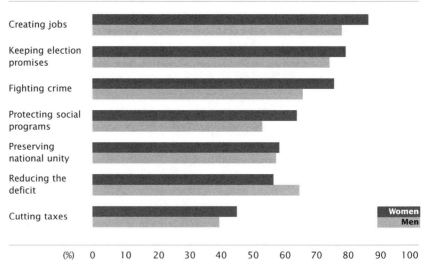

social programs, but women placed the emphasis on social programs, and they were even more persuaded than men of the importance of job creation. Women and men also differed over how they would go about solving these problems (see Figure 9.5). Women were even less persuaded than men that job creation should be left to the private sector; they clearly saw a role for government. They were also more sceptical than men that the deficit had to be eliminated if social programs were to be maintained. Underlying these differences were greater doubts about the fairness of federal spending cuts and a more widespread belief that the quality of education and health care has deteriorated in recent years. Not only did women and men differ in their concerns, but these issues had a stronger effect on women's vote. Indeed, the impact of opinions on the jobs issue on NDP voting was confined to women.

The election of 1997 was the first to reveal a significant gender gap in support for the NDP, but there was already evidence that women have a greater affinity for social democratic prescriptions (Brodie 1991; Everitt 1998; 1999; Gidengil 1995; Gidengil et al. forthcoming; Kopinak 1987; O'Neill 1995; Wearing and Wearing 1991). To be sure, even in 1997, more women voted Reform than voted NDP. None the less, in an electorate not known for its strong cleavages in voting (Leduc 1985), sex has emerged as one of the more important social predictors. Add to this the fact that sex is the 'fault line of maximum potential cleavage', dividing the electorate almost in half (unlike, say, religious affiliation or ethnicity, which applies only to a minority of voters) (Jennings 1988: 9). For these reasons, it is important to ask why women are more

Figure 9.5: Sex Differences in Policy Preferences and Beliefs about Free Enterprise, Outside Quebec (% taking position indicated)

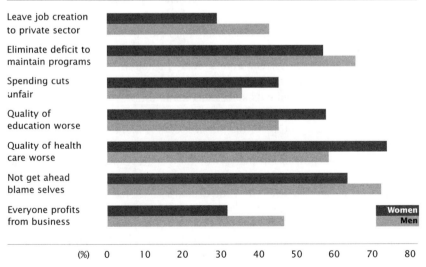

attracted than men to social democratic positions and, finally in 1997, to the political party that promotes them.

One possible explanation lies in the so-called 'welfare state dismantlement hypothesis' (Erie and Rein 1988). At the heart of this explanation is the idea that women are more likely than men to be either clients or employees of the welfare state. Whether the welfare state is providing them with a social safety net or with a job, women will be more reluctant than men to support cuts in social programs. The hypothesis proves half right when it is extended to voting for the NDP. Family income is a strong correlate of women's support for the NDP. Those with family incomes in the lowest quintile are significantly more likely to vote for the party than women whose family income is in the highest quintile. The gap in NDP voting between women in these two income groups is 12 percentage points. There is no comparable income effect for men.[15] Indeed, the income effect that we noted earlier (see Appendix C) turns out to be almost wholly due to the women in the sample. The other half of the hypothesis, however, finds no support. That is, employment in the public sector does not have any significant effect on women's likelihood of voting for the NDP.

A second possible explanation for the gender gap in NDP voting is suggested by Carol Gilligan's (1982) work. Rather than women's material interests, this explanation focuses on sex differences in fundamental ideological outlook that predispose women to be more supportive of the welfare state. Whether by nature or by upbringing, the argument goes, women are less individualistic than men and more likely to adhere to a collectivist conception of society. That outlook is reflected in a greater scepticism about the capitalist system and a greater reluctance to allow market forces to work without restraint. The implication of this argument is that women will be more supportive of government intervention to help those in need and this support will cut across income groups. It turns out that women were indeed even more sceptical than men that everyone benefits, including the poor, when businesses make a lot of money (see Figure 9.5). They were also less likely than men to believe that those who don't get ahead should blame themselves rather than the system. These beliefs about the free enterprise system were strongly related to their vote, even after income differences were taken into account. In fact, women's scepticism about the workings of the system cuts across income lines.

The other ideological question that had a particularly strong effect on women's likelihood of voting for the NDP was continentalism. In fact, the effect observed earlier for the whole sample was almost wholly attributable to women. And we know from analysis of the gender gap in support for the Canada–US Free Trade Agreement in the 1988 federal election that women's resistance to closer ties with the United States is related to their scepticism about the workings of market forces and concerns about welfare provision (Gidengil 1995).

Finally, there is an important non-finding that emerges. The belief that more should be done for women had no significant effect on women's vote for the

NDP. That finding casts doubt on the sex-roles explanation of the gender gap, an explanation that sees women's social democratic leanings as an extension of their traditional roles as wives and mothers. The assumption has been that this will be reflected in a preoccupation with so-called women's issues. Instead, the effect, such as it was, was confined to men.[16]

The key to the gender gap in support for the NDP is clearly women's greater scepticism about the workings of the free enterprise system. These ideological differences between women and men account for over three points of the gender gap in NDP voting. They are far from being the whole story, however. An additional point is due to differences in opinion on the issues of the day, and almost two points to women's greater liking for McDonough. Ideological differences are less of a factor in the gender gap in Reform voting, but at one and a half points, they are a factor none the less. At just over two points, issues assume greater importance in the Reform gap. And the fact that women like Manning less than men do accounts for another two points.

Conclusion

The NDP increased its vote share over 1993 by a wider margin than any other party, and that, coupled with its long-awaited breakthrough in the Atlantic region, was cause for celebration. The party would be spared the recriminations and soul-searching that followed the two previous federal elections. And yet in important respects the NDP's success was very partial. Only in the Atlantic provinces was it able to take advantage of voters' general sense of political malaise. The issue that it had sought to make its own—jobs—failed to win the party many votes, and even in Atlantic Canada, it was unable to capitalize on dissatisfaction with the Liberals' performance in office.

In concentrating on jobs, the NDP had certainly chosen the right issues, and, judging from our respondents' issue positions, it was offering what were, to many voters, the right solutions. Moreover, Alexa McDonough was a potential asset going into the campaign and did, indeed, help the party. Even outside Quebec, however, only two voters in five said they knew anything at all about her, while only slightly more than one in ten associated the promise to cut unemployment in half by the year 2000 with the NDP. And voters who expressed no familiarity with the party's campaign promise and who knew nothing about its leader were significantly less likely to vote NDP, regardless of their issue positions, ideological outlooks, or political evaluations. In short, lack of visibility was a serious obstacle for the party. As the analysis of campaign coverage in Chapter 3 clearly demonstrated, on as many as a third of the evening newscasts on CBC and CTV, there was not a single story about the NDP.

Now that McDonough has a seat in the House of Commons and leads a party that enjoys official status, her visibility should increase and, along with that, her value to the party. Among women, at least, she was able to project an image of being in touch with the times, an image that could well help to counter the party's own image problem of being out of touch. The NDP's appeal to women is a second potential asset as it approaches the next federal election. From that standpoint, the challenge, of course, is to build on this support base among women without compromising its support among men. Finally, the party must be encouraged by the fact that even in the immediate aftermath of the election (and before the cracks began to appear within the Reform party), the NDP was the second choice of 18 per cent of voters, ahead of Reform at only 11 per cent.

The party's problems, however, go beyond lack of visibility. The NDP also has to deal with the impression that it is out of touch. It does help to have a leader who is considered to be in touch with the times, but it is not enough. Chapter 4 provides graphic evidence of the NDP's problem. It is not simply the fact that New Democrats are located so far from the median Canadian voters that should give party strategists pause. Even more worrying for the party is the relatively small number of voters who form its ideological constituency. And now in this chapter we have seen the lukewarm commitment of even its own voters to some of the party's traditional social democratic prescriptions. It is hard to escape the conclusion that these principles are simply not very relevant in the minds of Canadian voters in the 1990s.

The party is currently engaged in a policy review aimed at refashioning the party more in the image of Britain's New Labour. Even the issue of the NDP's organizational ties to the trade unions has been put on the table. It remains to be seen what will emerge from the party's national convention in August 1999, but the opposition from within the party to any changes to its principles or to its relationship with organized labour suggests that the NDP leadership will face formidable obstacles to adapting its social democratic principles to the new political realities. For the party's hardliners the problem is not that the party is too far to the left of the median Canadian voter, but that it is not left enough. The price of ideological purity, however, may be continued marginalization.

Chapter 10

Why Did the Bloc Québécois Lose Ground?

On 2 June 1997, the Bloc Québécois received 38 per cent of the votes cast, thus losing about a quarter of the support it had received four years earlier (49.5 per cent). The Bloc lost one-fifth of its seats in Parliament (10 MPs out of 54) and, in the process, its status as the official Opposition in Ottawa. By these benchmarks the outcome of the 1997 election was a setback for the Bloc.

An examination of the causes of the Bloc's setback thus takes the analysis in several different directions. We must first determine whether, at the beginning of the campaign, the Bloc could count on as large a core of sovereignist voters as in 1993 and whether a significant number of Quebeckers were still convinced of the need for a sovereignist party in Ottawa in 1997. Then we must determine whether there was any link between the performance of Lucien Bouchard's government and support for the Bloc. Finally, on the matter of leadership, it is possible that the Bloc's setback was mainly due to the unpopularity of its leader, Gilles Duceppe.

An Autopsy of the Setback

One useful way of understanding the Bloc Québécois's relatively weak performance in 1997 is to examine electoral choices in relation to the constitutional preferences of the voters. Table 10.1 shows that Gilles Duceppe's party had difficulty maintaining the allegiance of its natural clientele of sovereignists. In fact, nearly one sovereignist in five supported a federalist party in 1997. Significantly, three-quarters of these defections were to Jean Charest's Conservative party. Moreover, the party proved incapable of making significant inroads among federalists, of whom barely one in 20 voted for Lucien Bouchard's old party.

These findings stand in marked contrast with those of 1993. In that election, not only did the Bloc Québécois attract almost all the sovereignist votes, but it also managed to persuade more than one federalist in five (23 per cent, Table 10.1) to vote for a sovereignist party in Ottawa. Led by Lucien Bouchard, the

Table 10.1: Vote and Constitutional Preferences, Quebec, 1993 and 1997

	1993		1997	
	Sovereignists	*Federalists*	*Sovereignists*	*Federalists*
Bloc Québécois	94%	23%	80%	7%
Conservatives	3	20	15	28
Liberals	3	58	5	66
N	648		547	

Bloc Québécois not only enjoyed a solid consensus of support among the sovereignists, but it also attracted a significant number of federalist votes.

The Decline of Sovereignty?

The profile of the Bloc's clientele during the last election illustrates once again just how important the constitutional preferences of Quebec voters are to their electoral choices. The typical Bloc supporter is francophone, relatively young, and unionized. He or she identifies naturally with the Bloc Québécois but is, above all, a sovereignist (see Appendix C). The profile of the Bloc's support base closely resembles that of the PQ, and that underscores the extent to which support for the Bloc depends in part on the climate of opinion in Quebec, particularly on the strength of nationalist sentiment at election time (Blais et al. 1995; Nadeau et al. 1995).

Given these essential features, it is reasonable to suppose that the Bloc's setback may have been the result of a decline in support for Quebec's sovereignty between 1993 and 1997. But the data in Table 10.2 do not justify that interpretation; in fact, support for Quebec sovereignty was virtually the same as during the 1993 election. But, though there was no change in the relative number of sovereignists and federalists between the last two federal elections, there were significant changes in the voting behaviour of the members of these blocs (see Table 10.1). In 1993 there were four times as many defections from the federalist camp as there were from the sovereignist camp; four years later there were three times as many defections from the sovereignist camp as there were from the federalist camp.

How can the stability of constitutional preferences and the changes in electoral behaviour between the two elections be explained? An examination of the determinants of support for sovereignty in 1997 shows that the dividing lines between federalists and sovereignists remained relatively stable over these years, with support for sovereignty more pronounced among francophones (53 per cent versus only 8 per cent among non-francophones), younger voters (49 per cent in the 18–54 age group versus 29 per cent for those 55 and

Table 10.2: Support for Sovereignty, Quebec, 1993 and 1997

	1993	*1997*
Very favourable	16%	22%
Somewhat favourable	30	23
	46	45
Somewhat opposed	22	17
Very opposed	32	38
	54	55
N	809	737

older), as well as among those more attached to Quebec than to Canada or who foresaw positive consequences (economic or linguistic) from sovereignty. These opinions and perceptions have changed little in recent years (Blais and Nadeau 1992; Clarke and Kornberg 1996; Nadeau and Fleury 1995; Nadeau et al. 1999; Pinard et al. 1997). Support for the Bloc seems to have been affected by more immediate factors, three of which deserve particular attention: opinions about the need for electing a sovereignist party in Ottawa; the performance of the Bouchard government; and the popularity of the leaders.

The Utility of a Sovereignist Party in Ottawa

The debate over the need for a sovereignist party in Ottawa is not new. The opinion of sovereignist leaders as to the correct strategy in federal elections has varied, but it has been dominated by René Lévesque's opposition to the direct participation of sovereignists on the federal scene. Originally this strategy was pursued through abstention and the voiding of ballots. Later the Parti Québécois gave tacit support to the political party most favourable to Quebec's interests. In 1979 it even expressed fairly explicit support for the Social Credit leader Fabien Roy and, in 1984, more implicit support for Brian Mulroney. The attempts to launch a federal sovereignist party outside of the Parti Québécois were unsuccessful (the ephemeral Parti nationaliste of the early 1980s obtained little support) until the creation of the Bloc Québécois in the early 1990s.

Because of the success of the Bloc Québécois in 1993 it is easy to overlook the ambiguity of its place in the federal arena. During the 1993 campaign, Lucien Bouchard presented the Bloc as an ephemeral political party whose purpose was to prepare the way for Quebec's sovereignty and whose presence in Ottawa was to be short-lived. That is still the official position of the Bloc's leaders, although a growing number of party members seem to think that the party's presence in Ottawa could be extended if the party stops short of choosing the sovereignty option.

What was the view of Quebeckers on this question during the 1997 election? Is there evidence of reduced interest in having a sovereignist party in Ottawa? Does this explain the decline in support between the two elections? The answers to these questions are complex. Although Quebeckers are divided over the necessity of a sovereignist party on the federal scene (45 per cent of respondents agreed with the statement 'There is no reason to have a sovereignist party in Ottawa' and 43 per cent were opposed), the vast majority still spontaneously named the Bloc Québécois as the party best able to defend Quebec's interests in Ottawa (63 per cent as opposed to only 14 per cent for the Conservatives and 11 per cent for the Liberals). Our analysis of Bloc support suggests that scepticism about the need for a sovereignist party in Ottawa did not affect support for the Bloc Québécois in 1997. Nor does it explain the Bloc's setback; the reservations that some voters have about the presence of the Bloc in Ottawa are outweighed by the other parties' difficulties in presenting themselves as defenders of Quebec's interests. Finally, the relative stability in the number of Bloc partisans in 1993 and 1997 (23 per cent and 20 per cent respectively) also suggests that the Bloc setback could not be attributed to a substantial decrease in the long-term reservoir of support for a sovereignist party in Ottawa.

The Economy

Beyond its sociological profile and ideological roots, support for the Bloc Québécois is also linked to what are usually thought of as short-term factors. These factors involve issues debated during the campaign as well as the popularity of the various leaders. And paramount among these is the state of the economy. The case of the economy raises two questions in the context of federal elections in Quebec. First, is it the performance of Quebec's economy, or of Canada's economy as a whole, that influences Quebec voters the most? Second, if the Quebec economy is most influential, is support for the Bloc Québécois hurt or helped by its ideological association with Lucien Bouchard's PQ government?

The data in Appendix C shed light on this question. The first point to observe is that perceptions about Quebec's economy are significantly linked to the probability of supporting or not supporting the Bloc Québécois. The more satisfied a Quebec resident is with the Quebec economy, the more likely he or she is to vote for the Bloc Québécois.

The coefficient linking support for the Bloc to the economic variable is .05, which means that, other things being equal, the probability that a voter satisfied with the performance of Quebec's economy supports the Bloc Québécois is 10 points higher than for an unsatisfied voter.[1] To appreciate how that affected the 1997 election, we need to examine what the economic perceptions were at the time of the elections.

Table 10.3 shows, first of all, that the economic perceptions of Quebeckers concerning their own province were more negative (–26) than those concerning Canada as a whole (–5). This difference is significant. If the assessments of the economic situation in Quebec had been the same as those for all of Canada, then the Bloc would have gained an extra percentage point.[2]

This estimate of the economic impact is probably too conservative. Not surprisingly, both federal and provincial politicians often take credit for any improvements in the economy but blame each other when there are none. The voters, however, make their own assessment of who deserves the credit and the blame. In the 1997 election, Quebec voters punished the Bloc for the performance of Quebec's economy. If they had held the federal government responsible, the Bloc would have increased its electoral support to about 40 per cent.[3]

Overall, the impact of economic perceptions in Quebec on the Bloc's vote was real but relatively weak (one to two points). These findings, coupled with the preceding analysis of support for sovereignty, the usefulness of the Bloc, and its partisan base, strongly suggest that political leadership may well have played a crucial role in the decline of Lucien Bouchard's former party between 1993 and 1997.

The Popularity of the Political Leaders

The evidence displayed in Appendix C shows that, all else being equal, a voter very favourable to Gilles Duceppe (evaluation of 100) and very unfavourable to all the other leaders (evaluation of 0) sees his or her probability of supporting the Bloc rise 45 percentage points. The impact of this variable, a bit weaker than that observed for the Liberals (the coefficient of the variable LEADER is .52 for Jean Chrétien) and significantly less than in the case of the Conservatives (the coefficient is .66 in this case), shows that the effect of the LEADER variable in electoral choices was less for the Bloc Québécois than for the other federal parties in 1997.

What explains the relatively unfavourable opinions about Gilles Duceppe? According to our data, the Bloc leader's popularity was damaged most by an appearance of weakness. The ratings of the leadership strength of Gilles Duceppe, Jean Chrétien, and Jean Charest are striking (see Table 10.4). Of

Table 10.3: Perceptions of Economy in Last 12 Months, Quebec, 1997

	Provincial	National
Better	13%	24%
Same	47	48
Worse	39	29
	(–26)	(–5)
N	1,021	1,022

Table 10.4: Percentage of Respondents Saying That the Statement 'He Is a Strong Leader' Describes (Gille Duceppe/ Jean Chrétien/ Jean Charest) Very Well, Fairly Well, Not Very Well, or Not at All

	Duceppe	Chrétien	Charest
Very well	6	16	29
Fairly well	25	42	54
Not well	69	41	16

Note: 'Not very well' and 'not at all' categories are collapsed. 'Don't know's' and refusals (7% for Charest and Duceppe and 3% for Chrétien) are excluded.

those who expressed an opinion, only 6 per cent strongly agreed with the statement that Gilles Duceppe was 'a strong leader'. That compares with 16 per cent for Jean Chrétien and 29 per cent for Jean Charest. When the percentages of those who believe that this trait describes the leaders very well or fairly well are added, Jean Charest had a 52-point edge over the Bloc leader (83 per cent versus 31 per cent) and a 25-point lead over Jean Chrétien (83 per cent versus 58 per cent).[4] The image of Gilles Duceppe as weak and indecisive is probably linked to the erratic character of the Bloc electoral campaign (see Chapter 3). Duceppe's stature may well have suffered also from the inevitable comparisons with Lucien Bouchard, and this, as will become obvious,[5] was clearly a problem for the Bloc.

The figures in Table 10.5 (which are for francophones only) also point to the conclusion that Gilles Duceppe was burdened with a serious image problem. Among sovereignists, the average evaluation of Gilles Duceppe was only 53. Among this same group four years earlier, Lucien Bouchard's rating had been 73. In fact, among the sovereignists, the evaluation of Gilles Duceppe was barely higher than that of Jean Charest (53 compared to 49). The lack of enthusiasm generated by the Bloc's leader among his own troops was shared by federalists. In fact, Gilles Duceppe's popularity among the federalists was as low as Jean Chrétien's among the sovereignists. Undoubtedly, some sovereignists supported Gilles Duceppe's party despite their reservations about him.

Table 10.5: Ratings of Leaders and Constitutional Preferences, Quebec Francophones, 1993 and 1997

	1993		1997	
	Sovereignists	Federalists	Sovereignists	Federalists
Bouchard or Duceppe	73	56	53	30
Campbell or Charest	44	38	49	57
Chrétien	49	63	34	56

And among federalists, while aware of the presence of a party dedicated to the defence of Quebec's interests in Ottawa, hesitated to vote for this party because they shared these very same reservations about the Bloc's leader (Nadeau 1997; Nadeau et al. 1997).

Jean Charest's popularity gives credence to this explanation. Among francophone federalists Charest was as popular as Jean Chrétien, but what was particularly noteworthy was his success at gaining the respect of sovereignists, among whom he was nearly as popular as Gilles Duceppe. In this respect, Charest's accomplishment resembles Lucien Bouchard's in 1993: both Bouchard and Charest had the ability to establish high levels of popularity among their own supporters while being acceptable to others outside of that group.

The way in which Gilles Duceppe's lack of popularity affected the support for his party can be measured in two ways (see figures 10.1 and 10.2).[6] First, we can estimate what gains the Bloc Québécois would have made if its leader had been as popular as his competitors. That analysis shows that the party would have obtained six extra points.[7] But this measure underestimates the effect of the leaders' popularity on the Bloc's decline compared to 1993. To explain the full impact of the leader factor in the Bloc's setback, we need to replace Duceppe's rating (lower than for his opponents) with Bouchard's four years earlier (higher than for his opponents). That more sophisticated analysis shows clearly that if Duceppe had been as popular in 1997 as his predecessor had been four years earlier, the Bloc would have received nine more points.[8] This means that with a leader capable of rivalling his or her adversaries, the Bloc could hope to approach 45 per cent of the popular vote. But the Bloc could not hope to repeat its exceptional 1993 results unless it found a leader as dominant as Lucien Bouchard was in 1993.

Defections: Were Moderate Sovereignists Easy Prey for Jean Charest?

The ability of a leader to project an acceptable image to his most moderate opponents is often the source of defections to his party. Blais et al. (1995), for example, demonstrate that the most plausible explanation of the large federalist defections to the Bloc in the 1993 election was Lucien Bouchard's popularity among francophone federalists. It is equally plausible that Jean Charest's attractiveness to sovereignists played a very similar role in the 1997 election.

The figures in Table 10.6 provide some insight into the plausibility of this interpretation. The first part of the table deals with federalist defections to the Bloc Québécois in 1993. Recall that there was a defection rate of some 23 per cent among federalists in 1993. The second part of the table examines the same phenomenon among sovereignists in 1997, when there was a 20 per cent defection rate among sovereignists. The data illustrate the impact of the relative popularity of the leaders and the respondents' firmness in their constitutional

Figure 10.1: Mean Ratings of Leaders, Quebec, 1993 and 1997

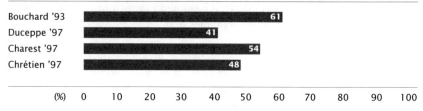

preferences. In the case of the federalists in 1993, it is useful to distinguish between those who were very opposed and those who were somewhat opposed to sovereignty ('hard federalists' and 'soft federalists' respectively). In 1997 a similar distinction is made between those who were very favourable to sovereignty and those who were somewhat favourable ('hard sovereignists' and 'soft sovereignists' respectively). If each of these variables really does have a distinct impact, we would expect to find the most defections among the moderates holding a positive view of the opposing camp's leader.

Overall, the figures in Table 10.6 support that interpretation. In 1993 defections of soft federalists were three times greater than those of hard federalists (40 per cent versus 12 per cent), and they were more than 10 times greater among those preferring Lucien Bouchard to the other federalist leaders (61 per cent versus 5 per cent). The combined impact of these two variables effectively produces the highest levels of defection; defections are eight percentage points higher among soft federalists preferring federalist leaders and 18 points higher among soft federalists preferring Lucien Bouchard. Viewed this way, the most important factor clearly appears to be the attraction of the leader of the opposing camp.

The impact of the leader's popularity is even more striking in 1997. Among those who preferred Gilles Duceppe, sovereignist defections were all but non-existent. That finding holds up regardless of the respondent's firmness with respect to sovereignty; among sovereignists preferring one of the federalist leaders to the Bloc Québécois' leader, defections reached 37 per cent. As one might expect, these desertions were a little more numerous among soft sovereignists than among the hard sovereignists. Perhaps the most surprising

Figure 10.2: Mean Ratings of Leaders, Quebec Francophones, 1993 and 1997

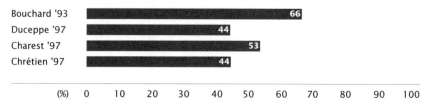

Table 10.6: Defection Rates, Constitutional Preferences, and Opinions of Leaders, 1993 and 1997

	1993: Defection Rates among Federalists (raw numbers in parentheses)			
	Soft Federalists	*Hard Federalists*	*All Federalists*	
Prefer a	11%	3%	5%	
federalist leader	(59)	(153)	(212)	67%
Do not prefer a	68	50	61	
federalist leader	(63)	(40)	(103)	33%
	40	12	23	
	(122)	(193)	(315)	100%

	1997: Defection Rates among Sovereignists (raw numbers in parentheses)			
	Soft Sovereignists	*Hard Sovereignists*	*All Sovereignists*	
Prefer Duceppe	0%	1%	1%	
	(76)	(41)	(117)	46%
Do not prefer	42	32	37	
Duceppe	(78)	(59)	(137)	54%
	28	15	20	
	(119)	(135)	(254)	100%

finding, however, is that a remarkably small percentage of sovereignists preferred their own leader to the federalist leaders. Compare that to the 1993 election, when 67 per cent of federalists preferred Jean Chrétien or Kim Campbell to Lucien Bouchard. In 1997 fewer than half of the sovereignists expressed a preference for the Bloc leader. It is thus the low percentage of sovereignists preferring Gilles Duceppe to the federalist leaders, rather than high defection rates among soft and hard sovereignists per se, that explains the Bloc's failure to retain its natural clientele in the 1997 election.

Conclusion

Support for the Bloc Québécois turns on a combination of short- and long-term factors. The intensity of nationalist sentiments in Quebec and the place occupied by the constitutional question on the political agenda are both prominent considerations for voters. In this respect, the Bloc Québécois benefited from an equally favourable environment in 1993 and 1997. The 1993 election followed on the heels of two substantial failures to arrive at an acceptable accord—Meech Lake and Charlottetown. Support for sovereignty, though on the decline, remained high. The 1997 election, 18 months after the very close 1995 referendum, took place in a context where the question of Quebec's political status retained an immediacy that seemed to justify the presence of a sovereignist party in Ottawa for a significant portion of the electorate. And the re-election of the Parti Québécois government in 1998 may well keep this question sufficiently high on the agenda that the Bloc will have another opportunity to run a campaign under the same favourable circumstances.

These considerations underscore the importance of short-term factors in determining the Bloc Québécois' support. The performance of Quebec's economy under a Parti Québécois government had a real, though modest, effect on support for the Bloc. The last and by far most important factor was the popularity of the leaders. The Bloc Québécois received a weak level of support in 1997 because its leader was less popular than the others, a situation that stood in sharp contrast with Lucien Bouchard's leadership in 1993. From this perspective, a more popular leader would certainly help the Bloc in the next election, either to consolidate its dominance if the federalist vote remains split in Quebec or at least to keep a strong position if this vote rallies massively behind the Liberals.

Chapter 11

Unsteady State

The main goal in this book has been to answer the kinds of basic questions that many concerned Canadians asked about the 1997 Canadian federal election. But in the process of searching for those answers we have also been interested in what the 1997 election data reveal more generally about the Canadian party system and about voting behaviour. The task now is to step back from the details of the evidence and to place the central findings in a broader context.

An Evolving Party System

Canadians have good reason to wonder about what has been happening to the Canadian party system during the 1990s. Though it is a very risky venture to interpret a decade of electoral dynamics on the basis of a single election, the 1997 election does give us an additional opportunity to understand some of these important developments. At the beginning of the 1997 election campaign, it seemed that the Canadian party system might move in any one of three directions. The election might mark a return to the historically recognizable two-party-plus system that prevailed during much of the post-war period. It might signify a consolidation of the new alignment that emerged in 1993. Or it might produce something else.

The simplest interpretation to rule out is the first one, and there are two pieces of evidence underscoring the point that the 1997 federal election patently did not signify any reversion to the pre-1993 party system. First, the revival of the Progressive Conservatives was far too modest to warrant the suggestion that the party had regained its status as the only logical challenger to the Liberals. Second, the two parties most responsible for shattering the old party system in 1993 managed to retain much of their support in 1997. Indeed, Reform was the most successful party in retaining its 1993 voters and the Bloc remains dominant in Quebec with almost 40 per cent of the vote and 60 per cent of the seats.

It is tempting to accept the second interpretation, namely, that the 1997 election represented the consolidation of the new alignment that had emerged in 1993. After all, the basic features of the 1997 result did look a lot like that of 1993, and there are two pieces of evidence for this interpretation.

First, the 1993 election outcome showed that Canada had two party systems, one in Quebec and one outside Quebec, and the 1997 election might be seen as a consolidation of a new order in the sense that it confirmed the presence of those two systems. Not only do the identities of the main contenders differ between Quebec and the rest of Canada, but the structure of opportunities and constraints facing parties in the two settings are also quite different. Outside Quebec, for reasons that have been outlined, the Liberals retain an enormous strategic advantage. To the Liberals' left, the NDP was able to achieve only a very modest revival. To their right, the competition between the Conservatives and Reform grew even keener. In Quebec, the Bloc enjoys a comparable advantage because the Liberals and the Conservatives contest the same federalist turf. But the truly striking consequence of the emergence of the Bloc is that electoral competition in Quebec is now almost entirely structured around the divide between sovereignists and federalists. Other ideological dimensions, our analysis shows, are essentially irrelevant in determining the Quebec vote. Indeed, Liberal, Conservative, and Bloc voters in Quebec are hardly distinguishable on any of the other dimensions that structure citizens' ideological world views. The story could hardly be more different in the rest of the country, where these ideological outlooks clearly do separate supporters of the different parties.

A second argument that could be mustered in support of the consolidation-of-a-new-order interpretation has to do with regionalism. First, there is the character of regionalism, one face of which is the geographic concentration of party support. On that score, regionalism was no stronger in 1997 than in 1993, but it was still strong. The numbers are striking. All elected members of the Bloc are (obviously) from Quebec, all Reform MPs come from the West, and two-thirds of the Liberals and Conservatives are, respectively, from Ontario and the Atlantic provinces. Because of Reform's failure to make a breakthrough in Ontario, regionalism remained almost as pronounced in 1997 as in 1993. Regional parties failed to break out of their regional strongholds.

But there is another face to regionalism, and one of the most intriguing findings to emerge from our evidence has to do with regional differences in how citizens decide how to vote. It is significant that voter calculations even vary regionally for voters supporting the same party. Nowhere is this point more vividly illustrated than in the factors motivating the Reform vote in the West versus the Reform vote in Ontario. Recall that preferences about fiscal policy, orientations towards moral traditionalism, views about accommodating diversity, and above all attitudes towards Quebec, were all central for mobilizing the Reform vote in the West. Not one of these factors moved voters to support the party in Ontario.

The emergence once again of two different party systems and the repeated influence of the same regional forces both suggest that 1997 represented a consolidation of a new party system. The interpretation is a neat one, but if we dig deeper it becomes less convincing; in fact, the case can be made that the 1997 election produced 'something else', a fragile balance that will be hard to sustain, because alongside these elements of stability, there are significant sources of instability. This point needs further elaboration.

One element of instability to consider concerns some broader features of the current 'five-party' configuration. Three political parties are supported by three-fifths of the electorate and these do serve as stabilizing forces; the Liberals qualify more than ever as the natural party of government with the Bloc and the NDP qualifying as 'natural' parties of opposition. In this scheme of things, the Liberals and the NDP appear to be the most durable elements of this configuration in terms of their political orientations, clienteles, and type of appeal to voters. The future of the Bloc is tied to the fortunes of the sovereignist cause, and thus its status as a stabilizing force for the current party system appears uncertain. But for the time being the rhetoric and political appeal of this party seem quite predictable (e.g., a sovereignist party competitive in about 50 Quebec ridings). Moreover, the recent re-election of the Parti Québécois keeps the sovereignty issue on the agenda (even if a referendum is not an immediate possibility) and improves the chance that the Bloc will fight the next election on the same platform as the last election, that is, the defence of Quebec's interests and the promotion of sovereignty.

The unstable parts of the 'five-party' system in the short run feature those citizens supporting the Conservatives and Reform—voters that make up a substantial two-fifths of the electorate. The vital point here is the diversity of this segment of the voting public when it comes to policy preferences and ideology. Certainly, a significant portion of this group shares some common experience as erstwhile supporters of the federal or provincial Conservatives. They also share a common interest, namely, to defeat the Liberals. And that common interest understandably motivates party strategists to search for a way of co-ordinating the opposition forces. If they are ruled by the head, some version of the united alternative seems an attractive option. But there is a twofold problem: first, voters are also ruled by the heart and, second, the ideological hearts of Progressive Conservative voters and Reform voters are in different places. It is the absence of shared ideological visions and policy preferences that makes for fragmentation and instability. The different growth prospects (as shown by the voters' second choices) explain the eagerness of Reform and the cautiousness of the Conservatives about the united alternative and suggest that the centre of gravity of a viable alternative to the Liberals is much closer to the oldest right-wing party in Canada.

There is a third element that feeds into broader interpretations of the dynamics of the Canadian party system; it is one that attracts little attention partly because it concerns a far longer time horizon. There has been a gradual shift in what might be called the 'ballast' of the party system. In the past, Quebec has been crucial territory in federal elections for two major reasons. One was symbolic. Historically, the credibility of any party's claim that it was truly 'national' hinged on its ability to bring anglophone and francophone voters together under some sort of single consensual umbrella, and that imperative still exists. Herein lies one strength of the Liberal party, namely, that it can make a more credible claim that it is better placed to preserve national unity. This same reality is now simultaneously a source of strength and a liability for the Reform party. As the election study data show, Reform gains votes by being tough towards Quebec, but it also loses votes because it is seen as a threat to national unity.

The second reason that Quebec was once crucial territory in federal elections was its greater electoral cohesion. As Bakvis and Macpherson (1995, 666) explain, 'there is a clear difference between Quebec and Ontario, and between Quebec and most of the other provinces, in the propensity to concentrate its vote on one party'. That greater cohesion in Quebec results in overrepresentation in government: 'Quebec's mean share of seats on the government side from 1878 to 1993 inclusive was 32.9 per cent and its mean share of seats in the Commons for the same period was 28.1 per cent' (Bakvis and Macpherson 1995, 685). But with the advent of the Bloc this situation has changed. In 1997 Alberta and Ontario were the two most cohesive provinces, and it now seems that Ontario has replaced Quebec as the pivotal electoral battleground.

A comparison of the 1980 and 1997 election outcomes provides a stark illustration of this shift in political ballast. In 1980 the Liberals took 74 out of the 75 seats in Quebec. In 1997 they took 101 out of 103 seats in Ontario. In one sense, the 1993 and 1997 federal elections present something of a paradox: Quebec has remained as an important political issue while losing its electoral significance. The important point is that the shifting political ballast is woven into the changing party system and Ontario has realigned towards the Liberals, at least for now.

The main strength of the 'consolidation of a new partisan order' interpretation of the 1997 election is that it draws attention to the significance of the very real changes that have taken place in the Canadian party system over the last decade. But the main weakness of that interpretation, and the reason why it fails to be entirely compelling, is that it does not take into account the equally real sources of instability, which continue to stalk the present party system and to make the new status quo a fragile one.

It is entirely possible that the 1997 election represented the second phase of a transition period, a prelude to the emergence of a yet-to-be-defined party system. The precise structure of that system is a matter of speculation, but before we consider what those possibilities might be, it is useful to return to firmer ground and to consider what broader lessons about Canadian voting behaviour might be learned from our investigation of the 1997 federal election.

Lessons Learned: Short-Term Factors

Some lessons can be summarized quite briefly because they have been elaborated in greater detail in the preceding chapters. The place to begin is with the short-term lessons about what mattered to the vote. First, there is clear evidence that the economy mattered to the 1997 federal election result. Economic optimism contributed to the Liberals' re-election and this finding conforms to a pattern that has been observed in other Western democracies (Lewis-Beck 1988). But other issue areas mattered too. Centrist positions on issues, our data indicate, are rewarded. The pool of Liberal and Conservative support (respectively 60 and 40 per cent of first and second choices) demonstrates this point and shows that the pressure towards the restoration of two centrist parties are strong from the point of view of electoral rationality. Picking the right issue is important. Reform and the Conservatives chose to concentrate on tax reductions, but this emphasis was somewhat misplaced. Specifying precisely what the optimal mix of winning issues should be is further complicated by the fact that issues evolve, and so the ability of parties to adjust to such changes is important. Reducing the deficit, for example, seems to have become a non-issue; what may count more now is how to manage budget surpluses. The position of the Liberals on this issue was closer to that of the median voter than were the positions of the Conservatives and the Reform.

Second, there is also evidence that leadership matters (McAllister 1996; Nadeau et al. 1996). The Bloc's setback is mainly attributable to the unpopularity of Gilles Duceppe. Charest's positive image helped the Conservatives, especially in Quebec. Manning's low rating was an obstacle to the growth of the Reform vote. The NDP was able to make a breakthrough in the Atlantic provinces partly because of its 'native-daughter' leader, Alexa McDonough. But the limits of this factor are seen in Jean Charest's inability to translate his popularity into more votes.

Third, there are various media-related factors that come into play in complex ways. One such factor concerns the tone of the coverage. Positive coverage helped the Conservatives, negative coverage hurt the Bloc, and media coverage may also have worked to limit the growth of Reform. The influence of the media on voting intentions is harder to verify, and in the cases analysed here the effects seem to have been short-lived. Certainly the media can create opportunity (obstacles) for parties, but it is extremely difficult to isolate the precise influence of the media on an election. Media visibility has real consequences (Bartels 1988). The NDP suffered from being off the radar screen, whereas Reform probably suffered from being in the spotlight (and being covered so negatively). It is significant that the highs and lows in the parties' campaigns did correspond to highs and lows in the visibility of the parties, and with the possible exception of Reform, media coverage was not particularly negative during the campaign. The implications of that finding are far-reaching, but the evidence, which has to be read cautiously, is suggestive rather than conclusive.

The media are not the only actors that work at interpreting campaigns and issue positions. Political parties themselves have the opportunity to frame issues and parties may be more or less adept in the art of issue framing. The indications are, from the 1997 data, that the way the Liberals framed the deficit issue was important. The Liberals' message that the elimination of the deficit was a key to further economic improvements was well received by the voters, and it too contributed to their re-election.

Fourth, there are lessons about the influence of campaigns. Campaigns matter in many ways (Holbrook 1996). The 1997 Canadian Election Study data show that the front-runner decline, the Bloc setback, and the emergence of Jean Charest as a truly national figure were all consequences of the campaign. But campaigns are unpredictable. The rise of the unemployment rate during the campaign limited the Liberals' ability to sell their performance on job creation. That finding stands in stark contrast with the recent election in Quebec, where the unemployment rate fell below two digits for the first time in years.

A fifth area that seems to matter has to do with information. It is important to distinguish here between self-reported information and 'hard' information, that is, how well-informed the respondents claim to be as opposed to their ability to answer relatively simple questions about an election. The lack of basic knowledge among voters is worrying. Substantial proportions of voters admit to knowing nothing about one or another of the party leaders, particularly new ones. Similarly, many voters were unable to identify parties' major campaign promises. For example, although the NDP's policies on social programs and unemployment were close to voters' preferences, those policies went virtually unnoticed. And the Liberals were hurt by misconceptions about changes in the unemployment rate during the past few years.

The Long-Term Lessons

The party-centred approach taken here draws attention to the fact that a voter's decision is influenced by the choices available. Indeed, if there seems to be a lack of choice, some voters will simply abstain. As for those who do vote, one of the most striking findings to emerge from this investigation is the extent to which the decision about how to vote is shaped by ideological outlooks, at least for those parties that offer voters clearly defined ideological positions.

There are two vital findings here, namely, that many voters have coherent ideological beliefs and that these beliefs shape their vote. These findings are significant because they run counter to the conventional view that Canadian voters have little capacity for ideological reasoning. It is true that some voters may lack the political sophistication to understand and use left-right terminology, but that does not mean that they do not think ideologically. When it comes to the organization of fundamental beliefs about society and politics, it turns out that these beliefs are not only structured, but also are structured in ways that correspond closely to conventional understandings of left and right. In effect, a knowledge of where voters stand on these ideological dimensions helps us substantially to know how they are likely to vote. Voters who are on the left, whether defined as the 'old' left or the 'new', are significantly more likely to vote NDP, while those who are on the right, especially when defined as the 'new' right, are correspondingly more likely to vote Reform. Beliefs matter and they matter a lot. Knowing what voters believe is an important part of understanding why they vote as they do.

As well as knowing what voters believe, it is important to know who they are. This is another finding that challenges, or at least qualifies the conventional view that in Canada the relationship between social-background characteristics and the vote is weak. Usually the benchmark for comparison is evidence from other advanced electoral democracies. When the amount of variance explained by social background characteristics falls below 12 per cent, the effects of social structure qualify as weak (Franklin 1992). In the 1997 Canadian election, social-background characteristics explain 12 per cent and 15 per cent of variance respectively in Liberal (outside Quebec) and Reform voting. This means that, contrary to conventional wisdom, social structure is an essential starting point for understanding how people vote. The social-background characteristics that matter are not only the familiar Canadian ones of region, religion, and ethnicity, but also sex, which has clearly become more important. The 1997 federal election witnessed the emergence of a gender gap in NDP voting, mirroring the gender gap in Reform voting that had appeared in the previous election. What is particularly significant about these gaps— especially the NDP gap—is that they are rooted in more basic differences in ideology and issue positions. This means that they are likely to endure. Leadership is also a factor in these gaps, but it is only part of the story.

The findings for both ideological outlook and social-background characteristics have important implications for understanding the contemporary Canadian party system. Neither of these large findings concerning the effects of ideology and social structure is compatible with the notion that Canada still has a brokerage system. Such a characterization may have been accurate in the days when the Liberals and the Conservatives shared dominance of the system and routinely accounted for three-quarters or more of all the votes cast. But Reform and the Bloc both broke through in 1993 by refusing to follow the rules of the brokerage game. And support for both those parties in 1997 was too rooted in social-background characteristics and fundamental beliefs to qualify either party as a brokerage party. Having flirted with the brokerage model, to its cost, in 1988, the NDP also retains its ideologically distinctive base of support.

Finally, the election study reveals an important lesson about the role of partisanship. As much as half of the electorate do not have any real attachment to any party and are willing to float from one party to another. But it is equally important to appreciate that half of the Canadian electorate do feel a strong sense of attachment to a party. Although these 'partisans' do not automatically vote for 'their' party all of the time, they do so most of the time, that is, unless there are compelling reasons to support another party. Without considering the fact that the Liberals enjoy a substantial advantage with their large numbers of partisans, it is very difficult to make sense of the Liberals' 1997 election victory.

The image of the Canadian voter that emerges from the 1997 election does not entirely match the conventional picture. Short-term factors are important, but the Canadian voter seems more anchored by ideology and regional and group loyalties than previously thought.

What Does the Future Hold?

A central finding to emerge from this investigation is just how well the Liberals have survived the shattering of the old 'two-party plus' system. This element of continuity is a fundamental one. In both 1993 and 1997 the Liberal vote share was remarkably close to its average share in elections between 1968 and 1988, and as our analysis makes clear, the Liberal advantage in any election is formidable. The Liberal support base is both wide and deep. And no other party has anything even approaching this advantage in the size of its core of loyal support. Almost one in four electors is a Liberal partisan, which is almost as many as all of the other parties *combined*. More than that, the Liberals also have a substantial pool of potential recruits from which they can draw. The figures on second choices in 1997 are instructive: 60 per cent of Canadians either voted Liberal or picked the Liberals as their second choice. In short, the Liberal advantage is huge, and perhaps insurmountable. This formidable reality presents all of the other federal political parties with a monumental challenge: how can the Liberals be defeated?

The weight of the evidence clearly indicates that the Liberals are more vulnerable on their right flank than they are on their left. In the 1997 election the conditions were right for the NDP to regain some of the ground it had lost in 1993. The Liberal party's cuts in social spending, the broken promises, and the stubbornly high unemployment rate all played into the hands of the NDP. The NDP's inability to capitalize on these Liberal vulnerabilities suggests that any challenge from the left can be discounted, at least for the present. The Canadian electorate has shifted to the right, leaving the NDP out of sight and out of touch.

If any party is placed to defeat the Liberals, it may actually be the Conservatives. But to achieve that goal they would have to abandon the 1997 campaign strategy of contesting the space to the right of the Liberals. In 1997 the Conservatives focused their attention on winning back votes from Reform. Our analysis of voters' second choices indicates that the Conservatives might have won more votes if they had made the Liberals their main target. Recall that more Liberal voters than Reform voters identified the Conservatives as their second choice, and there were many more Liberal voters than Reform voters to be wooed.

But the Conservative Party has a critical problem of regaining its status as a plausible alternative to the Liberals. Our examination of the Liberals' support base drives home a crucial lesson for aspiring brokerage parties: while retaining their ideological flexibility, brokerage parties none the less need a solid core of partisans who will stay loyal. This core of loyal partisans was evident for the Liberals in terms of both the number of strong partisans and the support of identifiable social groups. What makes the Conservatives' future as a brokerage party uncertain is the absence of strong partisans and the difficulty of identifying those reliable social niches of support.

However problematic the Conservatives' prospects are, the Reform party is in a worse position. Reform's failure to establish an electoral foothold in Ontario was critical. Toning down the rhetoric and changing the leader might help, but that might not be enough. Once again, the evidence from second-choice preferences underscores the point that Reform may be too far away from the median voter on those dimensions that structure the ideological worlds of voters. This was true of every dimension except free enterprise. Then, there is no escaping the fact that Reform placed last in voters' second-choice preferences, behind even the NDP, which testifies to the limits on its growth. So, too, does the decline in political cynicism. Cynicism was one of the driving forces behind the rise of Reform, and Reform voters in 1997 were by far the most cynical of all about politics. All this suggests that Reform faces a strategic dilemma. If it wants to establish itself as the plausible alternative to the Liberals, then it has to consider positioning itself much closer to the median voter. In other words, Reform may have to act very much like a conventional brokerage party. But if it does, the voters who have found an antidote to their political malaise in the Reform party may simply abstain. It is significant that the Reform party has only a small core—smaller even than the Conservatives— of loyal supporters on whom it can count.

The obstacles facing both the Conservatives and Reform may seem to leave the united alternative as the most plausible strategy for unseating the Liberals. 'Unite the right' and 'fight for the right' make for catchy copy, but our evidence indicates that this may be the wrong advice. It is wrong because it suggests that the alternative to the Liberals should be located to the right and because it implies that Conservative and Reform voters could coalesce around a party that is ideologically positioned somewhere between the two. Conservative voters, however, are closer ideologically to the Liberals than to Reform, whether it is a matter of law and order, moral traditionalism, or accommodating diversity. Tellingly, many more Conservatives named the Liberals as their second choice than Reform. The clear implication of this line of reasoning is that the formation of a united alternative to the right of the Conservatives could well help to guarantee the continued electoral dominance of the Liberal party.

Appendix A

The 1997 Canadian Election Study

Data for the 1997 Canadian Election Study (CES) were collected by the Institute for Social Research at York University. The survey had three components: a campaign-period telephone survey, a post-election telephone survey, and a mail-back questionnaire.

The campaign survey began on 27 April, the day the election was called, and ended on 1 June, the last day of the campaign. A total of 3,949 interviews were conducted, approximately 110 per day of the campaign. A rolling cross-section sample release was employed. The total sample was broken down into 36 sub-samples, and a new sub-sample was released each day of the campaign. The sample (as well as the daily sub-samples) was stratified by province, to overrepresent smaller provinces. For the first time in a Canadian Election Study, the Northwest Territories and Yukon were included. Random digit dialing was used to select households, and the birthday selection method was used to select respondents. The response rate was 59 per cent.

The post-election survey was conducted with respondents to the campaign survey in the eight weeks after the election. A total of 3,170 persons, 80 per cent of the campaign survey respondents, were re-interviewed.

At the end of the post-election survey, respondents were asked if they would be willing to provide an address so that a mail-back questionnaire could be sent to them. A total of 2,627 did so and 1,857 people (59 per cent of the post-election survey respondents) completed the questionnaire.

All analyses in this book use weighted data to correct for the overrepresentation of small households and small provinces.

Reported vote in the post-election survey is 38 per cent for the Liberals, 22 per cent for Reform, 18 per cent for the Conservatives, 10 per cent for the NDP, and 10 per cent for the Bloc Québécois. Support for Reform is slightly overestimated.

The reported turnout was 82 per cent, whereas the official turnout was 67 per cent. That is not surprising, because surveys systematically overestimate electoral participation for three reasons. First, those who are not interested in politics and who are less likely to vote are less likely to agree to an interview (Wolfinger and Rosenstone 1980, 117). Second, responding to a survey increases the respondents' interest in politics and makes them more likely to vote (Blais and Young 1999; Granberg and Holmberg 1992). Third, some respondents do not want to admit they did not vote, because voting is considered to be a duty of a good citizen. Validation checks performed in the United States have shown that between 5 per cent and 10 per cent of non-voters claim to have voted. Fortunately, however, misreporting does not seem to bias the survey findings (Brady, Verba, and Schlozman 1995, 292; Cassell 1998).

Appendix B

Factor Analysis of Ideological Dimensions

Basic Outlooks

		Outside Quebec	
Items	Cynicism	Moral Traditionalism	Free Enterprise
Politicians lie to get elected	**.76**	.04	−.04
Government doesn't care what people like me think	**.74**	.16	−.15
Political parties don't keep their election promises	**.65**	−.01	−.02
Those elected to Parliament soon lose touch	**.63**	−.06	.05
Only married people should have children	.02	**.79**	.15
Society better off if more women stayed home with their children	.09	**.75**	.04
Abortion should never be permitted	−.04	**.69**	−.12
Businesses make money, everyone benefits	−.05	.02	**.76**
People who don't get ahead should blame themselves	.14	.05	**.68**
Feel positive about big business	−.22	−.03	**.62**
N = 2,909			
Eigenvalue	2.1	1.7	1.4
Variance explained (%)	21.3	17.0	13.7
Total variance explained = 52.0%			
Cronbach's Alpha	**.66**	**.60**	**.46**

| | | Quebec | |
Items	Cynicism	Moral Traditionalism	Free Enterprise
Politicians lie to get elected	**.76**	−.05	.10
Government doesn't care what people like me think	**.70**	.09	−.15
Political parties don't keep their election promises	**.61**	−.13	−.15
Those elected to Parliament soon lose touch	**.54**	−.04	.03
Society better off if more women stayed home with their children	.06	**.77**	.08
Only married people should have children	−.03	**.76**	.11
Abortion should never be permitted	−.15	**.62**	−.12
Businesses make money, everyone benefits	−.05	.19	**.68**
Feel positive about big business	−.10	−.15	**.67**
People who don't get ahead should blame themselves	.03	.03	**.66**
N = 1,021			
Eigenvalue	1.9	1.6	1.3
Variance explained (%)	19.4	15.7	13.4
Total variance explained = 48.6%			
Cronbach's Alpha	**.57**	**.56**	**.41**

Notes: Reported are the factor loadings of factor analyses using varimax rotation with pairwise deletion of missing cases.
'Don't know' responses are included in the analysis.

Communal Outlooks

		Outside Quebec	
Items	*Outgroups*	*Quebec*	*Canada/US*
Spending for aboriginal peoples should increase	**.84**	.08	–.02
Aboriginal peoples are worse off compared to other Canadians	**.68**	.14	–.10
More should be done for racial minorities	**.66**	.17	.01
Feel positive about Quebec	.07	**.84**	–.04
More should be done for Quebec	.34	**.61**	–.04
Quebec should be recognized as a distinct society	.18	**.58**	–.10
Canada should have closer ties with the United States	–.08	–.04	**.80**
A good thing if Canada and the US become one country	.06	–.22	**.74**
Feel positive about the United States	–.16	.52	**.60**
N = 2,899			
Eigenvalue	2.4	1.6	1.2
Variance explained (%)	26.3	17.7	13.2
Total variance explained = 57.1%			
Cronbach's Alpha	**.62**	**.60**	**.55**

Items	Sovereignty	Quebec Outgroups	Aboriginal Peoples	Canada/US
Defending the interests of Quebec is important	**.68**	.11	–.08	.06
French language is threatened in Quebec	**.67**	–.09	–.11	–.14
If Quebec separates, French language in Quebec will get better	**.66**	–.05	.06	–.10
Sovereignist party has the right to be in Ottawa	**.58**	–.21	–.04	.01
More should be done for racial minorities	.09	**.71**	.04	–.03
Feel positive about racial minorities	–.12	**.70**	.20	.00
Canada should admit more immigrants	–.13	**.54**	.12	.01
Aboriginal peoples are worse off compared to other Canadians	–.06	.10	**.81**	–.11
Spending for aboriginal peoples should increase	–.02	.17	**.80**	.02
Feel positive about aboriginal peoples	–.12	.46	**.52**	.05
Feel positive about the United States	–.10	.25	–.02	**.68**
Canada should have closer ties with the United States	–.03	–.21	.15	**.67**
A good thing if Canada and the US become one country	–.03	–.02	–.18	**.65**
N = 1,011				
Eigenvalue	2.6	1.7	1.3	1.0
Variance explained (%)	20.0	13.1	9.6	7.9
Total variance explained = 50.6%				
Cronbach's Alpha	**.57**	**.52**	**.66**	**.41**

Notes: Reported are the factor loadings of factor analyses using varimax rotation with pairwise deletion of missing cases.
'Don't know' responses are included in the analysis.

Question Wording of Items in the Modified 1993 and 1997 Ideological Scales Used in Figures 4.3 to 4.5

(* = in 1993 scale; ** = in 1997 scale; *** = in both 1993 and 1997 scales)

Moral Traditionalism

*** Only people who are married should be having children.
*** Society would be better off if more women stayed home with their children.
*** Now we would like to get your views on abortion. Of the following three positions, which is closest to your own opinion: abortion should NEVER be permitted, should be permitted only after NEED has been established by a doctor, OR should be a matter of the woman's PERSONAL CHOICE?

Free Enterprise

* When businesses are allowed to make as much money as they can, everyone profits in the long run, including the poor.
* Most people who don't get ahead should not blame the system; they have only themselves to blame.
** When businesses make a lot of money, everyone benefits, including the poor.
** People who don't get ahead should blame themselves, not the system.
*** How do you feel about big business?

Cynicism

* Politicians are willing to say anything to get elected.
** Politicians are ready to lie to get elected.
** Do political parties keep their election promises most of the time, some of the time, or hardly ever?
*** I don't think the government cares much what people like me think.
*** Those elected to Parliament soon lose touch with the people.

Outgroups

* Do you think Canada should admit more immigrants or fewer immigrants than at present?
** Do you think Canada should admit more immigrants, fewer immigrants, or about the same as now?
*** How much do you think should be done for racial minorities?
*** How do you feel about racial minorities?

Canada/US

*** Do you think Canada's ties with the United States should be much closer, somewhat closer, about the same as now, more distant, or much more distant?
*** How do you feel about the United States?

Quebec (Outside-Quebec sample)

* How much do you think should be done to promote French/for Quebec?
** How much do you think should be done for Quebec?
*** How do you feel about Quebec?

Appendix C

The Vote Regressions

Our analysis of support for each of the five main parties, as reported in chapters 6 to 10, is based on the regressions listed in tables C.1 to C.7. Because voters in Quebec and in the rest of the country were faced with a different set of choices—the latter did not have Bloc candidates and most Quebec ridings did not have Reform candidates—we performed separate analyses in Quebec and in the rest of the country (for a more detailed analysis of regional differences outside Quebec, see Gidengil et al. 1999).

For the purposes of this analysis we distinguish seven blocks of variables that may affect the vote. We start with the most distant factor, voters' socio-economic characteristics. We then move to their broad ideological orientations, which are examined in Chapter 4, and to their general partisan attachment. We finally look at more specific perceptions and opinions, first about the economy, then about the issues, the performance of the Liberal government, and the leaders.

For each party we present OLS estimations, which are easier to interpret than LOGIT or PROBIT estimations. The analysis was performed sequentially, starting with the most distant block, socio-economic variables. Only those variables that proved to be significant within a given block (and for a given party) were retained, and these variables were kept for all further analyses incorporating additional blocks of variables.

Such regressions allow us to estimate the impact of a given factor while controlling for a whole set of other variables. The numbers presented are the regression coefficients, which tell us how much difference a variable makes to the propensity to vote for a given party.

Let us illustrate how to make sense of the regression numbers, using the results concerning the NDP (Table C.3). Column 1 indicates the impact of those socio-economic variables that affect the NDP vote. All these variables are dichotomous and equal to 1 if the individual has a certain characteristic and 0 otherwise. The '–7.3' for male means that, even after region, age, education, income, ethnicity, religion, sector of employment, and unionization have been taken into account, the propensity to vote NDP is 7.3 percentage points lower among men than among women. This number gets lower as we move to columns on the right, suggesting that the lower propensity for men to support the NDP is partly explained by the attitudes and opinions included further on.

Column 2 includes ideological orientations. Most of the variables here go from 0 to 1, 0 corresponding to the lowest score possible on that dimension and 1 to the highest. The '–34.4' for free enterprise means that, controlling for a host of socio-economic variables, the propensity to vote NDP is 34.4 percentage points lower among those who score highest on free enterprise (and who are at 1), compared to those who are lowest (and who are at 0). Again, the effect of belief in free enterprise diminishes as we move to columns on the right, since those who are more critical of free enterprise tend to be more opposed to deficit reduction and tax cuts. Because it makes sense to assume that a general view of the virtues and vices of free enterprise produces specific opinions on spending, taxes, and deficits rather than the reverse, the first number that appears for a given variable, which controls for antecedent variables (socio-economic variables in this instance) but not for posterior ones, provides the most adequate estimate of its total effect.

Most variables introduced in blocks 3 to 7 range from –1 to +1. Their precise meaning is specified below. In the case of party identification, +1 refers to those individuals who identify with the NDP, –1 to those who identify with another party, and 0 to those who do not identify with any party. The '20.7' in column 3 indicates that, controlling for socio-economic factors and ideological orientations, the propensity to vote NDP is 20.7 points higher among those who identify with the NDP and 20.7 points lower among those who identify with another party, compared to those with no party attachment.

Table C.I: Liberal Voters, Outside Quebec

	1	*1–2*	*1–3*	*1–4*	*1–5*	*1–6*	*1–7*
				Block(s)			
Socio-economic Variables							
Atlantic	–24.3 [a]	–19.1 [a]	–15.6 [a]	–15.1 [a]	–14.4 [a]	–18.1 [a]	–14.8 [a]
Prairies	–20.7 [a]	–17.4 [a]	–8.6 [a]	–7.1 [a]	–6.0 [b]	–5.8 [b]	–3.4
British Columbia	–18.0 [a]	–13.3 [a]	–8.4 [a]	–7.9 [a]	–7.8 [a]	–6.7 [b]	–7.8 [a]
Rural–Urban	–5.0 [c]	–4.7 [c]	–2.8	–2.2	–0.7	–0.7	0.4
North European	–6.7 [b]	–7.0 [b]	–4.7 [c]	–4.4	–4.5 [c]	–5.1 [c]	–4.9 [c]
Non–European	18.2 [a]	17.3 [a]	13.9 [a]	13.6 [a]	12.8 [a]	11.2 [a]	9.2 [a]
Catholic	17.6 [a]	17.5 [a]	12.8 [a]	12.5 [a]	12.0 [a]	10.7 [a]	10.3 [a]
Dropout	6.5 [b]	7.9 [a]	6.8 [a]	7.8 [a]	6.8 [a]	5.9 [b]	5.5 [b]
Employed	9.7 [a]	9.7 [a]	9.2 [a]	8.3 [a]	8.2 [a]	7.9 [a]	7.1 [a]
Public employee	8.8 [a]	7.2 [a]	6.4 [a]	6.8 [a]	6.4 [a]	6.2 [a]	5.6 [a]
Union member (fam.)	–5.2 [b]	–4.5 [c]	–5.8 [a]	–5.2 [b]	–4.6 [b]	–5.4 [a]	–5.5 [a]

	1	1–2	1–3	1–4	1–5	1–6	1–7
				Block(s)			
Constant:							
block 1	35.6 [a]	—	—	—	—	—	—
Ideological Dimensions							
Regional alienation		−13.9 [a]	−10.4 [a]	−10.4 [a]	−10.2 [a]	−6.5 [a]	−4.0 [c]
Cynicism		−52.8 [a]	−36.8 [a]	−29.4 [a]	−29.9 [a]	−16.9 [a]	−14.4 [a]
Constant:							
blocks 1–2		73.9 [a]	—	—	—	—	—
Party Identification							
Party identification			30.7 [a]	29.7 [a]	29.1 [a]	26.3 [a]	21.9 [a]
Constant:							
blocks 1–3			62.6 [a]	—	—	—	—
Economic Perceptions							
Can. Econ. Retro.				2.7 [c]	2.9 [c]	1.6	1.0
Prv. Econ. Retro.				−4.5 [a]	−4.8 [a]	−4.7 [a]	−4.1 [a]
Unemployment Retro.				4.0 [a]	3.5 [a]	2.3 [c]	2.4 [c]
Can. Econ. Prosp.				8.3 [a]	7.8 [a]	7.0 [a]	6.3 [a]
Personal Fin. Prosp.				3.5 [b]	3.1 [b]	2.1	2.5 [c]
Constant:							
blocks 1–4				54.7 [a]	—	—	—
Issues							
Reducing deficit					4.9 [a]	4.3 [b]	3.9 [b]
Fighting crime					2.7 [b]	3.2 [a]	3.0 [a]
Gun control					5.4 [a]	4.3 [a]	3.1 [a]
Constant:							
blocks 1–5					52.4 [a]	—	—
Liberal Performance							
Liberals – national unity						6.5 [a]	3.2 [b]
Liberals – deficit						7.0 [a]	4.9 [a]
Liberals – jobs						5.2 [a]	2.3
Liberals – crime						5.9 [a]	5.2 [a]
Liberals – GST						−5.9 [a]	−4.3 [b]
Constant: blocks 1–6						48.5 [a]	—
Leader Evaluation							
Chrétien							44.2 [a]
Constant:							
blocks 1–7							48.1 [a]
Adjusted *R* square	0.11	0.19	0.38	0.40	0.41	0.44	0.49

a: significant α = .01   b: significant α = .05   c: significant α = .10

Table C.2: Conservative Voters, Outside Quebec

	1	1–2	1–3	1–4	1–5	1–6	1–7
				Block(s)			
Socio–economic Variables							
Atlantic	22.0 [a]	21.6 [a]	16.7 [a]	16.7 [a]	16.4 [a]	16.7 [a]	13.1 [a]
British Columbia	–10.0 [a]	–10.0 [a]	–6.8 [a]	–6.9 [a]	–6.6 [a]	–7.0 [a]	–6.4 [a]
North European	–5.9 [b]	–5.8 [b]	–5.9 [b]	–5.9 [b]	–5.3 [b]	–5.2 [b]	–4.6 [b]
Catholic	–6.8 [a]	–7.3 [a]	–4.9 [b]	–5.3 [a]	–5.3 [a]	–4.9 [b]	–5.8 [a]
No religion	–6.6 [b]	–6.6 [b]	–5.3 [b]	–5.3 [b]	–5.5 [b]	–5.6 [b]	–5.8 [b]
Dropout	–5.0 [b]	–4.8 [b]	–5.7 [a]	–5.8 [a]	–5.2 [b]	–5.0 [b]	–3.6 [c]
Employed	–5.9 [a]	–5.9 [a]	–5.8 [a]	–6.9 [a]	–7.0 [a]	–7.0 [a]	–6.6 [a]
Public employee	–7.8 [a]	–7.1 [a]	–5.9 [a]	–6.7 [a]	–6.8 [a]	–7.0 [a]	–7.5 [a]
Highest quintile income	7.8 [a]	6.9 [a]	5.2 [b]	5.7 [a]	5.6 [a]	5.2 [b]	3.1
Constant: block 1	25.6 [a]	—	—	—	—	—	—
Ideological Dimensions							
Women		6.5 [a]	6.4 [a]	6.1 [a]	5.0 [a]	5.3 [a]	4.6 [b]
Free enterprise		17.2 [a]	11.4 [a]	12.6 [a]	15.0 [a]	15.7 [a]	16.0 [a]
Constant: blocks 1–2		14.3 [a]	—	—	—	—	—
Party Identification							
Party identification			21.6 [a]	21.6 [a]	21.7 [a]	21.2 [a]	16.7 [a]
Constant: blocks 1–3			22.5 [a]	—	—	—	—
Economic Perceptions							
Fear of losing job				5.9 [b]	5.7 [b]	6.2 [b]	5.8 [b]
Constant: blocks 1–4				21.6 [a]	—	—	—
Issues							
Creating jobs					4.9 [b]	4.9 [b]	5.9 [a]
Fighting crime					–2.0 [b]	–2.1 [b]	–1.6 [c]
Constant: blocks 1–5					19.0 [a]	—	—
Liberal Performance							
Liberals – national unity						–3.0 [b]	–3.4 [b]
Liberals – GST						3.3 [c]	3.1 [c]
Constant: blocks 1–6						16.4 [a]	—

Leader Evaluation

Charest							40.7 [a]
Constant:							
blocks 1–7							23.2 [a]
Adjusted *R* square	0.07	0.08	0.23	0.23	0.24	0.24	0.32

a: significant α = .01   b: significant α = .05   c: significant α = .10

Table C.3: NDP Voters, Outside Quebec

				Block(s)			
	1	1–2	1–3	1–4	1–5	1–6	1–7
Socio–economic Variables							
Male	–7.3 [a]	–4.0 [b]	–3.5 [b]	–3.5 [b]	–2.6 [c]	–2.6 [c]	–1.0
Atlantic	13.4 [a]	12.3 [a]	11.7 [a]	11.7 [a]	10.7 [a]	10.7 [a]	6.3 [a]
Generation							
baby–boomer	–3.9 [c]	–5.7 [a]	–5.1 [a]	–5.1 [a]	–3.6 [b]	–3.6 [b]	–3.6 [b]
Generation X	–5.1 [b]	–8.2 [a]	–7.5 [a]	–7.5 [a]	–5.6 [a]	–5.6 [a]	–5.4 [a]
Non–European	–4.9 [c]	–3.8	–5.2 [b]	–5.2 [b]	–4.4 [c]	–4.4 [c]	–3.8 [c]
No religion	7.8 [a]	5.4 [b]	2.5	2.5	2.5	2.5	1.2
Dropout	–4.3 [c]	–4.3 [b]	–4.1 [b]	–4.1 [b]	–2.8	–2.8	–2.9
Graduated –							
university	6.4 [a]	3.6 [c]	3.1	3.1	2.5	2.5	2.2
Traditional							
marriage	–4.1 [b]	–2.4	–2.2	–2.2	–1.2	–1.2	–1.9
Public employee	3.6 [c]	1.7	1.2	1.2	1.6	1.6	1.5
Union member							
(fam.)	8.9 [a]	7.0 [a]	5.6 [a]	5.6 [a]	4.6 [a]	4.6 [a]	3.4 [b]
Lowest quintile							
income	4.8 [c]	3.5	2.6	2.6	2.6	2.6	3.0
Highest quintile							
income	–5.5 [b]	–4.1 [b]	–3.6 [c]	–3.6 [c]	–2.9	–2.9	–1.5
Constant: block 1	15.6 [a]	—	—	—	—	—	—
Ideological Dimensions							
Women		4.3 [b]	3.8 [b]	3.8 [b]	3.0 [c]	3.0 [c]	2.8 [c]
Quebec		11.3 [a]	8.4 [a]	8.4 [a]	4.4	4.4	0.5
Canada–US relations		–14.3 [a]	–10.7 [b]	–10.7 [b]	–7.7 [c]	–7.7 [c]	–5.9
Moral traditionalism		–11.9 [a]	–10.2 [a]	–10.2 [a]	–7.2 [b]	–7.2 [b]	–5.4 [c]
Free enterprise		–34.4 [a]	–21.8 [a]	–21.8 [a]	–15.9 [a]	–15.9 [a]	–12.1 [a]
Constant:							
blocks 1–2		40.2 [a]	—	—	—	—	—

Party Identification

Party identification		20.7 ª	20.7 ª	19.2 ª	19.2 ª	15.7 ª
Constant: blocks 1–3		41.0 ª	—	—	—	—

Economic Perceptions

No significant variable		no variable	—	—	—	—

Issues

Spending				−5.1 ᵇ	−5.1 ᵇ	−3.9 ᶜ
Reducing deficit				−7.3 ª	−7.3 ª	−6.1 ª
Taxes				−4.6 ª	−4.6 ª	−4.1 ª
Creating jobs				3.0 ᶜ	3.0 ᶜ	1.9
Fighting crime				−3.6 ª	−3.6 ª	−2.6 ª
Constant: blocks 1–5				31.1 ª	—	—

Liberal Performance

No significant variable					no variable	—

Leader Evaluation

McDonough						31.8 ª
Constant: blocks 1–7						37.1 ª
Adjusted R square	0.07	0.15	0.29	—	0.32	—	0.37

a: significant α = .01   b: significant α = .05   c: significant α = .10

Table C.4: Reform Party Voters, Outside Quebec

	Block(s)						
	1	1–2	1–3	1–4	1–5	1–6	1–7
Socio–economic Variables							
Male	9.4 ª	8.0 ª	6.8 ª	6.8 ª	4.7 ª	4.9 ª	3.0 ᶜ
Atlantic	−9.2 ª	−12.1 ª	−13.7 ª	−13.6 ª	−14.6 ª	−11.7 ª	−8.4 ª
Prairies	22.0 ª	15.9 ª	10.7 ª	9.5 ª	8.8 ª	7.9 ª	4.6 ᵇ
British Columbia	22.3 ª	18.8 ª	12.7 ª	12.6 ª	12.2 ª	10.2 ª	10.3 ª
North European	15.3 ª	11.4 ª	9.3 ª	9.3 ª	8.5 ª	9.0 ª	8.5 ª
Non–European	−11.9 ª	−10.3 ª	−9.7 ª	−8.9 ª	−9.2 ª	−8.0 ª	−7.8 ª
Catholic	−10.5 ª	−10.1 ª	−8.7 ª	−8.3 ª	−8.1 ª	−6.9 ª	−5.0 ª
Graduated – university	−10.8 ª	−3.1	−4.5 ᵇ	−4.7 ᵇ	−3.8 ᶜ	−4.3 ᵇ	−3.0
Public employee	−5.7 ᵇ	−3.4	−2.4	−1.5	−1.1	−0.6	0.0
Constant: block 1	23.5 ª	—	—	—	—	—	—

Ideological Dimensions

Women	−10.1 [a]	−6.8 [a]	−7.0 [a]	−4.9 [b]	−3.6 [c]	−1.8	
Regional alienation	11.0 [a]	8.6 [a]	8.4 [a]	8.1 [a]	5.9 [a]	5.9 [a]	
Quebec	−23.8 [a]	−20.1 [a]	−20.1 [a]	−18.1 [a]	−16.9 [a]	−8.5 [b]	
Outgroups	−15.6 [a]	−12.0 [a]	−12.1 [a]	−7.8 [b]	−7.1 [b]	−5.6 [c]	
Canada–US relations	12.7 [b]	12.6 [b]	11.8 [b]	9.5 [c]	9.2 [c]	−0.7	
Cynicism	38.2 [a]	23.5 [a]	22.1 [a]	20.2 [a]	12.1 [a]	6.2	
Moral traditionalism	17.1 [a]	12.4 [a]	11.7 [a]	8.7 [a]	8.7 [a]	6.6 [b]	
Constant: blocks 1–2	4.5	—	—	—	—	—	

Party Identification

Party identification		28.3 [a]	28.0 [a]	27.3 [a]	25.6 [a]	16.8 [a]	
Constant: blocks 1–3		25.8 [a]	—	—	—	—	

Economic Perceptions

Fear of losing job			−5.0 [c]	−4.0	−3.4	−5.1 [b]	
Can. econ. retro.			−2.9 [b]	−2.7 [b]	−1.5	−0.3	
Prv. econ. retro.			3.2 [a]	2.7 [b]	2.2 [c]	1.4	
Unemployment retro.			−4.5 [a]	−4.6 [a]	−3.6 [a]	−3.6 [a]	
Constant: blocks 1–4			27.7 [a]	—	—	—	

Issues

Taxes				4.7 [a]	3.9 [b]	2.3	
Creating jobs				−9.6 [a]	−9.1 [a]	−6.2 [a]	
Fighting crime				2.1 [b]	1.7 [c]	1.6 [c]	
Gun control				−3.8 [a]	−3.1 [a]	−1.6 [c]	
Constant: blocks 1–5				33.6 [a]	—	—	

Liberal Performance

Liberals – national unity					−5.5 [a]	−3.8 [a]	
Liberals – deficit					−8.0 [a]	−4.9 [a]	
Liberals – crime					−6.5 [a]	−4.4 [a]	
Liberals – social program					4.0 [b]	3.7 [a]	
Liberals – GST					3.6 [b]	2.7 [c]	
Constant: blocks 1–6					35.8 [a]	—	

Leader Evaluation

Manning							51.0 [a]
Constant: blocks 1–7							46.2 [a]
Adjusted R square	0.15	0.29	0.43	0.44	0.45	0.48	0.57

a: significant α = .01   b: significant α = .05   c: significant α = .10

Table C.5: Liberal Voters, Quebec

	1	*1–2*	*1–3*	*1–4*	*1–5*	*1–6*	*1–7*
				Block(s)			
Socio–economic Variables							
Not francophone	48.8 [a]	25.8 [a]	20.3 [a]	19.5 [a]	19.0 [a]	19.3 [a]	16.8 [a]
Traditional marriage	9.8 [a]	3.9	2.0	1.9	2.2	2.2	2.7
Union member (fam.)	−13.0 [a]	−5.1	−3.7	−4.0	−4.4	−4.6	−3.0
Constant: block 1	27.0 [a]	—	—	—	—	—	—
Ideological Dimensions							
Regional alienation		−14.6 [a]	−9.9 [a]	−10.2 [a]	−10.2 [a]	−9.5 [a]	−6.1 [c]
Quebec sovereignty		−60.8 [a]	−39.8 [a]	−38.0 [a]	−38.3 [a]	−37.1 [a]	−28.5 [a]
Aboriginal peoples		13.5 [c]	6.4	5.2	5.3	7.1	8.1
Canada–US relations		15.7 [c]	11.7	14.2 [c]	14.7 [c]	15.1 [c]	12.7
Cynicism		−15.8 [c]	−12.3	−13.6 [c]	−12.4	−8.8	−2.8
Moral traditionalism		23.8 [a]	19.8 [a]	18.9 [a]	20.9 [a]	18.3 [a]	14.1 [b]
Constant: blocks 1–2		61.7 [a]	—	—	—	—	—
Party Identification							
Party identification			25.2 [a]	24.8 [a]	24.8 [a]	24.1 [a]	19.0 [a]
Constant: blocks 1–3			54.5 [a]	—	—	—	—
Economic Perceptions							
Prv. Econ. Retro.				−5.6 [a]	−5.3 [b]	−5.4 [b]	−4.1 [c]
Constant: blocks 1–4				52.9 [a]	—	—	—
Issues							
Creating jobs					3.8 [b]	3.5 [c]	4.0 [b]
Constant: blocks 1–5					51.4 [a]	—	—
Liberal Performance							
Liberals – national unity						6.3 [b]	2.5
Constant: blocks 1–6						47.9 [a]	—
Leader Evaluation							
Chrétien							43.7 [a]
Constant: blocks 1–7							44.3 [a]
Adjusted *R* square	0.19	0.36	0.45	0.46	0.46	0.47	0.52

a: significant α = .01   b: significant α = .05   c: significant α = .10

Table C.6: Conservative Voters, Quebec

	1	1–2	1–3	1–4	1–5	1–6	1–7
				Block(s)			

	1	1–2	1–3	1–4	1–5	1–6	1–7
Socio–economic Variables							
Not francophone	–8.5 [c]	–10.3 [b]	–7.4 [c]	–7.4	–7.1	–7.0	–3.6
Employed	8.6 [b]	8.5 [b]	6.9 [b]	6.9 [b]	6.4 [b]	5.9 [c]	3.8
Constant: block 1	17.0 [a]	—	—	—	—	—	—
Ideological Dimensions							
Sovereignty		–26.5 [a]	–22.1 [a]	–22.1 [a]	–22.1 [a]	–22.6 [a]	–13.6 [b]
Aboriginal peoples		–20.6 [a]	–14.1 [b]	–14.1 [b]	–13.5 [c]	–14.6 [b]	–11.4 [c]
Cynicism		19.3 [b]	15.5 [b]	15.5 [b]	16.7 [b]	13.5 [c]	9.4
Free enterprise		17.9 [b]	15.0 [b]	15.0 [b]	15.9 [b]	15.4 [b]	12.0 [c]
Constant: blocks 1–2		18.6 [c]	—	—	—	—	—
Party Identification							
Party identification			25.5 [a]	25.5 [a]	25.0 [a]	25.0 [a]	17.0 [a]
Constant: blocks 1–3			27.0 [a]	27.0 [a]	—	—	—
Economic Perceptions							
No significant variable				no variable	—	—	—
Issues							
Spending					3.1 [c]	3.2 [c]	3.3 [c]
Gun control					–3.7 [c]	–3.6 [c]	–3.3 [c]
Constant: blocks 1–5					26.4 [a]	—	—
Liberal Performance							
Liberals – GST						6.0 [c]	5.1 [c]
Constant: blocks 1–6						26.5 [a]	—
Leader Evaluation							
Charest							63.4 [a]
Constant: blocks 1–7							26.5 [a]
Adjusted *R* square	0.01	0.07	0.20	—	0.20	0.21	0.33

a: significant $\alpha = .01$ b: significant $\alpha = .05$ c: significant $\alpha = .10$

Table C.7: Bloc Québécois Voters, Quebec

	1	1–2	1–3	1–4	1–5	1–6	1–7
				Block(s)			
Socio–economic Variables							
Not francophone	−40.6 a	−16.2 a	−6.8 c	−5.9	−6.1	−5.9	−1.8
Traditional marriage	−10.6 a	−5.1	−2.6	−2.5	−2.5	−1.7	0.0
Union member (fam.)	14.9 a	6.6 b	5.0 c	5.2 c	5.3 c	4.6	2.5
Constant: block 1	46.0 a	—	—	—	—	—	—
Ideological Dimensions							
Women		10.4 a	6.9 b	7.1 b	6.8 b	6.9 b	5.9 b
Regional alienation		10.0 a	4.8	5.1	5.5 c	5.2	4.3
Sovereignty		91.6 a	59.7 a	58.2 a	57.6 a	53.8 a	33.3 a
Canada–US relations		−32.8 a	−25.9 a	−28.1 a	−28.4 a	−26.0 a	−20.6 a
Constant: blocks 1–2		−4.0	—	—	—	—	—
Party Identification							
Party identification			33.5 a	33.0 a	33.3 a	33.2 a	26.3 a
Constant: blocks 1–3			15.1 b	—	—	—	—
Economic Perceptions							
Retro. prov. economy				4.9 b	5.3 b	5.3 b	4.2 b
Constant: blocks 1–4				17.7 a	—	—	—
Issues							
Gun control					3.2 c	2.6	2.5
Constant: blocks 1–5					17.6 a	—	—
Liberal Performance							
Liberals – Quebec interest						−5.0 c	−2.3
Liberals – social programs						−5.3 b	−4.8 b
Liberals – fighting crime						5.6 b	5.0 b
Liberals – GST						9.1 a	−8.7 a
Constant: blocks 1–6						22.2 a	—
Leader Evaluation							
Duceppe							45.4 a
Constant: block 1–7							40.6 a
Adjusted *R* square	0.14	0.40	0.56	0.56	0.57	0.58	0.63

a: significant α = .01   b: significant α = .05   c: significant α = .10

Description of Variables[1]

Ideological Dimensions

Variables were coded on a scale from 0 to 1, unless specified otherwise.

1.A. QUEBEC FEELING (outside Quebec only) is an index made up of three questions:

- How do you feel about Quebec? On a scale from 0 to 100, where 0 means you really dislike and 100 means you really like. (pesf12)
- How much do you think should be done for Quebec: more, less, or about the same as now? (cpse3a)
- Should Quebec be recognized as a distinct society? (cpsj3)

The index is the sum of the three scores divided by 3.

1.B. QUEBEC SOVEREIGNTY (Quebec only) is an index made up of four questions:

- In your opinion, is the French language threatened in Quebec? (pese10d)
- If Quebec separates from Canada, do you think the situation of the French language in Quebec will get better, get worse, or stay about the same as now? (pese10e)
- Do you strongly agree, somewhat agree, somewhat disagree, or strongly disagree with the following statements: There is no reason to have a sovereignist party in Ottawa? (pese21g)
- To you personally, in this election, is it very important, somewhat important, or not very important: defending the interests of Quebec? (cpsa2h)

The index is the sum of the four scores divided by 4.

2.A. OUTGROUPS (outside Quebec only) is an index made up of three questions:

- In general, would you say that Canada's aboriginal peoples are better off, worse off, or about the same as other Canadians? (cpsj9)
- Should the federal government spend more, spend less, or about the same as now for aboriginal peoples? (cpsj10)
- How much do you think should be done for racial minorities: more, about the same as now, or less? (cpsf1)

The index is the sum of the three scores divided by 3.

---

[1] The parentheses refer to the question number in the survey; 'cps' refers to the campaign survey and 'pes' to the post-election survey.

2.B.   OUTGROUPS (Quebec only) is an index made up of three questions:

- Do you think Canada should admit more immigrants, fewer, or about the same? (cpsj18)

- How do you feel about racial minorities? On a scale from 0 to 100, where 0 means you really dislike them and 100 means you really like them. (pesf8)

- How much do you think should be done for racial minorities: more, about the same as now, or less? (cpsf1)

The index is the sum of the three scores divided by 3.

3.   ABORIGINAL PEOPLES (Quebec only) is an index made up of three questions:

- In general, would you say that Canada's aboriginal peoples are better off, worse off, or about the same as other Canadians? (cpsj9)

- Should the federal government spend more, spend less, or about the same as now for aboriginal peoples? (cpsj10)

- How do you feel about aboriginal peoples? On a scale from 0 to 100, where 0 means you really dislike them and 100 means you really like them. (pesf6)

The index is the sum of the three scores divided by 3.

4.   CANADA–US is an index made up of three questions:

- How do you feel about the United States? On a scale from 0 to 100, where 0 means you really dislike them and 100 means you really like them. (pesf13)

- Do you think Canada's ties with the United States should be much more closer, somewhat closer, about the same as now, more distant, or much more distant? (pese4)

- Do you strongly agree, somewhat agree, somewhat disagree, or strongly disagree with the following statements: It would be a good thing if Canada and the United States became one country? (pese25)

The index is the sum of the three scores divided by 3.

5.   CYNICISM is an index made up of four questions:

- For each of the following statements, please tell me if you strongly agree, somewhat agree, somewhat disagree, or strongly disagree:

a) Those elected to Parliament soon lose touch with people. (cpsb10a)

b) I don't think the government cares much what people like me think. (cpsb10d)

c) Politicians are ready to lie to get elected. (cpsb10e)

- Do political parties keep their election promises most of the time, some of the time, or hardly ever? (cpsj13)

The index is the sum of the four scores divided by 4.

6.   MORAL TRADITIONALISM is an index made up of three questions:

- Do you strongly agree, somewhat agree, somewhat disagree, or strongly disagree with the following statements:

a) Only people who are married should be having children. (cpsf2)

b) Society would be better off if more women stayed home with their children. (cpsf3)

- Now we would like to get your views on abortion. Of the following three positions, which is closest to your own opinion:

1. Abortion should never be permitted.

2. Should be permitted only after need has been established by a doctor.

3. Should be a matter of the woman's personal choice. (pese5a, b, and c)

The index is the sum of the three scores divided by 3.

7.   FREE ENTERPRISE is an index made up of three questions:

- Do you strongly agree, somewhat agree, somewhat disagree, or strongly disagree with the following statements:

a) People who don't get ahead should blame themselves, not the system. (pese19)

b) When businesses make a lot of money, everyone benefits, including the poor. (pese20)

- How do you feel about big business? On a scale from 0 to 100, where 0 means you really dislike them and 100 means you really like them. (pesf1)

The index is the sum of the three scores divided by 3.

8.   WOMEN

- How much do you think should be done for women: much more, somewhat more, about the same as now, somewhat less or much less? (pese1)

The variable is a −1 to +1 scale where −1 means 'much less for women' and 1, 'much more'.

9.   REGIONAL ALIENATION is a dummy variable. It takes the value of 1 when the respondent answers 'worse' to the following question:

- Do you think the federal government treats your province better, worse, or about the same as the other parts of the country? (cpsj12)

Party Identification

- In federal politics, do you usually think of yourself as a Liberal, Conservative, NDP, Reform, Bloc, or none of these? (cpsk1)

- How strongly (name of the party) do you feel: very strongly, fairly strongly, or not very strongly? (cpsk2)

Four variables were created, one for each party. Each variable takes the value of 1 if the respondent has a strong or a fairly strong party identification with the party, −1 if the respondent has a strong or a fairly strong party identification with another party, and 0 otherwise.

Economic Perceptions

Variables were coded on a scale from −1 to +1, unless specified otherwise.

1.   FEAR OF LOSING JOB

- How worried are you about losing your job in the near future: a lot, somewhat, a little, or not at all? (cpsm8a)

The variable FEAR OF LOSING JOB is on a 0-to-1 scale, where 1 means the respondent worried a lot and 0 means not at all.

2.   PERSONAL FINANCE (RETROSPECTIVE)

- Financially, are you better off, worse off, or about the same as a year ago? (cpsc1)

3. PERSONAL FINANCE (PROSPECTIVE)

    • Do you think that a year from now you will be better off financially, worse off, or about the same as now? (cpsc2)

4. PERCEPTION OF UNEMPLOYMENT RATE (RETROSPECTIVE)

    • Do you think the unemployment rate in Canada has gone up, gone down, or stayed about the same since the Liberals came to power? (cpsc5)

5. PERCEPTION OF UNEMPLOYMENT RATE (PROSPECTIVE)

    • And in the next few years, do you think unemployment will go up, go down, or stay about the same? (cpsc6)

6. PERCEPTION OF CANADIAN ECONOMY (RETROSPECTIVE)

    • Over the past year, has Canada's economy gotten better, gotten worse, or stayed about the same? (cpsg1)

7. PERCEPTION OF CANADIAN ECONOMY (PROSPECTIVE)

    • What about the next 12 months? Will Canada's economy get better, get worse, or stay about the same? (cpsg3a)

8. PERCEPTION OF PROVINCIAL ECONOMY (RETROSPECTIVE)

    • Would you say that over the past year (province)'s economy has gotten better, stayed about the same, or gotten worse? (cpsg2)

9. Variable PERCEPTION OF PROVINCIAL ECONOMY (PROSPECTIVE)

    • And in the next 12 months, will (province)'s economy get better, get worse, or stay about the same? (cpsg3b)

Issues

Variables were coded on a scale from −1 to +1, unless specified otherwise.

1. SPENDING is an index made up of four questions on cutting spending in four areas. The following question has been used for each of the four areas:

    • If you had to make cuts, would you cut spending in the following areas a lot, some, or not at all? Pension and Old Age Security, Health Care, Unemployment Insurance, Education. (pese6c, d, e, f)

The index is the sum of the four scores divided by 4.

2. TAXES is an index made up of three different questions on the importance of cutting taxes:

   - How important are the following issues to you personally in this election: very important, somewhat important, not very important? Cutting taxes (cpsa2d).

   - We face tough choices. Cutting taxes means cutting social programs and improving social programs means increasing taxes. If you had to choose, would you cut taxes, increase taxes, or keep taxes as they are? (cpse1a)

   - What is the most important issue to you personally in this election? (cpsa1)

If the respondent said 'cutting taxes', the variable equals 1; if the respondent named another issue, the variable equals –1. Respondents who didn't know were given a score of 0.

The index is the sum of the three scores divided by 3.

3. DEFICIT is an index made up of three questions on the importance of reducing the deficit:

   - How important are the following issues to you personally in this election: very important, somewhat important, not very important? Reducing the deficit (cpsa2b).

   - Do you strongly agree, somewhat agree, somewhat disagree, or strongly disagree with the following statements? To maintain our social programs we must eliminate the deficit. (cpsf5)

   - Which is the best way to fight unemployment: eliminate the deficit or reduce taxes? (cpsf8)

The index is the sum of the three scores divided by 3.

4. JOBS is an index made up of three questions on the importance for governments to create jobs:

   - Do you strongly agree, somewhat agree, somewhat disagree, or strongly disagree with the following statements?

     There's not much any government can do these days to solve the unemployment problem. (cpsf4)

     The government should leave it entirely to the private sector to create jobs. (cpsf6)

   - How important are the following issues to you personally in this election: very important, somewhat important, not very important? Creating jobs. (cpsa2c)

The index is the sum of the three scores divided by 3.

5. CRIME

- Which is the best way to deal with young offenders who commit violent crime: give them tougher sentences or spend more on rehabilitating them? (cpsj21)

6. GUN CONTROL

- Do you strongly agree, somewhat agree, somewhat disagree, or strongly disagree with the following statement? Only police officers and the military should be allowed to have guns. (pese12)

Liberal Performance

Variables were coded on a scale from −1 to +1, unless specified otherwise.

1. NATIONAL UNITY

- How good a job do you think the Liberal government has done in preserving national unity: has the Liberal government done a very good job, quite good job, not good, or not good at all? (cpsf10a)

2. DEFICIT

- How good a job do you think the Liberal government has done in reducing the deficit: has the Liberal government done a very good job, quite good job, not good, or not good at all? (cpsf10b)

3. JOBS

- How good a job do you think the Liberal government has done in creating jobs: has the Liberal government done a very good job, quite good job, not good, or not good at all? (cpsf10c)

4. DEFENDING INTERESTS OF QUEBEC (Quebec only)

- How good a job do you think the Liberal government has done in defending the interests of Quebec: has the Liberal government done a very good job, quite good job, not good, or not good at all? (cpsf10e)

5. CRIME

- How good a job do you think the Liberal government has done in fighting crime: has the Liberal government done a very good job, quite good job, not good, or not good at all? (cpsf10f)

6.   SOCIAL PROGRAMS

- How good a job do you think the Liberal government has done in protecting social programs: has the Liberal government done a very good job, quite good job, not good, or not good at all? (cpsf10g)

7.   GST is a dummy variable. It takes the value of 1 when the respondent said the Liberals had promised to do away with the GST and that they didn't really try to keep their promise.

- In the 1993 election campaign, did the Liberals promise to do away with the GST? (cpsj2)

- Did the Liberals really try to keep their promise? (cpsj2b)

Leaders

Variables were coded on a scale from –1 to + 1.

The variable used in the regressions is the difference between the score (on a 0 to 1 scale) given for the leader of a given party minus the highest score among the other leaders.

- How do you feel about Jean Chrétien, Jean Charest, Alexa McDonough, Preston Manning, and Gilles Duceppe, on a scale from 0 to 100, where 0 means you really dislike him/her and 100 means you really like him/her? (pesc1a, b, c, d, e)

Appendix D

Explaining Turnout

Table D.1: The Determinants of Turnout

	Vote		
Age 18 to 29 years	−.16 (.02) ***	−.14 (.02) ***	−.13 (.02) ***
Age 30 to 39 years	−.06 (.02) ***	−.05 (.02) **	−.04 (.02) **
Did not complete high school	−.07 (.02) ***	−.05 (.02) ***	−.04 (.02) **
University graduate	.11 (.02) ***	.09 (.02) ***	.08 (.02) ***
Non-Christian	−.09 (.03) ***	−.09 (.03) ***	−.08 (.03) ***
Religiosity	.06 (.02) **	.06 (.02) **	.06 (.02) ***
Lowest household income quintile	−.06 (.02) ***	−.05 (.02) **	−.04 (.02) *
Atlantic resident	.03 (.03)	—	—
Quebec resident	.07 (.02) ***	.07 (.02) ***	.08 (.02) ***
West resident	.01 (.02)	—	—
Traditional marriage	.07 (.02) ***	.06 (.02) ***	.06 (.02) ***
Has children under 18 years	−.06 (.02) ***	−.05 (.02) ***	−.05 (.02) ***
Retired	.04 (.02) *	.03 (.02)	.03 (.02)
New immigrant	−.12 (.04) ***	−.13 (.04) ***	−.11 (.04) ***
Interest		.02 (.002) ***	.02 (.002) ***
Party identification		.07 (.01) ***	.06 (.01) ***
Cynicism		−.04 (.03)	−.05 (.03)
No issue			−.14 (.02) ***
No choice			−.09 (.03) ***
Constant	.81 (.02) ***	.67 (.04) ***	.73 (.04) ***
Adjusted R square	.10	.14	.16
N	2,703	2,676	2,676

* : $\alpha = 0.10$
** : $\alpha = 0.05$
*** : $\alpha = 0.01$

Table D.2: Turnout: Period, Life-Cycle, and Cohort Effects[a]

	Vote
1997 election	−.06 (.01) ***
1993 election	−.01 (.01)
1992 election	−.02 (.01) **
Age (log)	.38 (.06) ***
Cohort : 1945–59	.03 (.01) **
Cohort : 1960–9	−.01 (.02)
Cohort : 1970–9	−.06 (.03) **
Constant	.27 (.10) ***
Adjusted *R* square	.05
N = 10,717	

[a] 1988, 1992, 1993, 1997

Notes

Chapter 2   The Vote

1   Cramer's V was .34 in 1993.

2   For each party, we created a dummy variable indicating, for instance, how many people voted Liberal or for other parties in each province.

3   Cramer's V was .55 for the Bloc, .43 for Reform, .26 for the NDP, .19 for the Liberals, and .18 for the Conservatives.

4   We asked respondents what they thought were the chances, on a scale from 0 to 100, of each party winning the election in their constituency.

5   These analyses are reported in greater detail in Blais et al. (1999).

6   Perceptions of the race for the official Opposition seem not to have affected the vote in Quebec.

7   The only region where this pattern does not hold is Atlantic Canada. The Conservatives are the most popular second choice of Reform and NDP voters, and the NDP the most frequent second choice of Conservative voters. There seems to have been strong anti-Liberal sentiment in that region.

8   The English debate took place on 12 May and the French debate on 13 May. The latter was interrupted when the moderator fainted, and was continued on 18 May.

9   Each point represents the average of vote intentions for that day and for the two days before and after. Only 19 interviews were completed on 27 April, the day the election was called. Our first 'real' day of interview is 28 April. The first and last two days are omitted since five-day averages cannot be computed on those days.

10   The dependent variable is the percentage of respondents intending to vote for a given party on a given day of the campaign. We regress vote intentions on four independent variables: DEBATE, $DEBATE^2$, AD, and AD^2. The DEBATE variable equals 0 until 12 May, the day of the English debate, and takes the value of 1 to 20 afterwards. The AD variable equals 0 until 22 May, the day the ad was first aired, and 1 to 10 afterwards. If it takes some time for the debates to have their full effect, and if the effect then progressively decays, we should observe a positive coefficient on DEBATE and a negative one on $DEBATE^2$ (or the reverse for the party that lost the debate). As in Blais and Boyer (1996), we control for party identification (PI). The analysis suggests that the debates did not have an impact on Reform support nor the Quebec ad on Liberal or Conservative support. The results of the regressions are the following (for more details see Blais et al. forthcoming):

   LIBERAL VOTE: $45.32 - 1.14$DEBATE $+ 0.06$DEBATE^2 $+ 50.63$ PI.
   PC VOTE: $30.56 + 0.98$DEBATE $- 0.04$DEBATE^2 $+ 43.54$ PI.
   REFORM VOTE: $18.67 + 2.82$AD $- 0.29$AD^2 $+ 8.96$ PI.

11   The coefficients in note 10 imply that after 20 days the net impact was nil for the Liberals and $+2$ points for the Conservatives.

12   As many as 63 per cent of those with an opinion were of that view.

13 These points are examined in great detail in Blais, Nadeau, Gidengil, and Nevitte (1999).

14 There was no movement among those who did not think that the Liberals had failed to keep their promise. Note that the figures in this paragraph exclude Quebec, where Reform was practically nonexistent.

15 For details on the procedure see Blais et al. (1997a, 1997b).

16 See Mosteller (1968). Corrections were also made to the official turnout in 1993, which, for reasons explained in Chapter 3, overestimated actual turnout.

17 The table includes only those who voted in 1997. Abstention is examined in Chapter 4.

18 It should be kept in mind that because they had a larger 1993 base, the Liberals suffered more from similar proportional desertions. For instance, 10 per cent of 1993 Liberal voters went to the NDP in 1997, while 14 per cent of 1993 NDP voters went to the Liberals. In the exchange, however, the Liberals had a net loss, since a loss of 10 per cent of a 41 per cent base is much more than a gain of 14 per cent of a 7 per cent base.

19 Reform also did slightly better among those who were undecided at the beginning of the campaign.

Chapter 3 Television Coverage in the 1997 Election

1 This question is addressed in a recent study by Joslyn and Ceccoli (1996, 146), who concluded from their examination of the media coverage of the 1992 presidential election campaign in the United States that 'network news appraisal are volatile, reflecting campaign events, the dynamics of news organization, and the efforts of campaigns to curb the negatives and maintain and enhance the positives'.

2 Though related research in the United States demonstrates that television news commentary affect presidential popularity (West 1991), evidence of a systematic connection between shifts in media coverage and voting intentions during campaigns is still very limited (see Mendelsohn and Nadeau 1999).

3 The choice of the CBC News as representative of the Canadian news media is common. See Fletcher and Everett (1991) for a review, and Mendelsohn and Nadeau (1999) for an application to the 1993 federal election. In the United States, Zaller (1996, 1) noted that 'Network TV coverage of elections from 1968 to 1992 conforms to the same pattern as other media in this period.'

4 The composition of the groups of coders was as follows:

Sample composition

Network	Liberal	PC	NDP	Reform	Bloc	Non-voter	Total
CBC	2	2	2	1	0	2	9
CTV	2	2	2	1	0	2	9
Radio-Canada	4	3	0	0	4	3	14

5 For a complete description, see Nadeau et al. (1998). All documentation, including coding grids, is available from the authors upon request.

6 A comparative analysis of the evaluations of trained and untrained coders shows that the evaluations of the two groups follows the same dynamic but that trained coders' evaluations are systematically more negative. See Nadeau et al. (1998).

7 Another indicator of this reduced visibility is the order of the NDP's appearance on the

televised news. An analysis based on all news items, be they electoral or not, shows that the items dealing with the NDP were presented later in televised newscasts than those dealing with the other parties. The average order of appearance of the principal news item devoted to the parties on the English-language networks was 4.8 for the Liberals, 4.9 for the Conservatives, 4.7 for Reform, but 5.6 for the NDP.

8 As the results were very similar for the CBC and CTV networks, we have combined the results for the two networks for the sake of simplicity and clarity. We have also limited our attention to the seven competitive parties in the 1997 federal campaign, namely the Liberals, the Conservatives, and the Bloc in Quebec, and the four large federal parties (with the exception of the Bloc) in the rest of the country.

9 The front-page headlines of *La Presse* and *Le Devoir* after the first week of the campaign are particularly telling. *La Presse* ran the headlines reading 'Le Bloc cafouille encore' (The Bloc errs again) and 'Lucien Bouchard contredit Gilles Duceppe' (Lucien Bouchard contradicts Gilles Duceppe). Meanwhile *Le Devoir*, which is usually fairly sympathetic to the Bloc, evoked the 'dure semaine de Gilles Duceppe' (Gilles Duceppe's difficult week'). See *La Presse* and *Le Devoir*, 3 May 1997.

10 The first polls published after the debates on 17 May confirmed, both inside and outside Quebec, an improvement in Charest's image and a significant increase in his party's support.

11 'Conservative leader Jean Charest is the only leader who was applauded by the studio audience' (Julie Van Dusen, CBC, 12 May); 'It was the only time during the evening that there was spontaneous applause from the audience here' (Jason Moscowitz, CBC, 12 May); 'And then, the only part of the debate that drew applauses from the audiences' (Sacha Petrocik, CBC, 12 May).

12 'Winning the debate is one thing, winning seats is another' (Peter Mansbridge, CBC, 13 May); 'Jean Charest was the viewers' choice as winner of the English debate' (Dawna Friesen, CTV, 13 May).

13 Reform's visibility in the first three days after the commercial was broadcast was particularly striking. The party was featured in as many items as the Liberals and the Conservatives combined.

14 Chrétien's declaration was front-page news in Quebec's main newspapers, some of which, like *La Presse* and *Le Devoir* printed Gilles Duceppe's reply that this constituted 'an assault against Quebec'. Numerous commentaries by experts affirming that this declaration was likely to aid the Bloc were also published. See, for example, *La Presse*, Tuesday, 27 May, B1: 'Chrétien à l'aide du Bloc' (Chrétien to the aid of the Bloc).

15 The reaction on English-language television was also very similar. Peter Mansbridge prefaced Tom Kennedy's report on this subject by saying: 'The mood in the Bloc Québécois has suddenly become more upbeat. . . . The Bloc is getting a little help from its enemies' (27 May).

Chapter 4 Ideological Landscape

1 Factor analysis is particularly useful for searching through a large number of variables and for determining statistically which among those many items form part of an underlying ideological dimension. But there may be good reasons for including other ideological domains in the analysis of voting behaviour. In the Canadian Election Study surveys, some ideological dimensions were measured with only single items; there are

two in particular, one dealing with general orientations towards women and the other with regional alienation, that may be helpful for explaining the vote in the 1997 federal election (see Appendix C for the wording of these questions). There is evidence of sex differences in political preferences (Gidengil 1995; Gidengil et al. forthcoming; O'Neill 1995). Similarly, regional alienation has become part of the public discourse surrounding West-East regional cleavages that were so successfully harnessed by the Reform party in 1993 (Johnston et al. 1996c).

2   An additive scale is created for each ideological dimension. The choice of variables is based on the factor analytic solutions for respondents inside and outside Quebec. The scales, including the items contained in the scales, are standardized with values ranging from 0 and 1. *Refused* responses are excluded from the analysis, and *Don't know* responses are assigned a mid-point value of .5.

3   gamma = -.04 (1993), gamma = .07 (1997).

4   gamma = .16 (1993), gamma = .24 (1997).

5   For example, one out of three respondents outside Quebec said they were 'not sure' about where to place themselves on a standard 11-point left-right scale. Of those who did place themselves on the scale, one in three selected the mid-point. The data for Quebec are 31 per cent and 32 per cent respectively.

6   The correlations between self-placement on the left-right scale and each of the dimensions are: *Cynicism* = .08 (outside Quebec) and -.18 (Quebec); *Moral traditionalism* = .25 (outside Quebec) and .22 (Quebec); *Free enterprise* = .20 (outside Quebec) and .13 (Quebec); *Quebec* = -.10 (outside Quebec) and *Sovereignty* = -.15 (Quebec); *Outgroups* = -.22 (outside Quebec) and -.11 (Quebec); *Aboriginal peoples* = -.07 (Quebec); *Canada/US* = .17 (outside Quebec) and .16 (Quebec); *Women* = -.20 (outside Quebec) and -.22 (Quebec); and *Regional Alienation* = .18 (outside Quebec) and -.17 (Quebec).

7   Outside Quebec, New Democrats are more likely than others to see themselves in terms of left-right. Within Quebec, the Conservatives are most likely to use the scale.

Chapter 5   Low Turnout: A Sign of Disaffection?

1   The turnout figures for 1980 and 1993 have been adjusted to take into account the inflated number of electors on the electoral list. The list had been drawn up one year earlier and, as a consequence, the names of many people who had died or moved to another riding had not been deleted.

2   In Switzerland, the four major parties agree to share the collective executive, thus making electoral outcomes virtually meaningless, and elections and referenda are extremely frequent. In the United States, elections and referenda are also very frequent, and people have to register themselves on the electoral list. See Powell (1982; 1986) and Jackman and Miller (1995).

3   Seasonal influences on turnout are also observed by Eagles (1991).

4   We regressed turnout on two independent variables: season (S), a dummy variable that equals 1 for the elections held in the winter or summer, and distance (D), the difference in the vote shares of the two leading parties. Turnout = 77.4 - 5.6XS - 0.2XD (r^2 = .42).

5   We also thought that turnout might be lower in bad economic times but found no relationship between the rate of unemployment and turnout.

6   To gauge cohort effects, we constructed dummy variables that equal 1 for those born immediately after the war (usually called the baby-boomers), those born in the 1960s, and those born in the 1970s respectively. The life-cycle effect is captured by the age of the respondent at the time of a given election (preliminary analyses indicated that the logged variable performed better). And we finally have dummy variables for each election, which indicate specific 'period' effects.

7   This is so because the coefficient of cynicism (controlling for all socio-demographic variables) is .11.

8   Respondents were questioned about these two issues as well as about their interpretation of party policy. We used a seven-point scale from –3 to +3. Respondents were defined as considering a party to be close to their viewpoint on an issue if the distance between their own position and the party stand as they saw it was less than 2. We also created a variable that equalled .5 for those who did not consider any party to be close to their position on one of the two issues. This other measure was found not to be significant.

9   For evidence that sense of duty is a powerful determinant of voting, see Blais (1998).

Chapter 6   A Small Liberal Victory

1   Twice, in 1957 and in 1979, the Liberals got more votes but fewer seats than the Conservatives.

2   We did an experiment in the post-election survey and asked the following question to a random half of the respondents: 'In federal politics, do you usually think of yourself as close to any particular party?' This yields an estimate of 38 per cent with a party identification. This question has the advantage of being open-ended but the disadvantage of referring to 'closeness'. It is possible to think of oneself as a Liberal or a Catholic without feeling close to the Liberals or Catholics.

3   Note, however, that Ontario-Atlantic and Ontario-West comparisons show that differences in partisanship (*net* of socio-demographics and basic values) accounted for 4.5 points of the former gap and over 8 points of the latter gap.

4   That is, if the mean on each economic variable had been 0 on the +1 to –1 scale.

5   Fifty-seven per cent said that the Liberals had done a good job at reducing the deficit; the equivalent percentage on preserving social programs was 40 per cent.

6   The percentage was 52 per cent in 1993.

7   Almost all of the loss took place among those who felt angry about this. Opinions and feelings about the GST were similar in Quebec, but they did not have a significant effect on Liberal support.

8   When we controlled for socio-demographic variables, values, party identification, economic perceptions, and opinions on issues, the propensity to vote Liberal was four points higher among those who did not say that the Liberals had been elected to create jobs (this pattern holds only outside Quebec). This result suggests that the Liberals may have won two points thanks to the voters' poor memory.

9   An even larger majority of sovereignists (87 per cent) thought that Quebec has such a right.

10   The same difference holds among those without party identification.

11   For an analysis of the sources of leader evaluations and a more detailed comparison of the images of Chrétien and Charest, see Chapter 7.

Chapter 7 The Progressive Conservatives: A One-Man Show

1 The figure was 56 per cent in Quebec and 53 per cent in the rest of the country.

2 We should be careful not to overstate the extent of this perception of Charest as the winner of the English debate: 40 per cent of voters said they did not know who won. Similarly, 34 per cent of Quebeckers said they did not know who won the French debate.

3 We performed linear regression analyses, with leader rating on a 100-point scale as the dependent variable and each of the traits for that leader as independent variables. Thus, the effect of each trait is measured net of every other trait. Since trait evaluations might be shaped by partisanship, we added a control for party identification. The results were affected little by the addition of this control.

4 This question was asked only in Quebec.

5 In Quebec, the coefficient for the effect on Conservative voting of this perception of undue closeness to Mulroney was of borderline statistical significance.

Chapter 8 The Reform Party and the Limits to Growth

1 On Reform support in 1993, see Nevitte et al. (1998).

2 There are two different ways that gaps in vote share between regions can occur (and they are not mutually exclusive). First, there can be regional differences in issue positions. Second, there can be differences in the importance of those issues. For a more extended analysis of this question, see Gidengil et al. (1999).

3 The average scores on 0 to 1 scales for both regions are .62 for deficit reduction and .35 for tax cuts.

4 The average score on our jobs scale was .74 in Ontario and .71 in the West.

5 The average score on our moral traditionalism score was .39 for Ontario and .40 for the West.

6 Reform voters in the West had an average score of .42 on our outgroups scale, compared with the average outside Quebec of .54. The average score for all Westerners was .50 versus .57 for Ontarians.

7 This is also true of beliefs about free enterprise. The average score for the West and Ontario is the same at .55. Beliefs about free enterprise were not associated with Reform voting in either region.

8 It should be emphasized that this estimate is net of differences in party identification and issue positions.

9 The average scores on our cynicism scale are .71 for the West and .68 for Ontario.

10 The average score of Reform voters on the deficit scale was .64, compared with .62 for Conservative voters and .66 for Liberal voters (and .44 for NDP voters). On the spending scale, the scores were .33, .31, and .29, respectively (and .16 for NDP voters). Reform voters are more distinct on the jobs issue, though, with a mean score of .65 to the Liberals' .73 and the Conservatives' .75 (and the NDP's .83). All these figures are for voters outside Quebec.

11 It should be noted, however, that at least one in four (27 per cent) of those who opposed recognizing Quebec as a distinct society would change their mind if recognition would keep Quebec in Canada.

12 According to our calculations, the appearance of trustworthiness increased Manning's average rating by 13 points, compared with 22 points each for Charest and McDonough (and 8 points for Chrétien).

13 There were only 62 Quebeckers among the 1,500 plus people attending the United-Alternative Conference.

Chapter 9   The NDP: Off the Radar Screen

1   For information on the pre-campaign period and the campaign itself, see Whitehorn (1997).

2   The NDP's vote share increased from 5.4 per cent to 23.7 per cent, while the Conservatives' share rose from 26.2 per cent to 33.8 per cent and Reform's share barely increased from 8.4 per cent to 9.0 per cent. The vote for assorted minor political parties dropped from 3.1 per cent to 0.7 per cent.

3   Studies of women and representation have contended that women have historically had a lower success rate than men because they have been disproportionately chosen to run in ridings that the party has no hope of winning. See, for example, Megyery (1991). Studlar and Matland (1994), however, have disputed the 'sacrificial lamb' thesis.

4   There is evidence, though, of class cleavages in federal voting at the subnational level. See Gidengil (1989).

5   Household incomes were adjusted to take account of household size. A single person earning $20,000 is in a very different material position than a single parent with two children living on the same amount.

6   Whether this is the case in Canada depends on the definition of 'working class'. Manual workers score only slightly higher than Canadians at large on our moral traditionalism scale, but low-income Canadians score significantly higher.

7   The average score of Atlantic Canadians was .33 on a 0 to 1 scale (where 1 indicated the maximum willingness to countenance cuts), compared with a score of .49 in the rest of Canada outside Quebec.

8   When the analysis reported in Appendix C was repeated just for Atlantic Canadians, the coefficients were –.50 for free enterprise and –.26 for Canada–U.S. integration, with standard errors of .14.

9   The coefficient was .28 for cynicism, with a standard error of .14.

10   The figure for New Brunswick was 54 per cent.

11   The figures for Prince Edward Island and New Brunswick were 45 points and 44 points respectively.

12   When we ran separate regression analyses for women and men, set up just like the regressions reported in Appendix C for women and men combined, the coefficient for women was .38, compared with only .22 for men. The respective standard errors were .05 and .04, confirming that the results are robust.

13   Men ended the campaign with a similar level of professed lack of knowledge about McDonough. Indeed, McDonough was the only leader about whom men did not profess a higher level of information than women. In men's case, however, there was some apparent knowledge gain across the campaign, with the number saying they knew 'nothing at all' dropping from 69 per cent to 58 per cent.

14   Those who said they knew 'nothing at all' were not asked to rate McDonough on the various leadership traits.

15 The gap for men is a trivial one percentage point.

16 This raises a chicken-and-egg puzzle that we cannot resolve with survey data: do men support the NDP because they want to do more for women, or do they want to do more for women because they support the NDP (Bashevkin 1993)?

Chapter 10 Why Did the Bloc Québécois Lose Ground?

1 The economic-perceptions variable can take three values, namely –1 for negative perceptions, 0 for neutral perceptions, and +1 for positive perceptions. The effect of this variable is measured by multiplying the value of the coefficient, .05, by the corresponding category of the variable. This calculation allows us to observe that in comparison to voters with neutral perceptions of the economic situation (0 × .05), the probability that a voter with a negative perception of Quebec's economy will vote for the Bloc Québécois diminishes by 5 points (–1 × .05) while it rises by 5 points (+1 × .05) among those with a positive perception. From this one gets the total effect of 10 percentage points that is noted in the text.

2 This effect is calculated by multiplying the coefficient of the economic perceptions variable by the change in the distribution of this variable (.05 × 21 = 1.1).

3 The effect is calculated as follows: .05 × 31 = 1.6.

4 The perceptions of the Bloc leader on other traits was more positive. Duceppe was generally seen as a sympathetic leader (56 per cent), inspiring confidence (53 per cent) and lacking arrogance (54 per cent), while not being particularly 'in touch with the times' (45 per cent).

5 The figures for Lucien Bouchard in 1993 (the filter, or screening question, used was not the same that year; see note 6) stand in sharp contrast with 85 per cent saying that the statement 'he provides strong leadership' describes him very well (31) or fairly well (54).

6 Because of the filter used for the leader ratings in the interviews conducted during the 1997 election campaign, we use the post-election waves for 1993 and 1997 in this chapter. This explains the small discrepancies between the leader ratings in this Chapter and Chapter 6.

7 This effect is calculated by multiplying Gilles Duceppe's popularity deficit by the coefficient of the leader variable.

8 This effect is calculated by multiplying the difference between the popularity of Gilles Duceppe and Lucien Bouchard by the coefficient of the leader variable.

Bibliography

Abramson, Paul R., John R. Aldrich, Phil Paolino, and David Rohde (1992). 'Sophisticated Voting in the 1988 Presidential Primaries', *American Political Science Review* 86: 55–70.

Alford, Robert R. (1963). *Party and Society: The Anglo-American Democracies* (Chicago: Rand McNally).

Ansalobehere, Stephen, Roy Behr, and Shanto Iyengar (1993). *The Media Game* (New York: Macmillan).

Archer, Keith (1985). 'The Failure of the New Democratic Party: Unions, Unionists, and Politics in Canada', *Canadian Journal of Political Science* 18: 354–66.

Archer, Keith, and Marquis Johnson (1988). 'Inflation, Unemployment and Canadian Federal Voting Behaviour', *Canadian Journal of Political Science* 21: 569–84.

Bartels, Larry M. (1988). *Presidential Primaries and the Dynamics of Public Choice* (Princeton, NJ: Princeton University Press).

Bashevkin, Sylvia B. (1993). *Toeing the Lines: Women and Party Politics in English Canada*, 2nd edn (Toronto: Oxford University Press).

Betz, Hans-George (1993). 'The New Politics of Resentment: Radical Right-Wing Populist Parties in Western Europe', *Comparative Politics* 25: 413–27.

Betz, Hans-George, and Stefan Immerfall (1998). *The New Politics of the Right: Neo-Populist Parties and Movements in Established Democracies* (New York: St Martin's Press).

Black, Jerome (1991). 'Reforming the Context of the Voting Process in Canada'. In Herman Bakvis, ed., *Voter Turnout in Canada* (Toronto: Dundurn Press).

Blais, André (1998). *To Vote or Not to Vote?* Typescript, Montreal.

Blais, André, Antoine Bilodeau, and Christopher Kam (1997a). 'Constructing a Flow of the Vote Table, 1988–1993'. Typescript, Montreal.

—— (1997b). 'Déplacement des votes entre les élections de 1993 et 1997'. Typescript, Montreal.

Blais, André, Donald Blake, and Stéphane Dion (1990). 'The Public/Private Sector Cleavage in North America', *Comparative Political Studies* 23: 381–404.

Blais, André, and Martin Boyer (1996). 'Assessing the Impact of Televised Debates', *British Journal of Political Science* 26: 143–64.

Blais, André, and Agnieszka Dobrzynska (1998). 'Turnout in Electoral Democracies', *European Journal of Political Research* 33: 239–61.

Blais, André, and Richard Nadeau (1996). 'Measuring Strategic Voting', *Electoral Studies* 15: 39–52.

—— (1992). 'To Be or Not to Be Sovereignist: Quebeckers' Perennial Dilemma', *Canadian Public Policy* 18: 89–103.

Blais, André, Richard Nadeau, Elisabeth Gidengil, and Neil Nevitte (1999). 'Strategic Voting in the 1997 Canadian Election'. Typescript, Montreal.

—— (forthcoming). 'Campaign Dynamics in the 1997 Canadian Election', *Canadian Public Policy*.

Blais, André, Neil Nevitte, Elisabeth Gidengil, Henry Brady, and Richard Johnston (1995). 'L'Élection fédérale de 1993: le comportement électoral des Québécois', *Revue québécoise de science politique* 27: 15–49.

Blais, André, and Robert Young (1999). 'Why Do People Vote? An Experiment in Rationality', *Public Choice* 99: 39–55.

Blake, Donald E. (1982). 'The Consistency of Inconsistency: Party Identification in Federal and Provincial Politics', *Canadian Journal of Political Science* 15: 691–710.

Blizzard, Christina (1995). *Right Turn: How the Tories Took Ontario* (Toronto: Dundurn Press).

Brady, Henry, Sidney Verba, and Kay Lehman Scholzman (1995). 'Beyond SES: A Resource Model of Political Participation', *American Political Science Review* 89: 271–95.

Brodie, Janine (1991). 'Women and the Electoral Process in Canada'. In Kathy Megyery, ed., *Women in Canadian Politics: Toward Equity in Representation*. Vol. 6 of the research studies of the Royal Commission on Electoral Reform and Party Financing (Toronto: Dundurn Press).

Butler, David, and Donald Stokes (1969). *Political Change in Britain* (London: Macmillan).

Capella, Joseph, and Kathleen Hall Jamieson (1997). *Spiral of Cynicism: The Press and the Public Good* (New York: Oxford University Press).

Cassell, Carol A. (1998). 'Overreports of Voting and Theories of Turnout: The Nonvoting Voter Revisited'. Paper presented at the annual meeting of the Midwest Political Science Association, Chicago.

Clarke, Harold D., Jane Jenson, Lawrence LeDuc, and Jon Pammett (1984). *Absent Mandate: The Politics of Discontent in Canada* (Toronto: Gage).

—— (1979). *Political Choice in Canada* (Toronto: McGraw-Hill Ryerson).

—— (1991). *Absent Mandate: Interpreting Change in Canadian Elections*, 2nd edn (Toronto: Gage).

—— (1996). *Absent Mandate: Canadian Electoral Politics in an Era of Restructuring*, 3rd edn (Vancouver: Gage).

Clarke, Harold D., and Allan Kornberg (1992). 'Support for the Canadian Federal Progressive Party since 1988: The Impact of Economic Evaluations and Economic Issues', *Canadian Journal of Political Science* 25: 29–53.

—— (1996). 'Choosing Canada? The 1995 Quebec Sovereignty Referendum', *PS: Political Science and Politics* 29: 676–82.

Clarke, Harold D., and Marianne C. Stewart (1987). 'Partisan Inconsistency and Partisan Change in Federal States', *American Journal of Political Science* 31: 383–407.

Cox, Gary W. (1997). *Making Votes Count: Strategic Coordination in the World's Electoral Systems* (New York: Cambridge University Press).

Crête, Jean (1984). 'La Presse quotidienne et la campagne électorale de 1981', *Recherches sociographiques* 25: 103–14.

Dalton, Russell J. (1996). 'Political Cleavages, Issues, and Electoral Change'. In Lawrence LeDuc, Richard G. Niemi, and Pippa Norris, eds, *Comparing Democracies: Elections and Voting in Global Perspective* (Thousand Oaks, Calif.: Sage).

Dalton, Russell J., Paul Allen Beck, and Scott C. Flanagan (1984). 'Electoral Change in Advanced Industrial Democracies'. In Russell J. Dalton, Scott C. Flanagan, and Paul Allen Beck, eds, *Electoral Change in Advanced Industrial Democracies: Realignment or Dealignment?* (Princeton: Princeton University Press).

Dalton, Russell J., Scott Flanagan, and Paul Beck, eds (1984). *Electoral Change in Advanced Industrial Democracies* (Princeton, NJ: Princeton University Press).

Dalton, Russell J., Kazuhisa Kawakami, Holli A. Semetoko, Hiroshisa Suzuki, and Katrin Volmer (1998). 'Partisan Cues in the Media: Cross-National Comparisons of Election Coverage'. Paper prepared for presentation at the Annual Meeting of the American Political Science Association, Boston, September.

Dalton, Russell J., and Manfred Keuchler, eds (1990). *Challenging the Political Order: New Social and Political Movements in Western Democracies* (New York: Oxford University Press).

Eagles, Munroe (1991). 'Voting and Non-Voting in Canadian Federal Elections'. In Herman Bakvis, ed., *Voter Turnout in Canada* (Toronto: Dundurn Press).

Erie, Steven P., and Martin Rein (1988). 'Women and the Welfare State'. In Carol M. Mueller, ed., *The Politics of the Gender Gap: The Social Construction of Political Influence* (Beverly Hills, Calif.: Sage).

Everitt, Joanna (1998). 'The Gender Gap in Canada: Now You See It, Now You Don't', *Canadian Review of Sociology and Anthropology* 35: 192–219.

—— (1998). 'Public Opinion and Social Movements: The Women's Movement and the Gender Gap in Canada', *Canadian Journal of Political Science* 31: 743–65.

Fletcher, Frederick, and Robert Everett (1991). 'Mass Media and Elections in Canada'. In Frederick J. Fletcher, ed., *Media, Elections and Democracy* (Toronto: Dundurn).

—— (1996). 'Electoral Participation'. In Lawrence LeDuc, Richard G. Niemi, and Pippa Norris, eds, *Comparing Democracies: Elections and Voting in Global Perspective* (Thousand Oaks, Calif.: Sage).

Franklin, Mark N. (1992). *Electoral Change: Responses to Evolving Social and Attitudinal Structures in Western Countries* (Cambridge, UK: Cambridge University Press).

—— (1996). 'Electoral Participation'. In Lawrence LeDuc, Richard G. Niemi, and Pippa Norris, eds, *Comparing Democracies: Elections and Voting in Global Perspective* (Thousand Oaks, Calif.: Sage).

Frizzell, Alan, and Jon H. Pammett, eds (1994). *The Canadian General Election of 1993* (Toronto: Dundurn Press).

Frizzell, Alan, Jon H. Pammett, and Anthony Westell (1990). *The Canadian General Election of 1988* (Ottawa: Carleton University Press).

Gidengil, Elisabeth (1989). 'Class and Region in Canada: A Dependency Interpretation', *Canadian Journal of Political Science* 22: 563–87.

—— (1992). 'Canada Votes: A Quarter Century of Canadian National Election Studies', *Canadian Journal of Political Science* 25: 219–48.

—— (1995). 'Economic Man—Social Woman? The Case of the Gender Gap in Support for the Canada–US Free Trade Agreement', *Comparative Political Studies* 28: 384–408.

Gidengil, Elisabeth, André Blais, Richard Nadeau, and Neil Nevitte (1999). 'Making Sense of Regional Voting in the 1997 Federal Election: Liberal and Reform Support outside Quebec', *Canadian Journal of Political Science* 32: 247–72.

Gidengil, Elisabeth, Richard Johnston, André Blais, Henry E. Brady, and Neil Nevitte (forthcoming). 'A Missed Opportunity? Women, Voting and Canadian Parties'. In Keith Brownsey, ed., *Reinventing Political Parties* (Toronto: Irwin).

Gilligan, Carol (1982). *In a Different Voice* (Cambridge, Mass.: Harvard University Press).

Granberg, Donald, and Soren Holmberg (1992). 'The Hawthorne Effect in Election Studies', *British Journal of Political Science* 22: 240–8.

Happy, J.R. (1992). 'The Effects of Economic and Fiscal Performance on Incumbency Voting: The Canadian Case', *British Journal of Political Science* 22: 117–30.

Holbrook, Thomas M. (1996). *Do Campaigns Matter?* (Thousand Oaks, Calif.: Sage).

Huddy, Leonie, and Nayda Terkildsen (1993). 'Gender Stereotypes and the Perception of Male and Female Candidates', *American Journal of Political Science* 37: 119–47.

Ignazi, Piero (1992). 'The Silent Counter-Revolution: Hypotheses on the Emergence of Extreme Right-Wing Parties in Europe', *European Journal of Political Research* 22: 3–34.

Isaac, J.U. (1990). 'The New Right and The Moral Society', *Parliamentary Affairs* 43: 209–26.

Jackman, Robert, and Ross A. Miller (1995). 'Voter Turnout in the Industrial Democracies during the 1980s', *Comparative Political Studies* 27: 467–92.

Jennings, M. Kent (1988). 'Preface'. In Carol M. Mueller, ed., *The Politics of the Gender Gap: The Social Construction of Political Influence* (Beverly Hills, Calif.: Sage).

Johnston, Richard (1989). 'Générations politiques et changement électoral au Canada'. In Jean Crête and Pierre Favre, eds, *Générations et politiques* (Paris: Economica).

—— (1992). 'Political Generations and Electoral Change in Canada', *British Journal of Political Science* 22: 93–116.

Johnston, Richard, André Blais, Henry E. Brady, and Jean Crête (1992). *Letting the People Decide: Dynamics of a Canadian Election* (Montreal: McGill-Queen's University Press).

Johnston, Richard, André Blais, Henry E. Brady, Elisabeth Gidengil, and Neil Nevitte (1996a). 'The 1993 Election: Realignment, Dealignment, or Something Else?'. Paper presented at the annual meeting of the American Political Science Association, San Francisco.

Johnston, Richard, André Blais, Elisabeth Gidengil, and Neil Nevitte (1996b). *The Challenge of Direct Democracy: The 1992 Canadian Referendum* (Montreal: McGill-Queen's University Press).

Johnston, Richard, André Blais, Elisabeth Gidengil, Neil Nevitte, and Henry E. Brady (1996c). 'The 1993 Canadian Election: Realignment, Dealignment, or Something Else?' Paper presented at the annual meeting of the Canadian Political Science Association, St Catharines, Ont.

Joslyn, Mark, and Steve Ceccoli (1996). 'Attentiveness to Television News and Opinion Change in the Fall 1992 Presidential Campaign', *Political Behavior* 18: 141–70.

Kaase, Max, and Kenneth Newton (1995). *Beliefs in Government* (New York: Oxford University Press).

Kam, Christopher (1998). 'Party Identification in Canada: Re-Examining the Concept'. Paper presented at the annual meeting of the Canadian Political Science Association, Ottawa.

King, Desmond S. (1987). *The New Right: Politics, Markets and Citizenship* (Chicago: Dorsey Press).

Kirchheimer, Otto (1966). 'The Transformation of Western European Party Systems'. In Joseph LaPalombara and Myron Weiner, eds, *Political Parties and Political Development* (Princeton, NJ: Princeton University Press).

Kitschelt, Herbert (1994). *The Transformation of European Social Democracy* (New York: Cambridge University Press).

――― (1995). *The Radical Right in Western Europe: A Comparative Analysis* (Ann Arbor, Mich.: University of Michigan Press).

Kitschelt, Herbert (1997). *The Radical Right in Western Europe: A Comparative Analysis* (Ann Arbor, Mich.: University of Michigan Press).

Knutsen, Oddbjørn, and Elinor Scarbrough (1995). 'Cleavage Politics'. In Jan W. van Deth and Elinor Scarbrough, eds, *The Impact of Values* (New York: Oxford University Press).

Kopinak, Kathryn (1987). 'Gender Differences in Political Ideology in Canada', *Canadian Review of Sociology and Anthropology* 24: 23–38.

Krieger, Joel (1986). *Reagan, Thatcher and the Politics of Decline* (New York: Oxford University Press).

LeDuc, Lawrence (1984). 'Canada: The Politics of Stable Dealignment'. In Russell J. Dalton, Scott C. Flanagan, and Paul Allen Beck, eds, *Electoral Change in Advanced Industrial Democracies: Realignment or Dealignment?* (Princeton, NJ: Princeton University Press).

――― (1985). 'Canada'. In Ivor Crewe and David Denver, eds, *Electoral Change in Western Democracies: Patterns and Sources of Electoral Volatility* (New York: St Martin's Press).

Lemert, James B., William R. Elliott, James M. Bernstein, William L. Rosenberg, and Karl J. Nestvold (1991). *News Verdicts, the Debates, and Presidential Campaigns* (New York: Praeger).

Lewis-Beck, Michael S. (1988). *Economics and Elections: The Major Western Democracies* (Ann Arbor, Mich.: University of Michigan Press).

McAllister, Ian (1996). 'Leaders'. In Lawrence LeDuc, Richard G. Niemi, and Pippa Norris, eds, *Comparing Democracies: Elections and Voting in Global Perspectives* (Thousand Oaks, Calif.: Sage).

Megyery, Kathy, ed. (1991). *Women in Canadian Politics: Toward Equity in Representation.* Volume 17 of the research studies of the Royal Commission on Electoral Reform and Party Financing (Toronto: Dundurn Press).

Mendelsohn, Matthew, and Richard Nadeau (1999). 'Good People and Bad Politicians: TV News, Public Opinion and Election Outcomes', *Harvard International Journal of Press and Politics* 4: 63–76.

Monière, Denis (1994). 'Les Journaux durant les campagnes électorales québécoises', *Revue québécoise de science politique* 25: 115–34.

Mosteller, Frederick (1968). 'Association and Estimation in Contingency Tables', *Journal of the American Statistical Association* 63: 1–28.

Müller-Rommel, Ferdinand (1990). 'New Political Movements and "New Politics" Parties in Western Europe'. In Russell J. Dalton and Manfred Kuechler, eds, *Challenging the Political Order: New Social and Political Movements in Western Democracies* (New York: Oxford University Press).

Nadeau, Richard (1997). 'Le dilemme des Québécois: choisir le chef ou le parti?' *La Press*, 30 May, B3.

Nadeau, Richard, and André Blais (1993). 'Explaining Election Outcomes in Canada', *Canadian Journal of Political Science* 26: 775–90.

—— (1995). 'Economic Conditions, Leader Evaluations and Election Outcomes in Canada', *Canadian Public Policy* 21: 212–19.

Nadeau, Richard, André Blais, Elisabeth Gidengil, and Neil Nevitte (1997). 'Le chef et la cause, Pourquoi le Bloc québécois a-t-il perdu du terrain le 2 juin dernier?' *Le Devoir*, Friday, 4 July, A9.

Nadeau, Richard, and Christopher J. Fleury (1995). 'Gains linguistiques anticipés et appui à la souveraineté du Québec', *Canadian Journal of Political Science* 28: 35–50.

Nadeau, Richard, Elisabeth Gidengil, Neil Nevitte, and André Blais (1998). 'Do Trained and Untrained Coders Perceive Electoral Coverage Differently?' Paper prepared for presentation at the annual meeting of the American Political Science Association, Boston, September.

Nadeau, Richard, Pierre Martin, and André Blais (1999). 'Attitudes toward Risk-Taking and Modes of Political Choice in the Quebec Referendum on Sovereignty', *British Journal of Political Science* 29 (forthcoming).

Nadeau, Richard, Richard G. Niemi, and Timothy Amato (1996). 'Prospective and Comparative or Restrospective and Individual? Party Leaders and Party Support in Great Britain', *British Journal of Political Science* 26: 245–58.

Nevitte, Neil (1996). *The Decline of Deference* (Peterborough, Ont.: Broadview Press).

Nevitte, Neil, André Blais, Henry Brady, Elisabeth Gidengil, and Richard Johnston (1998). 'The Populist Right in Canada: The Rise of the Reform Party of Canada'. In Hans-Georg Betz and Stefan Immerfall, eds, *The New Politics of the Right: Neo-Populist Parties and Movements in Established Democracies* (New York: St Martin's Press), 173–202.

Nevitte, Neil, Richard Johnston, André Blais, Henry E. Brady, and Elisabeth Gidengil (1995). 'Electoral Discontinuity: The 1993 Canadian Federal Election', *International Social Science Journal* 47: 583–99.

Norporth, Helmuth (1996). 'The Economy'. In Lawrence LeDuc, Richard G. Niemi, and Pippa Norris, eds, *Comparing Democracies: Elections and Voting in Global Perspective* (Thousand Oaks, Calif.: Sage).

Offe, Claus (1987). 'Challenging the Boundaries of Institutional Politics'. In Charles S. Maier, ed., *Changing the Boundaries of the Political: Essays on the Evolving Balance between the State and Society, Public and Private in Europe* (New York: Cambridge University Press).

O'Neill, Brenda (1995). 'The Gender Gap: Re-evaluating Theory and Method'. In Sandra Burt and Lorraine Code, eds, *Changing Methods: Feminists Transforming Practice* (Peterborough, Ont.: Broadview Press).

—— (1998). 'The Relevance of Leader Gender to Voting in the 1993 Canadian National Election', *International Journal of Canadian Studies* 17: 105–30.

Pammett, Jon H. (1987). 'Class Voting and Class Consciousness in Canada', *Canadian Review of Sociology and Anthropology* 24: 269–89.

—— (1991). 'Voting Turnout in Canada'. In Herman Bakvis, ed., *Voter Turnout in Canada* (Toronto: Dundurn Press).

Pinard, Maurice, Robert Bernier, and Vincent Lemieux (1997). *Un Combat inachevé* (Sainte-Foy, PQ: Presses de l'université du Québec).

Powell, G. Bingham (1982). *Contemporary Democracies: Participation, Stability and Violence* (Cambridge: Harvard University Press).

—— (1986). 'American Voter Turnout in Comparative Perspective', *American Political Science Review* 80: 17–45.

Przeworski, Adam, and John Sprague (1986). *Paper Stones: A History of Electoral Socialism* (Chicago: University of Chicago Press).

Qualter, T.H., and K.A. MacKirdy (1964). 'The Press of Ontario and the Election'. In John Meisel, ed., *Papers on the 1962 Election* (Toronto: University of Toronto Press).

Rabinowitz, George, and Stuart Elaine Macdonald (1989). 'A Directional Theory of Issue Voting', *American Political Science Review* 83: 93–121.

Robinson, Michael J., and Margaret A. Shehan (1980). *Over the Wire and on TV* (New York: Russell Sage Foundation).

Rosenstone, Steven J., and John Mark Hansen (1993). *Mobilization, Participation, and Democracy in America* (New York: Macmillan).

Rothman, Stanley, and Robert S. Lichter (1981). 'Media and Business Elites', *Public Opinion* (October/November): 42–6.

Rucht, Dieter (1991). *Research on Social Movements: The State of the Art in Western Europe and the U.S.A.* Frankfurt/Boulder, Colo.: Campus Verlag/Westview Press.

Sarlvik, Bo, and Ivor Crewe (1983). *Decade of Dealignment* (Cambridge, UK: Cambridge University Press).

Smith, Gordon (1990). 'Core Persistence: Change and the "People's Party"'. In Peter Mair and Gordon Smith, eds, *Understanding Party System Change in Western Europe* (London: Frank Cass).

Stoker, Laura, and M. Kent Jennings (1995). 'Life-Cycle Transitions and Political Participation: The Case of Marriage', *American Political Science Review* 89: 421–36.

Strom, Kaare (1990). *Minority Government and Majority Rule* (Cambridge, UK: Cambridge University Press).

Studlar, Donley T., and Richard E. Matland (1994). 'The Growth of Women's Representation in the Canadian House of Commons and the Election of 1984: A Reappraisal', *Canadian Journal of Political Science* 27: 53–79.

Trent, John E. (1996). 'Post-Referendum Citizen Group Activity'. In Patrick C. Fafard and Douglas M. Brown, eds, *Canada: The State of the Federation 1996* (Kingston: Queen's University Institute of Intergovernmental Relations).

Verba, Sidney, Norman H. Nie, and Jae-on Kim (1978). *Participation and Political Equality: A Seven Nation Comparison* (Cambridge, UK: Cambridge University Press).

Verba, Sidney, Kay Lehman Scholzman, and Henry Brady (1995). *Voice and Equality: Civic Voluntarism in American Politics* (Cambridge, Mass.: Harvard University Press).

Wearing, Peter, and Joseph Wearing (1991). 'Does Gender Make a Difference in Voting Behaviour?'. In Joseph Wearing, ed., *The Ballot and Its Message: Voting in Canada* (Mississauga: Copp Clark Pitman).

West, Darrell M. (1991). 'Television and Presidential Popularity in the US', *British Journal of Political Science* 29: 198–214.

Whitehorn, Alan (1997). 'Alexa McDonough and Atlantic Breakthrough for the New Democratic Party'. In Alan Frizzell and Jon H. Pammett, eds, *The Canadian General Election of 1997* (Toronto: Dundurn Press).

Wolfinger, Raymond E., and Steven J. Rosenstone (1980). *Who Votes?* (New Haven, Conn.: Yale University Press).

Zaller, John (1996). 'The Good News Is the Bad News: How the Rising Tide of Negative Presidential Campaign Coverage Serves Democracy'. Paper prepared for presentation at the Annual Meeting of the American Political Science Association, San Francisco, September.

Zaller, John (with Mark Hunt) (1994). 'The Rise and Fall of Candidate Perot: Unmediated Versus Mediated Politics—Part 1', *Political Communications* 11: 357–90.

——— (1995). 'The Rise and Fall of Candidate Perot: Unmediated Versus Mediated Politics—Part 2', *Political Communications* 12: 97–123.

Index